COLD WAR FRIENDSHIPS

D1563266

COLD WAR FRIENDSHIPS

COLD WAR FRIENDSHIPS

Korea, Vietnam, and Asian American Literature

Josephine Nock-Hee Park

OXFORD
UNIVERSITY PRESS

OXFORD
UNIVERSITY PRESS

Oxford University Press is a department of the University of Oxford. It furthers
the University's objective of excellence in research, scholarship, and education
by publishing worldwide. Oxford is a registered trade mark of Oxford University
Press in the UK and certain other countries.

Published in the United States of America by Oxford University Press
198 Madison Avenue, New York, NY 10016, United States of America.

© Oxford University Press 2016

All rights reserved. No part of this publication may be reproduced, stored in
a retrieval system, or transmitted, in any form or by any means, without the
prior permission in writing of Oxford University Press, or as expressly permitted
by law, by license, or under terms agreed with the appropriate reproduction
rights organization. Inquiries concerning reproduction outside the scope of the
above should be sent to the Rights Department, Oxford University Press, at the
address above.

You must not circulate this work in any other form
and you must impose this same condition on any acquirer.

Cataloging-in-Publication data is on file at the Library of Congress
ISBN 978–0–19–025766–8 (hbk); 978–0–19–025767–5 (pbk)

1 3 5 7 9 8 6 4 2
Printed by Webcom, Canada

CONTENTS

CONTENTS

ACKNOWLEDGMENTS

I am grateful to my colleagues in the English Department and the Asian American Studies Program at the University of Pennsylvania. Special thanks are due to those who read and commented on portions of the manuscript—Nancy Bentley, David Eng, David Kazanjian, Suvir Kaul, and Ania Loomba—and I am most indebted to my mentor Amy Kaplan. Beyond my home department, Siyen Fei and Xiaojue Wang graciously shared their expertise. My students have helped me think through this material over the years, and I thank them for their interest and their questions.

I have been fortunate to find my scholarly tribe in the profession, and I thank those friends who have endured my presentations of this work: Tina Chen, Eric Hayot, Joseph Jeon, Sue-Im Lee, Colleen Lye, Warren Liu, Jena Osman, Crystal Parikh, James Salazar, and Edlie Wong. My most heartfelt thanks go to Daniel Kim, who is a shining example of how to be in academia. Many other collegial souls formed audiences for this material over the years at an array of venues, and I am grateful for so many instances of generosity. This book finally exists because I heard from Brendan O'Neill at Oxford

University Press at the exact point when I most desperately needed a brilliant editor, and I thank his assistant Steve Bradley as well.

And for J and J, you kept me going while I was mired in this dark stuff—and now that it's done, let's go play!

COLD WAR FRIENDSHIPS

COLD WAR FRIENDSHIPS

Introduction

Making Friendlies

In 1950, when he was a twenty-six-year-old surgical intern, Dr. Richard Hornberger was drafted to serve in the Korean War, at a Mobile Army Surgical Hospital in Korea. Years later, Hornberger—writing under the name Richard Hooker—published his account of the "extremes of hard work, leisure, tension, boredom, heat, cold, satisfaction and frustration" (5) endured by the doctors who "performed the definitive surgery on all the major casualties incurred by the 8th Army, the Republic of Korea Army, the Commonwealth Division and other United Nations forces" (5). Hornberger's 1968 novel *MASH* was a bestseller, and his episodic tales of young surgeons at work and play during wartime—some of whom "flipped their lids"; most "just raised hell" (5)—became a major cinematic event and, of course, a television staple.

Hornberger's *MASH* presented gifted surgeons whose pranks were directed against "Regular Army" types—and whose most outlandish acts ultimately served noble causes. In the book, Hawkeye Pierce (a thinly veiled version of Hornberger himself) and Trapper John are at their zaniest in their care of a young Korean, Ho-Jon. Hornberger opens the episode by explaining that "Each doctors' tent at the MASH had a young Korean to clean it, keep the stove going, shine shoes, and do the laundry and other chores. He was

1

called a houseboy," and the boy who serves the tent known as "The Swamp" forms a special bond with the irreverent doctors he serves:

> Unlike other houseboys, he was allowed to spend a lot of his spare time in the tent. The Swampmen helped him with reading and writing English, had books sent to him from the States, and gave him a good basic education in a few short months. Ho-Jon had a mind like a bear trap. It engulfed everything that came its way. During bull sessions in The Swamp, he sat quietly in a corner and listened. (66)

Ho-Jon's American education ultimately transports him out of Korea and into the United States. At seventeen, the boy is drafted into the Republic of Korea Army, only to return to the MASH unit as a gravely wounded soldier. He is saved by his beloved Swampmen, who are determined to rescue him from the war. Hawkeye secures a place for Ho-Jon at his alma mater in Maine, and he arrives at Androscoggin College on September 10, 1952— and, as Hornberger puts it, "Soon after, Hawkeye Pierce's old fraternity, assured by Hawkeye that Ho-Jon's prep school education had included martini mixing and crapshooting, pledged him" (77). The Swampmen have educated the Korean houseboy to become an American, and Ho-Jon graduates from The Swamp to Hawkeye's fraternity.

Hornberger metes out charity with a dose of blasphemy: in order to raise the funds for Ho-Jon's tuition, Hawkeye comes up with a scheme to photograph Trapper John as Jesus Christ, and the Swampmen put on a traveling Passion play, complete with signed pictures for purchase—antics that at once trumpet and skewer their benevolence. Their perverse virtue is peculiarly suited to Ho-Jon, who had previously "attended a church school in Seoul. He was a Christian. His English was relatively fluent" (66). Trapper John's

impersonation of the savior thus extends Ho-Jon's American tute-
lage in Christian schools (established by American missionaries
who won the favor of the Korean court at the end of the nineteenth
century) to present an all-too-fitting illustration of the wartime
political alliance between the United States and South Korea—
itself spun as a rescue operation. Ho-Jon's American education
spans the missionary school and the Swampmen's tent, but it is only
after he has served on the battlefield that he may be accorded a place
in an American fraternity. His wounds bind him to the American
doctors who complete his education; and in saving him, they fashion the boy-turned-soldier into their American brother.

Hornberger's book was written in the antiauthoritarian context
of the late 1960s, and MASH's commentary on the absurdity of war
clearly resonated in the Vietnam era. Robert Altman's 1970 film
adaptation of Hornberger's book was intended, and understood, to
be about Vietnam;[1] in the new context Altman created for MASH,
the natives were no longer opportunities to showcase American
goodness, even of the profane variety exhibited by Hornberger. In
the film, Ho-Jon cannot be rescued; he is only corrupted. Though
he may venture into the dissolute arena of the Swamp, the Korean
houseboy is never permitted to graduate to become an American.

In Altman's M*A*S*H (as it was styled on the film's promotional poster), we first meet Ho-Jon in the clutches of Major Frank
Burns, who has plucked him from the rest of the "mess hall boys"
for Christian inculcation. Breaking into Burns's dreary lesson, the
Swampmen offer Ho-Jon a "book" with "lots of pictures in it"—a
girlie magazine, which the boy swiftly accepts. Later, to a disap-
proving Burns, Hawkeye explains that they are training Ho-Jon to
be a bartender—and in this scene, Ho-Jon takes in their laundry,
the first intimation of his duties as a houseboy. Against the cold
instruction offered by Burns, the Swampmen's teachings inspire
Ho-Jon to offer them his service. The film jettisons the Christian

education that prepared Ho-Jon for the Swampmen's lessons in the novel; rather, Altman's Swampmen seduce the houseboy away from the possibility of uplift. Ho-Jon later reappears in the film drugged by Hawkeye in a botched attempt to save him from the draft—an effort that fails to save the Korean, but winks at American efforts to do the same in Vietnam.[2] If Hornberger's Hawkeye made a new fraternity brother out of his Korean houseboy, the "frat-party antics"[3] of Altman's Swampmen ultimately close the ranks of the film's counterculture heroes.

The first American film to win the Grand Prize at Cannes, Altman's *M*A*S*H* was a stylistic triumph: his maverick techniques—particularly his play with sound—announced an aesthetic daring that contended with those of European auteurs. Altman famously brought together his chaotic vignettes through a critical postproduction addition: a flat, wry voice piped through loudspeakers that announces sundry events throughout the film and finally concludes it by intoning, "Tonight's movie has been *M*A*S*H*." The film's unifying device evinces a self-reflexive turn that marks the shift from Korea to Vietnam: while Hornberger's Swampmen bemoan their service with black humor, Altman's wild young doctors serve themselves—and his movie turns inward. Subsequent Hollywood representations of the war in Vietnam featured varieties of the self-contemplation Altman made so fashionable, and the mirror of Vietnam tantalized a generation of American filmmakers, who found their own aesthetic powers in its reflection.

M*A*S*H, however, is best known as a long-running television show, so perennially popular that its reruns often outperformed first-run programming.[4] The show cashed in on the film's success by returning to Hornberger and cleaning up the Swampmen for prime time. The 1972 pilot retrieves Ho-Jon, taking up the storyline that Altman cut out: Hawkeye has secured a place for Ho-Jon at his alma mater, and the episode presents Hawkeye's attempt to raise tuition money by putting together a benefit party. The television version replaces Hornberger's blasphemous Passion play with Hawkeye's amiable sexism—he raffles off a weekend pass with the prettiest nurse in the outfit—and swaps Hawkeye's fraternity ties for a familial one: once in America, Ho-Jon will board with Hawkeye's parents. The show carefully calibrated its pranks as essentially good works to win remarkably broad appeal—indeed, it played off its two wartime contexts to placate both hawks and doves: "Korea was the perfect mechanism of disavowal: for opponents of the war the resemblance to Vietnam was obvious, while for supporters of the war the differences would be crucial."[5] And in overlaying Korea with Vietnam, M*A*S*H not only secured a divided audience; the analogy it made between the two wars reminded viewers that both wars were simultaneously utterly meaningless and fought with genuine goodwill—and thus if antiwar humor extended back to Korea, then the spirit of charity could touch Vietnam.

M*A*S*H became "the most moral show on TV":[6] two decades after the Korean war ended, television returned to Korea for eleven seasons to rediscover orphans and dispossessed peasants. In the pilot episode, Hawkeye's efforts on Ho-Jon's behalf introduce the particular mix of care and humor that would eventually anoint Alan Alda with "pop cultural sainthood"[7]—and Hawkeye's affection for what were called "local indigenous personnel"[8] in military lingo culminates in a bittersweet romance between his character and a Korean woman, played by Vietnamese American actor Kieu Chinh in a 1977 episode entitled "In Love and War."[9] Kieu's appearance incorporates small nods to Vietnam, including her character's fluent French and a knowing mention of an "Uncle Ho" (purportedly the name of a bombed-out restaurant). From the pilot episode's bright young houseboy to this failed romance, we may sketch out the long arc of America's not-so-cold war in Asia, which began by securing friends but ended in heartbreak. Over its eleven-year run, M*A*S*H featured virtually every Asian American actor of any prominence in Hollywood, who played feeble elders and wounded peasants (and, far less often, members of the MASH outfit).[10] This extraordinary after-life of the Korean War, channeled through Vietnam, fixed these "local indigenous personnel" as the guarantors of "quality television"[11]—and as the friendly faces of the Cold War.

Ho-Jon is not quite a friend; he is a "friendly," attached to his American big brothers by wartime service and sympathy. An adjective first turned into a noun to describe unthreatening natives, "friendlies" became military terminology most often used to distinguish among raced others.[12] To make friendlies is to make provisional and weak alliances, and this study considers these friendships in the twin conflagrations of the Cold War, Korea and Vietnam: two civil wars hitched to superpower rivalry, in which the United States first settled for half and then lost all. Korea and Vietnam were the first and second acts of a theater of combat kept at arm's length from Cold War–era America. In dramatic contrast to the preceding World Wars, these conflicts were meant to remain offstage: against the vast propaganda machines of the First and Second World Wars, Korea and Vietnam were packaged as safeguards against a third World War. Yet there still had to be something to save: though the wars remained dangerously murky—commentaries on both wars asked again and again, why are we in Korea? why are we in Vietnam?—the Cold War's grand wager for alignment churned out friendlies whose appeal diminished from one fight to the next.

In the words of one jaundiced critic, superpower conflict was merely "an *ideological* conflict like the one between Ford and General Motors!";[13] the true "fundamental clash of perspective on modern political history" instead belonged to the chasm between neocolonial agents and decolonizing subjects.[14] The Cold War between the United States and the Soviet Union—two competing versions of universalizing modernity[15]—faced the postwar wave of decolonization. Against the Manichean superpower conflict between East and West, communism and capitalism, stood decolonizing wars: struggles between North and South, colonizer and colonized. It was in Asia that these axes collided, and the disjunctions between them presented a formidable challenge to representation: every account of Asia's hot wars verged on incoherence because of the other axis that loomed in its shadow.[16]

China had been a valuable and perplexing epistemological object from the start of America's empire, and its "loss" to communism shattered decades of imperial fantasy.[17] The shock of Mao's 1949 revolution, in which a vast peasantry leaped from agrarian to communist modes of production to stand at the vanguard of an international movement, "altered the orientation of the Cold War by shifting its actual focal point from Europe to East Asia," a geographical shift that kept the West cool by inflaming the East.[18] US involvement in China's civil war, marked by "schizophrenic" aid to Jiang Jieshi (Chiang Kai-shek), entailed "increasing the amount of aid while doubting the survivability of the state," which "set the pattern for future problems in US policy, not least in Indochina."[19] With this pattern of intervention in place, parts of Asia in which the United States had virtually no economic or political stakes before 1945 became graveyards for American soldiers, who laid waste to these distant lands and annihilated populations.

The struggle to understand the wars that seemed to follow China's revolutionary lead became a major problem in American politics and culture. In the wake of China's astonishing revolution, Korea and Vietnam were decolonizing civil wars conscripted into the Cold War; it was in these unknown hinterlands that American military might was unleashed and transformed. Erupting out of the political vacuum left after the collapse of imperial rule, newly postcolonial rulers in Korea and Vietnam imagined divergent political futures, and they aligned their efforts to competing super-powers for vital material support. The novelty of the Cold War lay in the shared superpower strategy of securing alliances: both sides championed "an ideology around which to rally supporters and clients,"[20] and each "believed that friends or enemies on the international stage were defined by proximity or nonproximity to the specific ideological premises" they brandished.[21] The curious stability and remarkable duration of the Cold War have long been attributed to its novel policy of containment—in which both sides sought to preserve, rather than challenge, often fragile lines of political demarcation[22]—but ideological proximity was extraordinarily difficult to establish for regions long deemed unfathomable to the West.

A thick haze of Orientalism settled over every representation of America's Cold War incursions into Asia. The signal example of Karl A. Wittfogel's hallucinatory 1957 *Oriental Despotism* retraced a familiar path from Hegel's Orient as "the realm of theocratic despotism"[23] to Marx's Asiatic Mode of Production—a vague and contradictory pre-capitalist mode—to portray Mao's communist China as the exact rendering of despotic time and space.[24] Whether Chinese, Korean, or Vietnamese, the enemy was an Oriental fiend, updated as a Cold War despot. While the Asiatic enemy was entirely recognizable, however, the friend presented an acute crisis of representation. Faint and contradictory efforts were made to shelter Asian friends from prevailing codes of Oriental enmity;[25] for allies doomed to racial and cultural nonproximity, the political enlistment of the proxy—an agent authorized to work in the service of another—had to suffice.

8

In the Cold War, "proxy" became inseparable from "war," and while proxy states were inflamed, the superpowers unleashed a proliferation of geopolitical calculations. Indeed, once proximity gave way to proxy, material conditions gave way to figuration. Every war is fought with figures of speech, but proxy war launched a new logic of substitution. Recasting internal conflicts within states as miniature versions of the war between superpowers required a series of matching figurations—perhaps best exemplified in Eisenhower's metaphor of falling dominoes, which justified both overt and covert intervention on an unprecedented scale.[26] This order of substitution was itself perpetually on the verge of collapse, however, as neocolonial regimes coaxed and chastened client states that threatened to spin out of their control.

The proxy governed by metaphors of alliance, treated with open contempt, and militated into service: this is the Cold War friendly. Posited at the safe overlap of cold and decolonizing war, Korean and Vietnamese allies expose—and, critically, deploy—the politics of Cold War friendship. Derrida's *The Politics of Friendship* meditated upon Carl Schmitt's "friend-enemy distinction," the core formulation of Schmitt's 1923 treatise *The Concept of the Political*, to reveal that each "concept bears the phantom of the other" (72). Derrida critically destabilizes the absolute enemy defined by Schmitt as "existentially something different and alien, so that in the extreme case conflicts with him are possible"[27] by turning to the intensified context of civil war, in which, as Derrida notes, "the friend and enemy pass through into one another" (150). Considering the crisis of fratricidal war, Derrida traces the shape-shifting quality of the friend, who can morph from friend to enemy and back again. Cold War friendlies, superpower proxies in the nightmare of civil war, never had the luxury of the pure friendship or enmity theorized by Schmitt, however. Their American friendships had always already been destabilized by imperial racism—and under this erasure, they were rendered indistinct from the enemy: they, too, were "existentially something different and alien." The friendly perpetually deconstructs the friend-enemy distinction to lay bare the politics of friendship.

Thus consigned to expose political machinations, the friendly takes on the extraordinary task of fashioning a coherent self out of criss-crossing vectors of affiliation. She is fully cognizant of neo-colonial designs, but it is manifestly not in her interest to indict late-imperial fancy; instead, she seizes upon it. Her complex negotiations select and recombine deeply charged attachments. It goes without saying that the friendly is a politically suspect figure—what is remarkable, however, is her willed integrity: she devises her own, singular cohesion. As a political encumbrance and necessity, she is constantly subject to betrayal by her more powerful friends, and she betrays her brothers and sisters in turn. Following Crystal Parikh's compelling analysis of betrayal as a rupture that opens a critical window onto the ethics of "the minority subject as it wrestles with the implications of its own existence,"[28] this study, too, explores difficult acts of self-making that unveil incommensurable yet interlocking structures. Indeed, the neocolonial power, too, came to depend upon the friendly to justify political intervention, both during and after the fight. As a wartime convenience who outlasted the war, the friendly extended her claim on her powerful ally to make her way to America—even though proxies were always meant to stay offshore.

The field of American Cold War cultural studies has shifted from a longstanding focus on the culture of containment and anti-communist demonization in the domestic scene, to a more recent turn toward global contexts and the implications of decolonization abroad for domestic civil rights.[29] My study builds upon this expanding frame, and it is especially indebted to Christina Klein's *Cold War Orientalism*, which flipped the coin of containment to reveal its other side: namely, integration. Her readings of middle-brow American culture during the mid-twentieth century, replete with friendly Asians, significantly explore a logic of affiliation between the United States and Asia that sent Americans abroad and eased immigration restrictions at home. My study, however, considers those on the receiving end of American gestures of "tolerance and inclusion."[30] It is the friendly's task to shield her friends from the charge of neocolonialism, even though her very existence perpetually belies such attempts. Yet though she may be devastated by superpower interests, she also knows and insists upon her centrality to the Cold War's logic of integration.

II

The dissolution of the friend-enemy distinction on overseas battlefields thoroughly imbricated Asian America: the distant civil wars meant to keep the home front cool implicated a domestic population presumed to possess transnational ties, whether or not they claimed links to Asia. [31] Caught in the Cold War's crisis of representation, Asian Americans keenly felt figural constraints, and the grim events overseas covered in the news day after day presented a political and affective dilemma. As Judith Butler points out in *Frames of War*, "perception and policy are but two modalities of the same process" (29) which targets enemy populations "cast as threats to human life" (31). Butler elaborates on war's deadly divisiveness: "War sustains its practices through acting on the senses, crafting them to apprehend the world selectively, deadening affect in response to certain images and sounds, and enlivening affective responses to others" (51–52). Cast within a deadening frame, Asian America had to perform and proclaim its own enlivening acts.

The intertwining of domestic perception with wartime foreign relations in the experience of Asian Americans complicates the familiar liberal narrative, which traces a developing arc from exclusion to citizenship, in which once-barred groups are eventually incorporated into the nation. This story of progress is itself a product of the Cold War, in which the United States advertised its liberal ideals to a global audience. Yet in the shadow of this broadcast teleology of inclusion stood whispered stories of those hunted, locked up, or chased out. Keenly aware of the local repercussions of global political crises, Asian Americans understood a very different genealogy: the mere fact of their American existence recalled often calamitous US-Asian relations, which confounded the liberal trajectory from outsider to citizen.

In tangling linear histories, genealogies offer what Wendy Brown identifies in *Politics Out of History* "as an alternative ground for generating political aims" (94). Brown reads against progressive engines of history to argue that "Genealogy is uniquely suited to bring to light a specific democracy's historical attachments to and imbrications with nondemocratic principles" (135); such excavations ultimately provide "novel touchstones for a political consciousness that would mobilize and activate history" (173). Within the field of Asian American studies, this genealogical thinking uncovers a vexed political archaeology. Lisa Lowe's field-defining scholarship analyzes the terrain of minority culture as a site for erupting political contradictions, "an alternative site where the palimpsest of lost memories is reinvented, histories are fractured and retraced" (6). Retraced within the frame of war, a genealogy of such lost memories constellates a set of fraught political touchstones.

An Asian American genealogy of war links moments of intensified political contradiction. The Cold War problem of distinguishing friend from enemy calls forth two prior instances of debilitating friendship and enmity: US annexation of the Philippines at the turn of the twentieth century, which created a new category of friend for a budding imperial nation; and the bitter struggle against Japan in the Pacific War, which unleashed extraordinary enmity. These wars created caricatures of friends and enemies that defined Filipinos and Japanese within the United States—and established the political atmosphere for the neocolonial US-Asian wars that followed.

The controversial possession of the Philippines—an imperial acquisition that followed the script of preceding European scrambles—created a new kind of American: imperial subjects deemed "U.S. Nationals" but not full citizens.[32] Filipinos in the United States lived out the contradictions of imperial friendship: even as they were condescendingly embraced as "little brown brothers," they endured savage attacks. Compromised by colonial incorporation, they were doomed to be powerless friends—a caricature which rendered invisible major acts of anticolonial resistance, notably including the hard-fought war against the United States in the wake of annexation. At the other end of the spectrum, formerly timeless Japan marched into modernity as the enemy. With the attack on Pearl Harbor, the Japanese became, as anthropologist Ruth Benedict put it in 1946, "the most alien enemy the United States had ever fought in an all-out struggle" (1). Melding political enmity with racism, the intensity of wartime anti-Japanese sentiment fashioned a new breed of opponent, by turns sub- and super-human.[33] And for Japanese Americans, Japan's attack on US soil meant wholesale incarceration: internment revealed that simply resembling the enemy could strip Americans of their citizenship rights.

These contrasting imperial legacies shaped postwar Asian America: the wounding effects of US relations with the Philippines and Japan marked the ends of a hyperpoliticizing spectrum, and Asian Americans at midcentury found themselves caught in the complex span between them. In her discussion of the watershed of World War II, historian Mae M. Ngai emphasizes "the foregrounding of state relations in midcentury Asian immigration and race policy" in the United States: though Asian Americans were already deemed "unalterably foreign; war, hot and cold, imbued that foreignness with political implications of an unprecedented nature" (169). Asian Americans lived the contradictions of hot and cold war, as demonstrated by the exemplary case of San Francisco's Chinatown, where, as Ngai reports, "Rumors circulated that Chinese would be rounded up en masse and deported, or, alternatively, put into 'concentration camps'" (213)—even as the ethnic enclave was cleaned up to serve as a stage for dramas of assimilation. The specter of internment haunted a community in the throes of being remade into an exhibit for Cold War export.[34]

The Cold War political contortions on display in Chinatown demonstrate a complex interpellation at odds with the teleology of inclusion, and in presenting a Cold War genealogy anchored by weak friends and inhuman enemies, this study insists upon the determining effects of war for Asian America. It is perhaps unsurprising that the lens of Cold War would bring the Spanish-American War and the Pacific War into its purview; as Michael H. Hunt and Steven I. Levine put it, "These four wars—in the Philippines, against Japan, in Korea, and in Vietnam . . . constitute a single historical drama in four acts" (1), and their eloquent observation that "war creates its own geography" (2) has a significant temporal counterpart; war fashions its own space and time, and the coordinates of Asian America have been, and continue to be, defined by wartime vectors. The place and time of America's imperial errands are the defining constraints of Asian America, whose subjects have been rendered out of a modern history of US-Asian clashes and collaborations. American imperial designs critically unfolded in the Pacific, and the contours of Asian America have been—and continue to be—shaped by a history of military intervention.

In her pointed meditation on the time of war, Mary L. Dudziak explains that wartime is in fact "the only kind of time we have" (8). Writing against theorizations of wartime as a state of exception,[35] Dudziak underscores "the ways that war has become part of the normal course of American life" (25) to catalogue the innumerable wars, particularly small wars, that have marked US military history. "It is in war that citizens see the state" (22) Dudziak writes—a revelation shared by Carl Schmitt, whose friend-enemy distinction was inextricably linked to war. Citing Clausewitz's famous definition of war as the "continuation of politics by other means," Schmitt explains in a note that war is "the *ultima ratio* of the friend-and-enemy grouping. War has its own grammar (i.e., special military-technical laws), but politics remains its brain" (34). War is a parade of political logic, and over the long course of the Cold War, a raced minority divided into friends and enemies was made to see—and feel—political operations by the state. The experience of Asian Americans makes it all too clear that wars are not the exception, but rather the means by which norms are set.

The fact of a century of US-Asian conflicts has made wartime scholarship a prominent feature of Asian American studies. The study of wartime internment provided a critical foundation for the field, and the activist scholars who undertook this labor to create a new field of study were themselves inspired by the antiwar movement of the Vietnam era. Asian American studies is thus a wartime creation, and its activists, artists, and scholars have long traced—and embodied—the reverberating effects of American wars. The dramatic rise of Asian American populations, of course, is part and parcel of America's Cold War policies, and an Asian American perspective lends a significant counterweight to the recent global turn in Cold War cultural studies. Jodi Kim's *Ends of Empire* refocuses Cold War cultural studies to offer a vital reconsideration of Asian American subject formation. Kim explains that the

> protracted Cold War imperialist relation between Asia and America contradictorily configures the "Asian American" subject not only as immigrant, racial (minority) formation, or putative liberal citizen-subject of the U.S. nation-state, but also as postimperial exile or "refugee" who simultaneously is a product of, bears witness to, and critiques imperialist and gendered racial violence. (6)

Situating the Asian American subject within the critical turn toward Cold War integration, Kim reads "the relative 'inclusion' of Asians in the Cold War era ... as an imperial governmentality" (20). The Cold War subjects who are products of, witnesses to, and critics of this imperial violence, however, are also active participants in the logic of the Cold War. The friendly exposes political contradictions that are not only indictments of the state, but also potential sources of self-definition. Why and how this critical figure sustains extravagantly unequal alliances are the animating questions for the readings that follow.

III

Cold War Friendships examines Asian American narratives that position themselves squarely within the representative constraints demarcated by mainstream frames of war. The Asian American literary texts considered here vie for a place within the consensus created as a result of the Cold War—even as this accord crumbled. None of these works resists the political straits created out of Cold

War alliance; instead, it is from within these constraints that these Asian American voices discover imaginative forms for rendering the fraught creation of friendly subjects. The strangeness—and richness—of these texts lies in the modes they employ to confess their alliances, and my readings attend to the form and texture of these highly wrought literary creations.

The lively debates within Asian American studies about the status of literature are a product of the political underpinnings of the formation of the field, in which literary texts have served as living documents of marginalized experience as well as aesthetic opportunities to, as Kandice Chuh put it, "imagine otherwise." In 1993, Sau-ling Wong's defining argument for Asian American literature as a "textual coalition" challenged literary scholars to uncover historical contexts and, crucially, cultivate intertexts—that is, a web of literary thematics and tropes—through which "texts grouped under the Asian American rubric build upon, allude to, refine, controvert, and resonate with each other" (12). The generation of scholars who responded to her call created resonating literary clusters and, in key instances of field formation, took on the very contours of "the Asian American rubric." The tendentious and tenuous nature of the category "Asian America"—as unnatural as any political alliance—has inspired literary scholars both to question its founding premises, and to revel in the critical possibilities afforded by this very instability. From Susan Koshy's 1996 unmasking of Asian America as itself a fiction (a necessary but catachrestic rubric, with "no literal referent" [342]) to Chuh's 2003 welcoming of "subjectlessness" as a way of comprehending Asian American literature as "a space of theory" (18), Asian American literary study has identified a potential for undoing at the heart of its textual coalition.

Thus vulnerable to definitional collapse and amenable to critical reopening, every constellation of Asian American literary texts reconsiders a minority subject whose founding political assumptions waver, and whose forms query the politics of representation. While this critical climate belongs to a "post-identity turn,"[36] the subjects of this study may be better understood as "pre-identity": that is to say, these fictions and testimonies present the cognitions—and feelings—of proto-Americans. The friendly is entirely recognizable as a model-minority-to-be; her political integration on the global stage mirrors assimilationist strictures at home,[37] and in case after case, the friendly became an American. And though the friendly's insistence on becoming American peddles in essentialist identitarian claims, the aesthetics of her longing express the politics of being Asian American in often startling terms.

The ability to present inchoate selves and social formations is, of course, the province of aesthetics, and my examination of literary texts flows with Raymond Williams's "structures of feeling" (132), which possess a "special relevance to art and literature" (133). Williams's exhortation to read for "a social experience which is still *in process*, often indeed not yet recognized as social but taken to be private, idiosyncratic, and even isolating, but which in analysis (and rarely otherwise) has its emergent, connecting, and dominant characteristics, indeed its specific hierarchies" (132) crystallizes my interest in the friendly, who in every case appears "private, idiosyncratic, and even isolating," but whose experiences, upon close inspection, reveal an emergent formation—or, better, "pre-formation," to cite Williams again (134). For these figures of becoming, the necessity—and primacy—of the literary is abundantly clear, and it is the critical ambition of this book to work through elusive, contradictory, and even perverse social articulations by exploring their formal guises.

MASH's Ho-Jon inhabits and exemplifies three major roles assumed by the Korean War friendly: as the war unfolds, he is at first an adopted child, then a friendly soldier, and finally a foreign student—the three paradigmatic subjects of Part I, "Securing the

Korean War." For the vast majority of Americans—including those enlisted to fight—the Korean War was a bewildering morass, and Chapter 1 elucidates popular, albeit meager, attempts to portray and justify the war. Reading mainstream attempts to provide a motivation for an increasingly unpopular skirmish, Chapter 1 considers both journalistic portrayals of South Korean soldiers and Hollywood fantasies of rescue during the war—representations all marked by a grimness at odds with the consolidating technicolor portrait of 1950s-era America.

From this reading of the Korean War's narrowed frame of representation, Part I goes on to read three Korean American novels which return to the war. Chapter 2 considers Richard E. Kim's 1964 bestseller, *The Martyred*, in which a soul-searching South Korean soldier questions the role of the faithful ally, only to transform the military and political failures of the war into a complex expression of allegiance to US objectives. Abandoning his people for a solitary redemption, the friendly soldier ultimately marks an apotheosis of service, in which he calibrates his faith to the American mission. Chapter 3 turns to Susan Choi's 1998 novel *The Foreign Student*, in which a young Korean utterly broken by the war contrives to free himself from it by transporting himself to the United States as a foreign student, a figure newly visible during the Cold War as a manifestation of military alliance. Once in America, the wartime friend chafes against the strictures of his political condition: he frees himself from his abject position through a romantic union—which, we discover, is no less imbricated within the frames of Cold War alliance. Chapter 4 reads Chang-rae Lee's 2010 novel *The Surrendered*, which reimagines the Korean War orphan as a strangely indomitable girl who, perversely, wants to stay orphaned. The novel returns to a primal scene of the Cold War—the encounter between lost orphan and savior GI—in order to skewer both stock figures and reverse their roles. Lee's restaging empties the scene of sympathy, and the novel instead fabricates an angel of mercy to bring child and soldier together. Yet this good woman ultimately exposes the troubling depoliticization that attends this creative effort to recast wartime dependence. All three of these narratives are careful balancing acts that reveal the difficulty of imagining US-Asian alliances; their Korean protagonists are terribly hurt in the service of American aims and ideals, but these wounds only deepen their allegiance to those very ideals.

In dramatic contrast to the generally forgettable nature of popular representations of the Korean War, Vietnam, of course, became an aesthetic enterprise that drove a renaissance in American cultural production—and created a new cinematic genre. Part II, "Reviving the War in Vietnam," is devoted to both troubling and therapeutic American-Vietnamese friendships. Chapter 5 traces the fate of the American special agent as the diminishing means of alliance in Vietnam, from the bright idealists of the 1950s and 1960s— ingenious Americans who fostered alliances with the natives—to the wayward Green Berets of the 1970s and 1980s—who demonstrated a dark reverence for the enemy. In considering the meteoric rise and spectacular fall of the American agent, this chapter provides a frame for comprehending the forsaken Vietnamese ally, who would press her claims of friendship all the way to America.

From this initial reconsideration of an oeuvre whose fascination with a lost American innocence sacrificed Vietnamese innocents, Part II turns to Vietnamese American refugee testimonials that revive dismissed friendly relations. Chapter 6 reads Le Ly Hayslip's popular pair of autobiographies, *When Heaven and Earth Changed Places* (1989) and *Child of War, Woman of Peace* (1993), in which she presents herself as a reconciling spirit by claiming the power to grant absolution to the tormented GI. In rehabilitating the American soldier, Hayslip rehumanizes the Vietnamese, and ultimately restores Vietnamese suffering as a central reality of the war. She returns to

Vietnam to offer a new model of alliance to the wounded GI, as partner to a humanitarian mission. Chapter 7 examines Lan Cao's 1997 *Monkey Bridge*, a fictionalized account of her childhood experience of the war and her subsequent teenage years in the United States. Cao wields fictional license to detach her protagonist from both a Vietnamese past and a disappointing refugee community, and American friends become a necessary fiction in order to free this figure, who ultimately rehabilitates the Green Beret as a caring father figure. Cao's second novel, *The Lotus and the Storm* (2014), renarrates the war to secure a portrait of her father—a prominent member of the South Vietnamese military leadership—as its ultimate friendly. Chapter 8 considers Andrew X. Pham's 1999 memoir-cum-travelogue *Catfish and Mandala*, which recounts his return to Vietnam in the mid-1990s, and is spliced with vivid accounts of his family's wartime travails and harrowing passage to the United States. Pham's narrative uncovers a family secret of shameful US relations during the war, but in Vietnam he discovers a persistent Cold War structure of friendship that renders him a neocolonial agent. His subsequent literary acts devise safer modes of returning to the war, and ultimately transform sordid dependency into miraculous love. All of these Vietnamese American testimonies recuperate the lost category of the wartime friendly, and their deeply personal accounts recenter the refugee within the frame of the war in Vietnam.

From Korea to Vietnam, the Asian American texts I consider are bids for popular sympathy which shackle themselves to the modes of alliance scripted in mainstream renderings of these two conflicts. Every one of them presents a difficult military alliance that must be transformed, but never jettisoned. Between these Korean American novels of alliance and Vietnamese American testimonials of friendship, my readings chart a series of significant resonances: Kim's novel and Hayslip's autobiographies broke new ground by offering the ally's perspective onto these deeply unpopular wars, and both secured broad readerships by transcending the confines of their respective wars to offer far-reaching, trenchant philosophical and spiritual truths. The narratives by Choi and Cao, examined in the matched middle chapters, both dwell on the aftermath of the war in order to transpose US-Asian military alliances into personal ones. The efforts to recast a political alliance into a romantic union, on the one hand, and a familial bond, on the other, require imaginative labors that introduce speculative modes. And in the closing chapters of both halves, Lee and Pham self-consciously return to war in order to imagine Asian American subjects who spurn and transcend the wartime alliances that formed them: both disclose secret after secret in the hope of reversing and undoing wartime bonds— only to harden them instead.

I remember watching the epic 1983 television finale of *M*A*S*H* in rapt attention at age eleven, six years after my own arrival in the United States from Korea. Though my sisters and I occasionally squirmed at the "local indigenous personnel," we were all moved by Hawkeye's kindness—and *M*A*S*H* remains my father's favorite show. Returning to the series as an adult, I found myself watching episode after episode, entranced by its perfect alchemy of warmth and one-liners. *M*A*S*H*'s unflagging goodwill effortlessly sutured Korea and Vietnam together through doctoring and laughs, and my study explores the friendlies that Hawkeye patches up and forgets. These wounded souls are revived within a healing bond with imperial dimensions they fully comprehend—but whose balm they nevertheless claim as a means of restoration and, ultimately, self-creation.

PART I

SECURING THE KOREAN WAR

1

Lesser Friends

Americans have forgotten war after war, from the Philippine-American War to the Gulf Wars, and the oft-noted forgetting of the Korean War is in some respects unexceptional. But what is remarkable about this forgotten war is its centrality to America's postwar predominance. Citing diplomat Charles Bohlen's statement that "It was the Korean War and not World War II that made the United States a world military-political power," historian Robert J. McMahon underscores the "uncommon unanimity" of scholars in "identifying the Korean War as a key turning point in the international history of the postwar era."[1] Sixty years on, now-burgeoning scholarly interest in the Korean War resituates this conflict—recognized at the time as a serendipitous opportunity for implementing postwar containment policy[2]—as the signal event in militarizing foreign and domestic policy alike to shape and define the Cold War.

The Korean War was ripe for revisionist history from the moment that North Korean forces made their fateful strike across the 38th parallel on June 25, 1950. The roiling postwar situation on the Korean peninsula—liberated from four decades of Japanese occupation in 1945, only to be divided between two occupying superpowers—complicated this purported start of the war, whose layers of colonial and civil strife instigated Bruce Cumings's major reassessment of the origins of the Korean War in the early 1980s. The clarifying achievement of Cumings's history was to restore the conflict's origins as a civil war and recalibrate great-power politics within the region, which in turn prompted reconsiderations of the war's international dimensions as well as its legacy.[3] Contestation over the start of the war ultimately gave rise to scholarly accord on its significance, in large part because of this critical attention to the multiple and competing interests that transformed a local skirmish into a global scene. And so, after long being consigned to regional specialists, Korea has been rebranded in Hajimu Masuda's 2015 *Cold War Crucible* as the event that, in fact, made the Cold War happen. In squarely identifying Korea as the crucible—which triggered frenzy at home and dire prophecies abroad—Masuda's history lesson restores the Korean War to the larger sweep of Cold War cultural studies.

The present scholarly consensus echoes Truman's argument for Korea's importance. As he put it in his 1951 State of the Union address, Korea was a "symbol,"[4] and Truman's case for the war was built on an analogy: as he later wrote in 1956, "Communism was acting in Korea just as Hitler, Mussolini, and the Japanese had acted fifteen and twenty years earlier . . . If this was allowed to go unchallenged it would mean a third world war."[5] Truman's argument was accepted by the UN—and continues to be advanced by scholars and politicians today[6]—and his analogy at once downgraded the conflict itself and magnified its importance. Korea was nothing in and of itself, and so understanding this war required an expansion of both space and time: what mattered were the lands to the north and west, namely the USSR and China, and it was the future—the threat of yet another world war—that hung in the balance.

"Truman's war," however, cost him his reelection bid, but only after he had taken down a grand old warrior: General Douglas MacArthur, who was famously sacked by Truman in the spring of 1951. Months earlier, the general had triumphantly outflanked the enemy and marched into North Korea with Truman's backing, but with the entry of Chinese troops and the potential for a wider war, MacArthur's continued calls to roll back the enemy and take the fight all the way to China became dangerous insubordination. Against Truman's presentation of Korea as a means of averting a larger war, MacArthur insisted that the Korean War was the beginning of a major contest against communism. And while Truman's poll numbers sank, MacArthur was welcomed home in parade and song, and in his famous 1951 address to a joint session of Congress, famously declared, "In war, indeed, there can be no substitute for victory."[7] But MacArthur's dream of victory was an anachronism: his bluster was a relic of the last World War, and in the wake of his fall, Truman's "police action" became a model for a new era of containment.[8] Truman's argument for Korea as a symbol made the war itself a substitute, and its substitution of victory for enforced limits defined the Cold War.

Packaged as a symbol, Truman presented the Korean War as a preventive measure against World War III. When the dreaded all-out war froze in a strangely reassuring chill and America instead enjoyed an unprecedented and virtually mythic prosperity, the symbol disappeared. The recent reemergence of the Korean War—a late restoration to Cold War scholarship—uncovers its buried centrality in enabling the transcendence of postwar American might. A limited conflict sparked militarization that expanded without limits, and proxy warfare transformed the world: substituting military victory with militarization, this peculiar war created a state of victory out of a fight to a standstill. The Korean War was a series of substitutions, and the Cold War was a proliferating logic of proxies, in which substitutes were dressed up as more than lesser copies: fashioned into a set of links, the bright side of containment could be rendered as integration on a new scale.

This framing chapter for Part I maps out substitute victory via substitute soldiers to trace the popular contours of the Korean War friendly. I consider a set of popular attempts to inscribe the Korean War into the glossy mainstream of midcentury. I begin with an arch and outmoded attempt to understand the war against a new argument for integration—and then move on to three very different cinematic explanations of the war that reckon with a new kind of ally. Moving through the 1950s, these representations mark a waning affection, from the appearance of a new friend to this figure's demise and ultimate replacement. My final exhibit is *The Manchurian Candidate*'s 1962 skewering of the friendly, a nativist send-up of the 1950s cold warrior that runs straight back into the arms of pulp-fiction demon Fu Manchu. John Frankenheimer's film was lowbrow entertainment made gorgeous, and its satire crafted a prisonhouse for friendlies—which would require novel writerly strategies to disarm.

In the spring of 1951, correspondent E. J. Kahn, Jr. spent three months in Korea to cover the war for *The New Yorker*. He collected his desultory musings in *The Peculiar War*, which begins by noting what he missed:

> This book is in no sense supposed to be a complete account of the war in Korea, for, of course, I was not present during a great deal of it—the retreat of the United Nations troops toward the south after the North Koreans started it all, the first swing back of the pendulum and the ensuing advance to the Yalu River, the hasty flight from there when the Chinese entered the picture, and the subsequent reorganization of the Eighth Army. (vii–vii)

Whether the "North Koreans started it all" has been a point of debate from the start—and the instigation for Cumings's major revisionist account—but Kahn provides a useful backstory of the war up to the spring of 1951, when, after a series of advances and retreats, the fighting returned to the initial dividing line, only to linger there in the trenches. Kahn left the country in June, just before the beginning of cease-fire negotiations—although the fighting would not actually cease for two more years.

What made the war peculiar for Kahn was the strangeness of the natives. His opening chapter presents a remarkably hardy group "known by the informal designation of the 'A-Frame Army'":

> nearly all the villagers customarily carry whatever they have to carry on their backs. They strap their loads to a wooden contraption that looks like the letter "A," and they can tote staggering burdens with this device—well over a hundred pounds up a steep mountain trail, for instance. The Koreans in the A-Frame Army lugged rations and ammunition up hills, helped the engineers build roads, and dug the graves in which the Communist dead were buried and, not infrequently, in which some of their own dead were, since the native bearers accompanied our most forward units and were subject to the same hazards the soldiers were. (11)

The A-Frame Army is an assemblage of refugees carrying their lives on their backs, but they also bear the burden of "our most forward units." A different portrait of this civilian army appears in an account by General James G. Van Fleet, who took command of the Eighth Army after the shake-up in military hierarchy instigated by MacArthur's ouster. In May 1953—two months before the cease-fire—the general penned a two-part series for *Life* titled "The Truth

About Korea," which featured a passionate defense of Korea and its people. Van Fleet describes a vital support network:

> our own U.S. troops and the other U.N. units have the invaluable help of the Korean Service Corps, the unsung heroes of the war. As far as I know there has never been anything like this outfit in military history. It represents a sort of conscription of civilian manpower; its members are men exempt from the military draft. From 35 to 60, all Korean men are subject to being called up into the Service Corps, where they serve for a minimum of six months, doing everything to help win the war short of actually firing a gun. I found the Service Corps existing in an informal way when I arrived in Korea, and I am happy that I was able to formalize and expand it. (160)

Upon his arrival in 1951, Van Fleet professionalized Kahn's A-Frame Army into the Korean Service Corps, a transformation that fixed allegiances: these men were conscripted, clothed, and fed by the US military—and after they completed their tour of duty, they were certified for their loyal service by the Republic of Korea (160). While Kahn describes the "apparently aimless wanderings" of the A-Frame Army, "with all their meagre belongings piled high on their extraordinarily strong backs" (12), Van Fleet streamlines them into service: in the general's corps, these "native bearers" have become a vital appendage to the Eighth Army.

Like Kahn, Van Fleet marvels over the burdens they can bear: "They are used to carrying things on their backs, these Koreans, and they can perform incredible feats of strength and endurance" (160). Under Van Fleet's orders, these men no longer carry their own bundles; he has harnessed their backs for American military use. Van Fleet reveals the extent of the military's reliance on these Koreans: "There are 100,000 men of the Korean Service

Corps attached to our Eighth Army. Without them we should certainly have to send another 100,000 men of our own to Korea and perhaps even more, for these allies of ours do things that we ourselves could never do" (160). Their labors free American soldiers: "Because the corpsmen perform practically all our housekeeping chores and manual labor, our own men can devote their full time to being professional combat soldiers, either in actual combat or in training for it" (162). The Korean Service Corps is, in effect, a massive contingent of conscripted servants. The corpsmen carry ammunitions and ice cream; they clean weapons and house—and in shouldering all of these duties, they are constant companions to the American combat soldier.[9]

From Kahn's "informal designation" to Van Fleet's "unsung heroes," we register civilian and military perspectives of the Korean population: Kahn sees foreign contraptions and practices, but Van Fleet disciplines and mobilizes this peasant force. Hence, where Kahn encounters strange natives, Van Fleet identifies an untapped potential for service. The condescension and occasional scorn that run throughout Kahn's account are entirely familiar: his "peculiar war" is just another imperial gentleman's account, and indeed, the threat of an imperial relationship loomed large over the friendship between the United States and the newly minted Republic of Korea. The initial postwar occupation of Korea, marked by a hostility more appropriate to captured enemy territory, preserved the leadership put in place by Japan's colonial administration; the Americans simply picked up the reins left by the Japanese empire.[10] By contrast, the general's glowing portrait of his civilian corps heralds the peculiarity of the Cold War, which was fought to nurture alliances. Hence, while Kahn's wandering natives elude the political frame of the war—he remarks upon the "peculiar" fact that the civilians above the 38th parallel who "happened to be enemy aliens didn't seem to make anybody pay special attention" (12)—Van Fleet has metamorphosed impassive peasants into friendly military subjects. Put simply, Van Fleet has created a shadow army of friendlies.

Between Kahn's bemused reportage for *The New Yorker*'s liberal elite and Van Fleet's stern defense of the fight in *Life*, whose pages were consistently devoted to conservative cold warriors, we can mark out an American political spectrum. Kahn's tone and detachment were typical of his milieu, for whom the stakes of the Cold War properly belonged in Europe; unpleasantness had to be confined to the periphery, which only became more distant in Kahn's observations. Van Fleet's defense of the hot war put him at the forefront of those who placed Asia first, and he believed that the United States should expand the fight. And while Koreans were politically illegible to Kahn, who betrays longstanding assumptions of Oriental inscrutability that made political alliances impossible to imagine, cold warriors pushed Americans to imagine a new kind of ally, one who both believed in the American cause and kept to her allotted place. Though these new dependents were often seen as little more than despised colonial subjects, the Cold War's logic of global integration nurtured its allies in the faith of freedom.

II

The most endearing of these allies were the littlest. Samuel Fuller's minor 1951 classic *The Steel Helmet*, the first—and, by most accounts, the best—American movie about the Korean War, introduced a new friend. Fuller made his film on a shoestring budget without the assistance or approval of the US military, which refused his request for wartime footage and generated an uproar over the film's portrayal of American soldiers.[11] The film opens with a bound and bedraggled American soldier, the only survivor of a

Red attack; such images of captivity would come to define the later stages of the war, which became figured as a nightmare of communist imprisonment.[12] As Sergeant Zack struggles to free himself, we see a pair of bare legs dragging a rifle. When this unknown body picks up a knife we fear the worst—but instead of the enemy, we discover a young boy, who wields the knife to free the soldier. The child identifies himself with his first words: "South Korean!" The young ally quickly makes himself useful: he helps Zack dress a wound and then sweeps the remaining bodies for ammunition. When Zack remarks upon the child's knowledge of weaponry, the boy explains, "G.I.s here four years," thus reminding the viewer of the US occupation that preceded the outbreak of the war. The boy further instructs Zack (and the viewer) on a crucial bit of terminology: when the American soldier says, "You talk more like a dogface than a gook," the child fiercely replies, "I am no gook! I am Korean." Adamantly resisting the racist term, he insists upon a national and political identity—thus rendering political alignment a corrective to anti-Asian racism.

In this figure of a Korean boy who assists an American sergeant, *The Steel Helmet* creates the paradigmatic friendly of the Korean War: the war orphan. We learn that his family has been killed by "Red artillery—big stuff": the child thus carries the heavy knowledge of the politics of the war, and just as he instructs Zack in anti-racism, his personal loss imparts meaning to an otherwise pointless skirmish. This orphan is in fact a walking emblem of faith: he begs to accompany Zack, who is reluctant to take him on, with spiritual pleading: "But your heart is in my hands. Buddha say when you save a friend his heart is in your hands." The hands first seen brandishing a knife now carry the heart of the American soldier. The orphan's painfully sincere speech binds these new friends, and, as the film proceeds, the boy predictably captures the sergeant's hard-bitten heart.

Sergeant Zack names the child "Short Round" after a bullet that does not go all the way through (a name notably recycled by director Steven Spielberg for the young Asian sidekick in the second installment of the Indiana Jones franchise), but Short Round's faith makes up for faulty ammunition. As they set off together, the sergeant notices a bit of paper pinned to the boy's back, which Short Round explains is a "prayer to Buddha asking him to heal me if I am wounded." Zack's reply, "Thought you forgot to take off the price tag," foretells the price of their alliance: though Short Round will inspire a spiritual awakening, he will not survive this friendship. Short Round quickly becomes a soldier: he dons helmet and boots, and his transformation is virtually complete when Zack makes up a set of promised dogtags for him. Just before Zack presents him with this gift, however, Short Round is killed by enemy fire. This ultimately tragic friendship exposes the spectacular vulnerability of the friendly: the orphan permits attachment and lends meaning to the fight, but his allegiance finally puts him in the line of fire.

In contrast to Fuller's stark black-and-white film, Douglas Sirk's 1957 *Battle Hymn* contrives a happy ending out of the Korean War orphan's abject dependence. Sirk's technicolor melodrama provides a telling contrast: while *The Steel Helmet* launched Fuller's career and became a critical darling, the lurid, Sirkean treacle of *Battle Hymn* was only appreciated in Korea, where it was broadcast as a rare feel-good Hollywood movie about the war.[13] Fuller's film was notable for its controversial failure to win the stamp of military approval, but *Battle Hymn* is plastered with official backing: the film opens with an awkward testimonial by General Earle E. Partridge, who explains that *Battle Hymn* is an "affirmation of the essential goodness of the human spirit." In lieu of such an endorsement, Fuller's film opened with a dedication to the US Infantry, and *The Steel Helmet* is a gruff yet lyrical paean to enlisted men on the ground—far below the Air Force officers of *Battle Hymn*.

Battle Hymn features the true story of Colonel Dean Hess, played by Rock Hudson, who went to Korea to lead a training program for the first cadre of Republic of Korea fighter pilots, but ultimately found a deeper mission in establishing the Orphans Home of Korea.[14] The ROK Air Force officers Hess is charged with training are introduced as a "hot bunch," but the film is not particularly interested in their exploits. The South Korean officers duly shadow their American teachers on flight runs, and the story quickly arrives at Thanksgiving dinner—the culmination of their alliance—only to veer away, to a group of hungry orphans huddled outside the mess tent. The film shows us the festivities from their perspective: they peek up from the bottom of the tent, and one daring child—who will go on to steal Hess's heart—snatches a piece of bread from under the table as an American officer says grace. Their gaze refocuses the film: if *The Steel Helmet*'s Short Round transformed a potentially menacing body into a faithful ally, *Battle Hymn* turns us away from a rare depiction of US-ROK military harmony in order to present these supremely needy friendlies.

These orphans steal the show: not only do the children divert the attention of the film's protagonist—they move us out of the film altogether. The children featured in the film were in fact brought to the United States from the orphanage Hess founded in Korea, and so these orphans played themselves. The studio proclaimed that they "were not recruited by Central Casting in Hollywood. They were sent directly from Korea as 'Ambassadors of Good Will' by President Syngman Rhee. They had no chance to be spoiled; they were just themselves."[15] Given the knowledge that these children were actual Korean orphans, a strange melancholy pervades the film. As they cluster around American soldiers and pretend to be hungry and hurt, we realize that they are not actors but promotional material, not only for the film but for the political alliance: they are abject political emblems who exceed the narrative bounds of the film. In addition to exposing the film as propaganda, these children rupture diegetic identification and redirect our gaze to their plight.

It is thus curiously sad to watch the performance of a native song and dance by two of the little girls.[16] They cannot be absorbed into the narrative: their performance is framed less to be seen by the lead actors within the diegesis than to appeal to our mercy. The Hollywood studio traded on their abject reality to claim "they were just themselves"—and yet orphans are never "just themselves."[17] To imagine an ally as orphan creates a model of utter dependence; indeed, independence is a tragedy for this ultimate friendly of the war. That the orphan is still called into service in 1957 is a measure of the unpopularity of Korea: they remain the only way to salvage an unwon war. The belated publicity stunt of *Battle Hymn* presents an apotheosis of the proxy logic of the Korean War, in which humanitarian rescue is made a substitute for victory—a formula which will reappear with redoubled force in the aftermath of Vietnam. This culminating substitution upends imperial models of mimicry, because in Cold War logic, proxies are not derided as lesser copies, but in fact championed precisely because of their weakness.

III

The substitution of the orphan for the South Korean soldier—presented in *The Steel Helmet* as an allied-soldier-in-training and in *Battle Hymn* as a critical swerve away from the ROK soldier altogether—is also a symptom of popular understandings of the South Korean fighting force. The second installment of General Van Fleet's "The Truth about Korea" in *Life*, which opens with a large photograph of smiling ROK soldiers, launches into a full-scale defense of these men: "Regardless of anything else you may have heard, the Korean is a great soldier and a wonderful ally" (158).

ROK soldiers were routinely derided—Kahn mentions "the view held by numerous Americans that practically all ROKs were martially incompetent" (108)—but the general presents them as a valiant force. In Van Fleet's estimation, the ROK soldier's "faith and morale are superb, and he knows exactly why he is fighting. He has seen the results of Communism with his own eyes; someone in his own family has been killed or kidnaped or had his property stolen or destroyed" (158). This emphasis on "faith and morale" transcends military skill: the Korean is a "wonderful ally" because he knows the stakes of the fight. Lauding the ROK soldier's indomitable faith, Van Fleet spells out his formula for winning the war: "Korean gallantry and American firepower" (169). The general matches spirit to technology in order to present a complementary ally, one who supplies faith and knowledge. Bereft orphans, of course, could do more on this front than any trained soldier, but Van Fleet's emphasis on faith and morale also highlights qualities that famously eluded American soldiers in Korea.

This absence of spirit is on full display in *Pork Chop Hill* (1959), a depiction of a long and deadly fight to claim a desolate hill in the last months of the Korean War. The film was based on an account of the battle by Army General S. L. A. Marshall, who analyzed infantry operations for the Eighth Army, and it presents the plight of Lieutenant Joseph Clemons, played by Gregory Peck, as he leads inexperienced and occasionally unwilling soldiers into enemy fire with little support from higher command. Between Marshall's account and the Hollywood adaptation, however, Van Fleet's "Korean gallantry" has simply disappeared. Marshall's book opens by insisting that Army officers "were wrong in suspecting that when the Red tide moved in, too many young Americans took refuge inside the bunker walls, neglecting to use their weapons," claiming instead that "it was unmistakeably true that at inordinate percentage of ROK soldiers behaved that way, and I so reported" (17–18).

His report is replete with condemnation of these soldiers: Korean soldiers "refused to budge" (85); they risked the lives of Americans because, in their words, "Me afraid" (269); and one Korean soldier, the infamous "Easy Ed," was "a first-class liar" (287). Such cases abounded because, as we learn in Marshall's account, "On all out-guard posts, it was the company custom to team GIs and Koreans" (121). Yet the film has dispensed with ROK soldiers, and North Koreans, too, are absent from its caricatures of Chinese enmity— the film has thus rid the Korean War of Koreans.

In jettisoning ROK soldiers from its narrative, the film presents an empty struggle: in the absence of the faithful proxy, *Pork Chop Hill* renders the Korean War a meaningless conflict. Against the melodramatic excesses of *Battle Hymn*, the streamlined elegance of *Pork Chop Hill* rids the battle of proxies to present a purified, Sisyphean struggle of soldiers trudging up a hill.[18] With the friendlies out of the picture, the film is an inward tale that ultimately presents a domestic scene. Marshall's cowardly ROK soldiers have been channeled into the figure of Franklin, a treasonous African American soldier. Feigning injury and hiding in a bunker, we see Franklin in the shadows as a silhouette of smooth pate and gleaming dagger, an eerie shape suggesting, in its outline, Fu Manchu. Though his cowardice renders him "Oriental," he is quickly redeemed by Gregory Peck's character, who responds to Franklin's disaffection: "A lot of men came up here last night. They don't care any more about Korea than you do. A lot of them had it just as rough at home as you did. They came up and fought and there's about twenty-five of them left. That's a pretty exclusive club, but you can still join up if you want to." In offering membership in this exclusive club, Clemons exhorts Franklin to give up his dangerous solitude and enter the fold, and his words do the trick: Franklin emerges from the darkness with his helmet on, and he pitches into the fight. Franklin's character was a fiction—no such character appeared in Marshall's account—and his unconvincing rehabilitation demonstrates a Cold War fantasy of domestic integration.

The civil rights gains of African Americans and Asian Americans won during the Cold War era were calibrated to foreign relations, and domestic race relations in the postwar era were never detached from the international scene.[19] Arthur Schlesinger's 1949 treatise, *The Vital Center*, famously expressed the weaknesses of the "free world"—"Against totalitarian certitude, free society can only offer modern man devoured by alienation and fallibility" (47)— to expound upon an integrating vision. Stating that "we have not freed Negroes, Jews and Asiatics of the stigmata of slavery" (190), he exhorted Americans to admit that "we must reform our own racial practices" in order to reveal "the essential strength of democracy": "its startling insight into the value of the individual" (248). The presentation of unit integration in *Pork Chop Hill* is keenly attuned to this liberal argument, and Truman's desegregation of the armed forces—which first went into effect in Korea[20]—renders Franklin a particularly significant exhibit for Cold War integration. That he stands in for South Korean allies, however, undoes the chain of substitutions that forges Cold War alliances and reveals an incommensurability between the vital center at home and the maintenance of friendlies abroad. The promise of membership cannot, in fact, be an enticement for the friendly, whose existence must remain complementary. The friendly can never join the club because its promise of belonging is anathema to proxy logic, whose replacements rely on strict divisions.

Pork Chop Hill features another prominent figure of postwar integration: Lieutenant Clemons was assisted by second Lieutenant Tsugi Ohashi, who is notably played by George Shibata, the first Japanese American graduate of West Point. After suffering heavy casualties, Clemons and Ohashi confer over a change in strategy, and they agree to try a tactic "right out of the stone age": a bayonet charge. Ohashi volunteers to lead the charge, saying, "you know, my ancestors were pretty good at this Banzai business." This "business" belonged to the last, most recent war, but it has already become ancient history—and Ohashi makes light of the enforced linking of Japanese and Japanese Americans, which had led to American concentration camps only a few years earlier. That Ohashi can banter about "Banzai business" demonstrates that his loyalty is no longer in question, but this reference simultaneously reattaches him to Japan.

Ohashi's reclaiming of his ancestors registers the about-face in US-Japan relations after the war: Japan lost the Pacific War, only to become America's best friend in the Korean War. Occupied by US forces for the majority of the Korean War—and Americans lingered long after the end of formal occupation—Japan was a major base of US military operations. Indeed, Japan's postwar recovery owed its jump-start to the Korean War, which became a major market for Japan's rapidly expanding heavy industry; and as Korea was reduced to a wasteland, Japan was reconstructed into an American playground. In thus signaling his continuing attachment to Japan, then, Ohashi is not a member of Clemons's club but a friendly: Ohashi is governed by proxy politics. And though the Japanese American officer clearly supersedes the enlisted African American, his service requires a different order of servility—but one that paradoxically affords Ohashi a standing that Franklin could never attain.

The Steel Helmet, too, strikingly featured African American and Japanese American soldiers in Sergeant Zack's company. A captured North Korean soldier singles out these two raced Americans as susceptible to his ideological campaign. To the black medic who attends to his wounds, the enemy reveals a careful study of Jim Crow laws in America—but the medic proves to be impervious to his arguments for communist justice. Tanaka, the Japanese American soldier, is more flappable. The enemy begins his attack by saying, "You've got the same kind of eyes I have," adding, "They hate us because of our eyes." Tanaka initially rebuffs this remark, but he is less able to fend off a subsequent question: when the prisoner asks, "They threw Japanese Americans in the prison camps in the last war, didn't they? Perhaps even your parents? Perhaps even you?," Tanaka replies, "You rang the bell that time. They did." The enemy's opening salvo of racial solidarity failed to realign Tanaka within a decolonizing axis, but the mention of internment resounds with Tanaka because that mass incarceration revealed how thoroughly foreign relations determined domestic standing. And so, like Ohashi, Tanaka is revealed to be little more than a friendly: though he refuses racial solidarity with the North Korean enemy, he resembles Short Round because he is unable to go much further than the orphan. The film never suggests any special bond or strife between Tanaka and Short Round,[21] but the enemy forces the Asian American soldier to acknowledge the politics of friendship that render him as bereft as the war orphan.

IV

Hollywood had little interest in Korea. Unlike the domestic mobilization campaigns that enlisted the studios during the world wars, US policymakers on the domestic front fought to keep the war small: in the words of a 1950 article in *U.S. News and World Report*, "Official Washington" aimed "to keep Korea in its place: a pint-sized incident, not a full-scale war" in order to "keep the home front cool."[22] No propaganda agencies were created to school Americans on their friends and enemies for this new war, and though military brass stamped their approval on films like *Battle Hymn* and *Pork Chop Hill* (while refusing to endorse films such as *The Steel Helmet*) neither film cared to explain the politics of the Korean War. And beyond these films, which featured A-list actors—Rock Hudson and Gregory Peck, two ends of a Hollywood spectrum of sympathy and dignity—the small and forgettable corpus of Korean War films were instead largely B pictures about POWs, dark and poorly rendered nightmares of captive soldiers at the mercy of diabolical captors.[23]

The cause célèbre explored by these narratives was the practice of "brain-washing," a term which first appeared during the Korean War. Purportedly a direct translation of a Chinese term—in the words of the American journalist who first published the neologism, "The plain people of China have coined several revealing colloquialisms for the whole indoctrination process"[24]—Oriental mind control was the only captivating aspect of the war in the popular imagination. Captivity narratives loomed large throughout the Cold War, and Korea lent a new salience to the POW because stalled negotiations over prisoner release and exchange deadlocked the conflict into trench warfare along the 38th parallel for two years.[25] US negotiators insisted upon a novel policy of voluntary repatriation for POWs of Korea as a way of attenuating the vast numbers of conscripted enemy soldiers, but American victory in securing this agreement was popularly overshadowed by the unforeseen consequence of twenty-three American GIs who chose to repatriate to Red China—shocking evidence for a popular lament over American weakness and demonic Orientals.

The perils of failed manhood and Asiatic control that gripped the popular imagination during the Korean War produced one great film: John Frankenheimer's 1962 *The Manchurian Candidate*, which has come to stand as a summa of 1950s America, in which every dark fantasy of anticommunism comes deliriously true.[26] Its nightmare of enemy mind control has lodged firmly into the American psyche and inspired multiple rehashings of its fantasy scenario—both on and off the screen.[27] The film enshrines the darkest of

Hollywood heroes: Raymond Shaw, the American brainwashed by communists—ultimately revealed to be controlled by his mother, with whom, it is implied, he has an incestuous relationship—who must destroy himself. His nightmare begins in Korea, where he is ensnared by a seeming friendly: Chunjin, the South Korean interpreter to Shaw's Army unit. Once captured, Shaw is programmed by the enemy and then returned to America, to be followed by Chunjin, who is sent to monitor this unknowing communist weapon. Chunjin appears at Shaw's door, where he gives a culminating performance of friendly servility: in broken English, he entreats his wartime friend, "I need job . . . I am tailor and mender. I am cook." The film's portrait of Chunjin signals the demise of the Korean War friendly: his eagerness to serve is an unsavory mask for dark allegiances, and in his wake, such service will no longer be a mark of loyalty, but rather of suspicion. In the skewering vision of *The Manchurian Candidate*, General Van Fleet's "unsung heroes of the war" have been channeled into General Marshall's "first-class liar."

Chunjin is the lesser of two varieties of Oriental villainy in the film: he assists Yen Lo, the Chinese mastermind who reconditions Shaw. *The Manchurian Candidate* is not coy about naming the source of this fantasy: Frank Sinatra's Ben Marco, the troubled protagonist of the film who uncovers its wild plot, plainly identifies Yen Lo as a latter-day Fu Manchu, thus installing this representation within the longstanding "stigmata" of American racism decried by Arthur Schlesinger. Frankenheimer's terrifying film flipped the coin of Cold War integration to insist upon the other side of its liberal imagination: total demonization. And while Yen Lo recalled fantastic Yellow Peril fears, Chunjin's treachery, significantly, cast aspersions on Asian immigrants within the United States. In his hidden loyalty to the enemy, Chunjin represents a perversion of both the South Korean ally and the Asian American: in making impossible both alliance and minority belonging within the United States,[28] he exposes the yoke that binds foreign ally and model minority, and thus reveals the dark underside to the friendly status shared by Short Round and Tanaka. Neither the orphan nor the Asian American soldier can go all the way, and from *The Steel Helmet* in 1951 to *The Manchurian Candidate* in 1962, we may trace an impossible Americanization.

Perceptions of these dependent allies played a determining role in the political debate instigated by the Korean War. The gentlemanly account in *The Peculiar War* wondered at the natives, but cold warriors championed their cause in order to fix them within America's orbit. The politics of substitution fashioned this new ally, at once celebrated and utterly dependent—and how to imagine this friendly marked a crisis of representation that would only deepen over the course of the Cold War. The problem of recuperating such a figure, whose power relied on fitting into a new American imperium, became a vexing question, and the next three chapters examine Asian American attempts to imagine a wartime ally in the wake of *The Manchurian Candidate*'s thrilling exposure of the Asian immigrant's false promise and, most tellingly, of a deeply illiberal America. This framing chapter has examined the extraordinary fragility of the wartime ally, and the remaining chapters of Part I turn to the formal adventure and difficulty of matching Asian friendlies to American friends.

2

Faithless Warrior

Richard E. Kim's The Martyred

In a 1990 lecture, novelist Richard E. Kim presented his literary awakening against the backdrop of a trans-Pacific passage:

> on my maiden voyage to the United States, in the middle of the vast Pacific Ocean, I came, alone, face to face with the sun emerging from the waves on the morning horizon ... and it was then as if I saw the sun for the first time in my life, it speaking to me and I speaking to it.
>
> I think it all went with my own, private exploration, discovery of my Self, now utterly alone, physically and psychologically, away from Korea and toward the unknown ...
>
> And, later when I began to write in English, the "I" in Korean gave way willingly and joyously to the "I" in English— and it was like discovering and assuming a wholly new identity of Being and, with it, a wholly new way of seeing, thinking, cogitating and understanding, having shed the Korean "I" that is not really "I" but that is subservient, always, to the Korean "we."[1]

Kim casts his voyage to the United States as a turn away from Korea and toward the Self: he sheds a cumbersome Korean "we" for a solitary exhilaration. Turning his back on a known subservience, he faces an "unknown" suffused with the light of Western freedom. Kim revels in his detachment; he has shed a lesser identity for a "wholly new way of seeing, thinking, cogitating and understanding," facilitated by the person he discovers in English.

This rapturous passage is shot through with a geopolitical order learned from the Cold War, which newly politicized the age-old notion of the West as a beacon of freedom against a dim, subservient East. Kim's account of his private dawn is a literary efflorescence grown out of the Cold War's hemispheric division and his own political alliance with the United States. Kim served in the South Korean military as a liaison officer to UN forces during the war, and this "maiden voyage" was his 1954 trip to Middlebury College in Vermont; after his studies ended, he stayed and made America his home. The revelation of the sun on the Pacific is a harbinger of his new identity as an American, which precedes his arrival—the Western sun itself was sufficient. That one may encounter this light before setting foot in America is a premise of the "free world," which purports to shelter nations in its light. In Kim's metaphysics, political alliance with the West is enshrined as a private revelation.

Kim's faith in the Western sun streams through this strange passage: he presents a moment of conversion in which images and words rush together and fall away. In reading the curious pauses amid his dramatic tones, we may register a tension between his overwhelming belief and a political alignment which renders his metaphysics partial. Indeed, we may read the excesses of this passage as an attempt to redress a lost universality: in discovering Being, Kim has identified its Western limits. He can become an American on the open sea, but his process of singular identification reveals both the rarefied nature of this awareness as well as the magnitude of faith required to attain it.

This new sun makes extraordinary demands: Kim must reorder his perceptions and thoughts. In Kim's words, "the 'I' in Korean gave way willingly and joyously to the 'I' in English": there is no battle between Korean and English because Korean readily cedes. This, too, is an order of acquiescence not so different from subservience to the Korean "we"; in bowing to this new sun, Kim may in fact be demonstrating a transcendent obeisance. If, following Kim's elucidation, being Korean means being subservient, then his own respect for the American "I" paradoxically marks the apotheosis of his subservient Korean "I." He has not shed his Korean identity; instead, he has revealed that the Korean must always acquiesce— and this new master requires a new kind of subservience.

This complex pose of subservience is a product of a new order of allegiance: not simple domination, but rather an existential superiority. In declaring his independence, Kim has in fact sketched out a dependence which dematerializes the substance of alliance. The rhetoric of the "free world" is inseparable from the promise of material gain, but it peddles its claims for bounty on the basis of moral values.[2] Kim's lecture elevates an unequal political alliance: a voyage to the neocolonial center is an epiphany, and the neocolonial subject extols the triumph of Western Being—through which the wartime friendly may imagine a future for himself beyond the frame of war. The current of belief that runs through Kim's words seems to transcend more base promises of wealth and security, but the immaterial is inseparable from the material of the "free world." Kim's metaphysical celebration is not a mere cover for political allegiance; the talk of Being belongs to the very heart of the Cold War vision of global integration.

Kim's "discovery of my Self" showcases the complexity of forging an ideological alliance across the Cold War divide between East and West. His alliance is at once effortless and impossible: it is simply a matter of turning to the West, but the turn itself is conditioned by an ineradicable foreignness. Indeed, Kim's exultation of solitude marks his incommensurability with the unknown world he welcomes: Cold War discourse rendered isolation a political liability, both on the global stage as well as within the domestic scene. Kim thus aspires to a condition widely lamented as a particular failing of the free world: pundits hailed the American perfection of individualism, at the same time that they cautioned against a melancholy solitude uniquely susceptible to the enemy's communal ideology. Popular accounts of Cold War culture fretted over the lonely American, but Asian Americans were not accorded this weakness precisely because they were never imagined to be detached from an Asian "we." Allies may be treacherous—they may even be unmasked as enemies—but they are never mere weak souls. They are not permitted the luxury of wavering in their faith; instead, they must make declarations of it.

Kim presents the sun over the Pacific as the wellspring of his writing, and the aesthetic products of his new faith imagine solitary journeys toward this light. Strikingly, Kim's books are not set in the New World, but rather in Korea at moments of political crisis: the period of Japanese occupation, the war, and a 1960 political coup. Within these settings, the narrators of these stories all express a consciousness of Self which aligns with Kim's 1990 declaration. Indeed, it is through these distant settings that Kim presents the emergence of a newly detached first person: in each case, the "I" that governs the telling of the story holds himself apart from the more charismatic actors who drive the action, and this detached observer painstakingly reveals the weaknesses of the stronger men—all the while strengthening a grand alliance that simultaneously underwrites and conscripts his detached protagonist. At the heart of each tale is a claim for the privilege of Being: the narrator keeps himself at a philosophical remove from actors who are beholden to a compromising "we" by forging a larger accord.

In this chapter, I explore the detachment of an "I" from a Korean "we" in Kim's first novel, *The Martyred* (1964). Set during the Korean War, the novel presents a crisis of Christian faith which ultimately frees its narrator to conduct his own solitary journey. Kim's presentation of the war takes little notice of the battlefield or the political negotiations between North and South, East and West; instead, *The Martyred* recounts a moral struggle. In tracing Kim's construction of an existential crisis against the backdrop of military intrigue, this chapter analyzes Kim's presentation of the war as an American interest backed by a history of Christian alignment between the two nations. The friendly preserves US interests in order to emerge as a new kind of "I" who, by the book's end, faces the unknown across the Pacific.

I

The Martyred opens with the arrival of the war:

> The war came early one morning in June of 1950, and by the time the North Koreans occupied our capital city, Seoul, we had already left our university, where we were instructors in the History of Human Civilization. I joined the Korean Army, and Park volunteered for the Marine Corps—the proud combat outfit that suited his temperament. In a short time— because junior officers died very fast in the early phase of the war—we were trained and battle-tested, and we both became officers. We survived, but we were both wounded. The shrapnel of a mortar shell had grazed my right knee during the defense of Taegu, and a sniper had shot Park in his left arm in the mopping-up operation in Seoul after the Inchon landing.

We both spent some time in the hospital, were both promised medals, and were returned promptly to our respective
duties. (1)

This rapid-fire opening introduces us to our narrator and his proud
friend, whose careers parallel each other from civilian to military life: from university instructors to junior officers, both are
wounded, patched up, and promised medals. Over the course of
the novel, however, these initially twinned young men will experience a profound divergence, and only one of them will survive
the war.

The bulk of the novel is set during a brief and extraordinary period
of the Korean War: the three-month occupation of Pyongyang, the
northern capital, by South Korean, US, and UN forces.[3] In the wake
of MacArthur's successful surprise landing at Inchon—a dramatic
reversal that checked the enemy's advance—South Korean and
allied forces pushed northward, all the way to the Manchurian border, until Chinese troops entered the fight and forced a headlong
retreat. The occupation of Pyongyang from October to December
1950 stands as "the only instance throughout the cold war period of
'rollback' in action, that is, the military occupation of a communist
territory by anticommunist forces led by the United States."[4] This
single instance of rollback was a failure, and the subsequent abandonment of rollback as a strategy by the Truman administration
marks the end of one era of warfare—exemplified by MacArthur's
drive toward conquering victory—and the beginning of a new era
of containment, which did not breach borders, but rather sought to
harden them.

Delving into this brief, unsettled period, Kim weaves a complex tale of intrigue. Upon his release from the hospital, Captain
Lee, the young narrator, is assigned to "Army Political Intelligence"
(1), whose headquarters are established in Pyongyang in the wake

of its capture by Southern forces. Lee describes their reception in the city:

> for the first few weeks I was in a state of buoyancy, partly because of the exciting novelty of finding myself in an enemy city that our victorious Army occupied, and partly because of the irresistible enthusiasm and affection with which the people of the city greeted all of us, their liberators. (2)

Lee's "state of buoyancy" is composed of two parts: he is both occupier of an enemy city and liberator of its friendly people. The "exciting novelty" of occupation belongs to the thrill of rollback, but the people's "irresistible enthusiasm and affection" remind us that we are in a civil war.

In the careful division of Lee's heady feelings, we may identify two different orders of conflict layered together: the war against communism and the war to reunite a divided nation. The South Korean leadership bound anticommunism to civil war, but the former was the only concern of the United States, for whom Korea became a testing ground for a new global contest between capitalist and communist blocs. Lee's sentiment showcases the alignment between the two types of conflict—but they did not always make a perfect match. These two kinds of war belonged to two different global axes: the anticommunist war pitted East against West, slave world against free; the war to reunite a divided country was, for North and South, a continuation of a nationalist struggle against Japanese occupation. Both halves of the Korean peninsula were governed by strident nationalists who achieved prominence for their resistance to Japanese imperialism, and each dreamed of reuniting the nation under his own political terms. The North-South axis of decolonization lent a fierce undercurrent to Korea's civil war: each side denounced the other as a puppet of empire, and the powerful allies of both sides stoked the fires of international and civil war.[5] In the two parts of Captain Lee's buoyancy, we witness the formal balance of these two orders of conflict: their paired construction in the sentence enforces an identity between them.

In contrast to Lee, Park's wartime experience opens a dark chasm. A letter from Park provides the novel's only glimpse of combat:

> we got into a bayonet fight with a company of North Koreans in a valley. Both sides charged and it was all right for a while—just regular hand-to-hand combat. Then somehow everything got all mixed up, and it was wild. The trouble was that it was pitch-black night and that we all spoke Korean. Devil only knew which side we were killing. Everyone was shouting in the same language, "Who are you? Who are you?" (26)

Park describes the nightmare of civil war, in which distinctions cannot hold. A black night strips away the distinction between friend and enemy; the desperate cries of "Who are you?" only reveal a single language. Park's wild scene presents a commentary on civil war: political distinctions fall away to reveal a shared problem of identification—and ultimately a shared identity. Park's parable demonstrates the invisibility of political difference at the deepest heart of the human condition; his abyss is a recognizably existential location which illustrates the futility of a fight between brothers. They fight at the expense of themselves; they lose their own identities in the chaos.

Park does not care to sustain the political distinctions lost in the fight; instead, by letting go of such distinctions, he finds a measure of peace and personal reconciliation. For Park, the nightmare of civil war ultimately dissolves the basis for all manner of distinctions, and it is unsurprising yet deeply affecting when, in the final hours of his life, he renounces worldly distinctions altogether. His critique of civil war establishes a capacity for political renunciation which makes his death an opportunity for letting go. By contrast, Lee soldiers on: he is meticulous in his distinctions, which he exacts throughout the novel—and this consistency becomes itself a virtue that preserves him. The initial parsing of his "state of buoyancy" into its component parts is thus indicative of Lee's character throughout the novel: he maintains distinctions which demonstrate his constancy, and ultimately register a deeper loyalty.

It is in the occupation of Pyongyang that a set of political and moral intrigues ensnares Lee and Park, and through the puzzle of an occupation that is at once a liberation, each comes to acquire an understanding of the war and his own role in it. The two young men befriended each other at the university, where both taught the "History of Human Civilization," but the wartime drama that arises out of occupation profoundly separates them: in a brief deathbed letter to Lee, Park announces, "I have been clinging onto the precipice of History, but I give up. I am prepared to take leave of it" (222). By contrast, Lee finds a way of enduring the trials of Cold War and civil war by identifying the matched aims of occupation and liberation; his steady gaze clarifies distinctions, and he ultimately embraces a conception of Being that belongs to history's latest and most far-reaching empire.

II

As part of the occupying force, Captain Lee is assigned to a propaganda campaign: he is to orchestrate a memorial service for Christian ministers tortured and executed by communist agents. These orders unsettle Lee, not least because his friend Park's father is among the murdered ministers. As he sets out to clarify and secure the story, Lee encounters a young protegé of Park's father who was incarcerated along with the murdered men, and has become deranged as a result. Regarding the ravaged face of the young minister, Lee recalls an earlier scene of wartime horror, when he was assigned to dig open a cave into which political prisoners had been forced by retreating communists. Working for hours before a growing band of spectators,

> At last we made an opening barely large enough for me to squeeze through into the black mouth of the cave. Something gave way under my boots—I had stumbled on a corpse. With a shiver I stood dazed in the darkness, nauseated by the hellish stench of decomposition and excrement, aware of faint groans and a whimpering that seemed no longer human. Something touched my arm; in a frenzy, I seized it, a human hand almost skeletal, and edged toward the opening and out into the world, pulling, carrying, dragging a man. And there he was, out in the flooding sunshine, lying on his back, his hollow eyes wide open, his spent flesh shrouded in tattered, rotting clothes, oblivious of everything around him as though his soul had not been dug out of the cave with his body. And I, too, was oblivious of everything, everyone around me as I squatted down beside him. Then I came to and saw them, those photographers, and heard the sharp, metallic clicking of the shutters of their cameras. A strange, terrible shame seized me, and I crouched over the man, staring into the limbo of his leaden eyes, as if trying to shield with my body the mute dignity of his suffering from the nonchalant prying eyes behind the cameras. (19)

The scene ends with Lee "blind with rage," "chasing those cold eyes from my man" (20). Lee doubly saves this barely living man: first,

RICHARD E. KIM'S *THE MARTYRED*

from the nightmare of his living interment; second, from the cameras. Lee experiences a strange communion with this skeletal figure—both are oblivious to the scene around them—and then comes to claim him as "my man." The shame and then the rage Lee cannot contain are products of his attachment; shielding this body from "cold eyes," he refuses to turn his man's suffering into an image to be manipulated and consumed by others.

It is unfathomably hellish inside the cave, but the scene outside the cave transforms the nightmare within into a source of shame and rage. In this stark presentation of the coldness of the camera eye, we are given a piercing indictment against propaganda: to capture human suffering for political use is the ultimate act of degradation. As he recalls this terrible memory while regarding the young minister, Lee remarks, "I do not know what it was about him that pierced my heart, but suddenly I felt again the same rage" (19). Like the figure from the cave, the fragility of the young minister pierces Lee's heart, and the rage that follows belongs to the second rush of feeling against the cold eyes. This time, however, Lee's assignment places him in the group of spectators, and in this new role, he cannot shield this young man.

In pursuing his assignment, Lee finds himself caught between two charismatic figures: his superior officer Colonel Chang, who is the most eager to sell the story of the martyrs; and Reverend Shin, the only other survivor of the ordeal, whose mysterious rectitude suggests that there is more to the story. *The Martyred* constructs a series of parallels between the colonel and the minister: both are singularly devoted to their calling, which they pursue with great severity and fervor. At the heart of the contest between Chang and Shin is a problem: the supposed purity of the martyrs. Over the course of the novel, we discover what both men knew from the start: the ministers, rather than stoically facing death, begged for their lives and abjured their faith. Colonel Chang is a skeptic, disdainful of

Christianity, but his political interests require the perfect piety of the martyrs; Reverend Shin, the only sane witness to the martyrs' last days, seeks to protect their virtue.

Colonel Chang vehemently defends his office. After presenting the argument of the propaganda campaign—"we are fighting this war for the glorious cause of our independence, our liberty, and, to make the matter more complicated, for the interest and preservation of our democratic system of government" (121–22)—he spells out the alternative: the wretched truth that

> this war is just like any other bloody war in the stinking history of idiotic mankind, that it is nothing but the sickening result of a blind struggle for power among the beastly states, among the rotten politicians and so on, that thousands of people have died and more will die in this stupid war, for nothing, for absolutely nothing, because they are just innocent victims, helpless pawns in the arena of cold-blooded, calculating international power politics. (122)

In placing "our independence" and "our democratic system of government" against "cold-blooded, calculating international power politics," Chang makes an impassioned claim for the high-minded interests of the people against the base machinations of cold warriors.

It is thus Chang's mission to fabricate "moral talks" (121) in order to shield "a bevy of sweet old ladies and housewives or a flock of young students" (122) from the cold of the international contest, and in so doing, he transforms them into something more than "innocent victims, helpless pawns": through the propaganda campaign, they may mature from helpless innocents to political crusaders. In Chang's view, popular mobilization shelters the people from the larger context of the Cold War, which would render their hardship meaningless. Chang's argument reveals the desperate plight of those burning at the global periphery of the Cold War: they must detach themselves from the international context which inflames their struggle, because to comprehend this "cold-blooded" frame would plunge them into despair.

Chang concludes his defense by saying, "The important thing, as far as I am concerned and as far as this job goes, is to tell them what is necessary for them to know, and what is demanded of them by this collective body called the state" (122). Yet this "collective body" is a particularly vexed formation: not only is this state roiled in civil war, the fact of political occupation adds a coercive undercurrent to his endeavors. In the context of rollback, the twofold project elaborated by Colonel Chang—arming the people with democratic political values and shielding them from the coldness of the international war—acquires a new political dimension: old ladies, housewives, and students are indoctrinated to serve an occupying force. When Chang yokes the people to the interests of the state, he reveals the priority of the state, which does not function to serve the people, but instead enlists them within the larger political contexts obscured by Chang's propaganda. The political maturation he espouses is, finally, an instrument of war: he is attacking the enemy state by mobilizing and blinkering its people.

Chang makes clear that the campaign to consecrate martyrs serves martial aims: as Chang explains to Lee, "What you don't understand is that there should be no doubt about the glory of the martyrs. They were good and saintly. Why? Because they *are* martyrs. Because they were murdered by the Reds. It is as simple as that" (86). Chang sacrifices the martyrs themselves to the interests of the state, and from his circular reasoning—the martyrs are good because they were martyred—we may register a tautology at the heart of his broader defense of the propaganda campaign: the people are to be manipulated because they are pawns in a much larger game.

If Colonel Chang ultimately sacrifices the people to the state, Reverend Shin sacrifices himself. Shin redeems his fallen colleagues by claiming to have betrayed them: though we discover that he was spared because he was the only one who defied their captors, Shin falsely confesses to betraying the others in order to purify them in the eyes of their followers. Shin confesses over and over again: first to a group of fellow ministers, then to his congregation, and then to congregations throughout the North. Shin's brand of sacralization magnifies the suffering of the martyred: to his congregation, he cries out his confession and then presents an astonishing narrative. As Lee notes, "To my surprise—and uneasiness—Mr. Shin, for the next twenty minutes or so, described to the congregation in the minutest detail how each minister was tortured, one after another, all twelve of them" (138). When the congregation revolts—one woman cries out, "You—a sinner! How dare you defile our martyrs!" (139)—Shin sternly rebukes them, shouting, "Sinners! Weaklings! Can you not share with your martyrs their suffering!" (139). Hushed, the congregation attends to the rest of Shin's terrible revelations, and the service concludes with an ecstatic repentance, in which the congregants fall to their knees.

In Shin's gruesome telling, we recall Lee's memory of the skeletal man pulled from the cave—but while Lee instinctively shielded his man from prying eyes, Shin parades the physical torment endured by his fellow clergymen. Lee lashed out at the camera's coldly sensational gaze, but Shin forces his congregation to see. In detailing their torture, Shin revives the martyrs in a way unimaginable to Lee: Shin's religious frame elevates suffering into a uniting virtue. In the light of Shin's Christian context, we see that Lee's memory could itself be redeemed: Lee's man clearly recalls Lazarus, but Lee's lack of faith makes his revival impossible. Yet Lee's rage against the cameras reveals a missing context for Shin's revival as well: in publicizing their suffering, Shin delivers his martyrs to the propaganda campaign. The cry of the woman against the defiling of the martyrs reminds us of Lee's disgust at publicizing suffering in the service of political aims. In brandishing the suffering of the martyred, Shin brings his congregation to its knees: he elevates the murdered men by reducing himself and his people to cowed, lowly sinners.

Shin's extraordinary performance earns him newfound respect from Colonel Chang as well as from Park, who has returned to the city to uncover the fate of his father, one of the martyred. Before the war, Park rebelled against his father's faith and was disowned as an apostate. Upon his return, Park falls under Shin's spell and finds himself serving Shin's cause. Park explains his change of heart to Lee: "It is Mr. Shin, don't you see?" Park says to his perplexed friend. "He persuaded me to go to the elders of my father's congregation. . . . Many will think that my return to my father, to my father's faith, is a miracle, as it were, born of the sacrifice of my father and the ministers" (154). Lee objects to Park's new fervor:

> "Why didn't you tell him you couldn't do it? How can you, when you don't believe in what you are doing?
>
> " 'Then, pretend,' he said to me," Park whispered. "Pretend!"
>
> "But why! Why!"
>
> "For the people, don't you see?" he said passionately. "For the poor, suffering, tortured people, can't you see?" (154)

Under Reverend Shin's guidance, Park sets out to tell a comforting lie in the service of the people: Park's return to the church is emptied of belief; conspiring with Shin, he manufactures a performance meant to succor the people. In Park's new religion, the people trump faith and in fact permit a desecration of religious belief: the interests of the people make a virtue of pretense.

In playing the prodigal son, Park sacrifices himself to "the poor, suffering, tortured people," because he belongs to them. Park's allegiance to the people reveals a significant political distinction between Park and Lee: while Lee's arrival in Pyongyang was balanced between occupation and liberation, for Park, it was a homecoming. Park's description of the chaos of combat stripped the war of its political frameworks, and his ultimate loyalty to the people turns a blind eye to the logic of war. The civil war finally divides these matched young men, even though they fight on the same side: Park claims an allegiance to the people that simply disregards the facts of occupation and liberation—and his attachment undermines the political machinations that drive both terms.

In contrast to the growing separation between Park and Lee, the novel plots a rapprochement between Colonel Chang and Reverend Shin. As Chang puts it, Shin "had his church and its reputation to protect and I had my state and its cause to guard. What I failed to realize was that he and I had a legitimate common interest to look after in this little affair" (130). Each fiercely protects and guards a collective entity, and the "little affair" of the martyrs reveals deep-seated similarities between them. In fact, one cause verges into the other. Near the end of the book, we see Shin marching in the street, taking part in an anticommunist rally "in the spirit of the twelve martyrs" (204); and Chang himself becomes a devotee of Shin's cause—when we learn of his death at the end of the book, we discover that he has left money for the purchase of Bibles for northern refugees. Neither man survives at the end of the book; both die for their causes.

Chang, Shin, and Park all express their subservience to a "we," and they each engage in deceptive acts aimed to protect the collectives they serve. In serving the people, Park claims them—but Lee only possesses the man he pulled from the cave. The widening rift between the two young men makes evident both the sway of the collective, and the singularity of Lee's detachment from them. While the other men guard their collectives, Lee shields his single man. We may read Lee's jealous guardianship of his man as not only a critique of propaganda, but also an inability to comprehend the interests of the people: against Park's feeling for the suffering mass, Lee shares the existential limbo of the man pulled from the deathly pit. In guarding against the deceptive uses of propaganda, Lee communes only with "the limbo of his leaden eyes"—a look which reveals an existence emptied of everything but the dull and vicious fact of war. We may read Lee's shame and rage as mute responses to war in the absence of a transforming passion capable of reviving the dead. Lee's bitter, empty feelings register the brutal truth that, as Chang put it, "more will die in this stupid war, for nothing, for absolutely nothing."

III

As the military propaganda campaign lines up with the beautiful fiction of Christian martyrdom, Lee reflects that

> I had been tricked into a sort of nice little game, in which both the pursuer and the pursued skillfully staged a clever play of intrigues, of plots and counterplots, all this only to reveal that they were fellow conspirators, after all. (145)

These "fellow conspirators" significantly echo a modern history of intertwined political and Christian aims in Korea. Protestant missionaries from the United States famously ingratiated themselves with the Korean court in the late nineteenth century, and over the course of the twentieth century, Christianity established itself as the religion of both the political elite and the dispossessed.[6] The church "was closely allied with a progressive reform movement in late Confucian Korea (1884–1905) and with nationalist activism in the colonial era (1905–1945)."[7] Indeed, despite missionaries' attempts to separate their religion from political turmoil, Christian churches became "a political training ground" for Korean nationalists during Japan's occupation.[8] With Korea's 1945 division, Christianity became a vital component of the South's political allegiance to the United States. The mass exodus of Christians from the North in the years before and during the Korean War attests to Christianity's identification with the US-backed South.[9] In the wake of the war, Christian refugees from the North vociferously denounced the Northern regime, and these strident anticommunists rose up the ranks of the Southern leadership.[10]

The northern regions of the country were particularly fertile ground for Christianity; because of a long history of missionaries in the region and a wealth of charismatic converts who grew sizable congregations, in the early twentieth century Pyongyang was known as "the Jerusalem of Korea."[11] In fact, Park's father's church, the Central Presbyterian Church, has a storied past: its legendary minister was a leader of the Great Revival of 1907, in which an outpouring of declarations of faith swept through the population.[12] These searing expressions of devotion convinced formerly skeptical missionaries that the natives were capable of true belief,[13] and revival followed revival: another great wave took place in the years immediately after the end of Japan's occupation. The revival led by Reverend Shin thus belongs to an established practice of charismatic Christian leaders; he follows a method proven to mobilize the people.

The Martyred registers the significance of Christianity for American interests. When Captain Lee is first given his assignment to investigate the martyred ministers, he immediately identifies its larger import: "You are suggesting that it may be good material for propaganda," he says to Colonel Chang. "A grave case of religious persecution by the Communists. Of international significance, if I may add, sir, particularly in America" (6–7). Chang waves off this bit of reasoning, but he goes on to lambast the wartime influence of Christians: "Everyone seems to be Christian nowadays; it seems fashionable to be one. From the President to cabinet ministers, generals, colonels, all the way down to privates. Why, even the Army has to have Christian chaplains, just to please the American advisors" (7–8). In discussing their mission, Lee and Chang identify the Americans as the true audience of the propaganda campaign. Hence, though Lee muses at the conclusion of the campaign that he "had been tricked into a sort of nice little game" by "fellow conspirators," the conspiratorial relation between Christianity and American interests was clear from the start.

Further, despite his critique of "plots and counterplots," Lee finds himself complicit in a far more damaging maneuver: the impending military evacuation of Pyongyang. The novel binds the resolution of its Christian intrigue to a new military operation—one which does not assuage the people, but simply abandons them. Even as plans are made for the memorial for the fallen ministers, Lee learns that Chinese forces have smashed through their lines, and a general retreat from the north is imminent. Under orders from above, Lee keeps this secret—even though, as he puts it, "I felt sick to find myself forced into taking part in this grand deception, as it were; and I was ashamed" (147–48). This "grand deception" reframes the dilemma of the martyrs: in the face of retreat, the drama surrounding the Christian ministers is rendered a futile, academic exercise. It ultimately does not matter whether the propaganda campaign succeeds—and, on the eve of their abandonment, the revival effort to mobilize the masses itself seems deceptive. In the end, the central drama of the novel is only a "nice little game" that unmasks the illusory aims of an occupying force: the grand mystery of faith opened by the propaganda campaign is a product of rollback—and its existential questions retreat along with the occupying forces.

In its utter detachment from the interests of the people, the military retreat reveals American interests. Against the clamor of the ROK leadership, which exhorted its allies to push on with the fight, Truman's administration drew the line to harden a division that neither Korean side wanted. Although Lee critiques the propaganda campaign, he remains faithful to the military deception— even when UN leaflets falsely promising democratic victory are dropped over the land. Lee keeps himself apart from Chang's and Shin's campaigns, but he holds fast to a larger alliance. In light of this "grand deception," then, we may reframe Lee's isolation from the people as itself an alignment with the United States. Lee critiques both military propaganda and Korean Christianity for seeking to curry favor with the Americans; yet he protects American interests at the expense of the people.

Cast in the shadow of the retreat, the final portion of *The Martyred* moves toward a singular denouement, in which both the weary populace and demanding congregants fall away. After Shin's two confessions—the first to fellow ministers, the second to his congregation—the minister makes a third, private confession to Lee in the waning days of the occupation. In a feverish exchange, Shin reveals that he himself does not believe and sees nothing after death—but he continues his work for the people in order to fight despair. When Lee asks, "What about you? What about your despair?" Shin cries, "That is my cross!" The faithless minister adds, "I must bear that alone." This revelation finally moves Lee—he embraces Shin, saying, "Forgive me! I have been unjust to you!" (185)—and releases a hidden reserve of feeling:

> And for the first time since the war, I abandoned myself to uncontrollable tears, my tears, my contrition—for my parents,

for my countrymen, and for those many unknown souls I had destroyed. (186)

This scene presents a perversion of confession—a negative image of Christian revival—but it also powerfully recalls Shin's previous performances, all of which inspire his auditors to acknowledge their own conduct. Perhaps we may read this final confession as Shin's greatest sacrifice:[14] he offers up his own belief in order to move the dispassionate Captain Lee. When Shin reveals his apostasy, Lee asks for forgiveness, conceding, "I have been unfair to you." Moved to contrition and tears, Lee follows the form of revival even in the absence of belief. In this strange scene, religious forms take in profane content.

This dark communion recalls Lee's shielding of his suffering man: in both cases, Lee is moved by gazing into solitary emptiness. Lee's tears have no redemptive value, and abandonment is itself a politically charged term in the context of military retreat: Lee's expression of abandoning himself significantly ties his individual action to the larger movement dictated by the American military leadership. Indeed, Lee's self-abandonment emerges out of a context overdetermined by American influence, given that the conversation between Lee and Shin takes place over a shared meal in Lee's quarters: "I had canned food and I could make some tea. I invited him to join me, if he did not mind tasting canned American food" (182). Shin's blasphemous confession belongs to the world of American orders and rations—and it is in this context that each man identifies a solitary burden. Lee later shares the secret of the military retreat with Shin, but the minister ultimately refuses to retreat. Lee takes his final leave of Shin at his church, and as Lee withdraws, he remarks, "I closed the door, leaving behind me the murmuring voices of those who had their god and the one who loved them" (206). Lee's final vision of Shin is thus a portrait of abandonment, in which Lee closes the door on Shin's devotion to his people to walk away, alone.

The Martyred generates a structure of persecution and revival that its protagonist interrogates and ultimately empties. The culmination of this hollowing-out of Christian redemption takes place when Lee finally departs from the city. He is part of the final convoy out of Pyongyang, after which the bridge to the city is bombed by American soldiers to halt enemy forces. As Lee nears the bridge, we hear Americans for the first time in the novel: Kim writes, "English mingled with Korean. Planes flew overhead in the dark heavens" (211). Upon hearing "a series of shattering explosions," we see the Americans:

> A few parka-clad American soldiers in the truck ahead of my jeep were looking out of the canvas cover. A voice cried out, "There goes the God-damned bridge!" Another shouted, "Oh, Jesus! Look at that!" I got out of my jeep and looked back toward Pyongyang. The doomed city was in flames. (211)

In their loose, profane way, the American soldiers identify the city as the ultimate martyr, as Christ himself. The casual blasphemy of these American voices mimics and undercuts the narrative of martyrdom laid out in the novel. Pyongyang will burn, but it will never be redeemed.

The fact that American soldiers voice these sentiments reveals an aspect of the occupation of Pyongyang largely unseen in the novel. *The Martyred* considers a failed occupation within the framework of spiritual renunciation, but the presence of the US at this critical juncture unmasks this occupation—which was no less brutal than those conducted by northern forces[15]—as an imperial one. Though Lee can match occupation to liberation in the context of civil war, US involvement can only be read as a colonial foray into enemy territory. The forsaken city, irredeemable within the novel's Christian context, lays bare the Cold War alliance—and as Lee looks on helplessly, American voices spell out the end of a failed program of rollback.

American influence is nowhere more evident that in the military retreat, and this large-scale movement instigates Lee's inward retreat. Shin's final confession refocuses Lee: no longer a reluctant witness to political maneuvers couched in religious terms, Lee moves into the center of the tale to ponder his own morality—but this individual focus is just as inseparable from the larger political context of the war. The conclusion of *The Martyred* is consumed by Lee's solitary journey, and he caps his self-exploration with another American meal: "On that Christmas Eve I withdrew early to my quonset hut, where I had a solitary supper of American rations. I was reading a Japanese translation of Aurelius' *Meditations*" (212). This "solitary supper" ties together multiple strands in the novel. In reading the private diary of a Roman emperor who contemplated stoic virtue in his daily life, Lee arrives at a discovery of Western, non-Christian morality. That Lee reads Aurelius on Christmas Eve clearly establishes his preference for stoic over Christian virtue, pragmatic survival over sacrifice.

Christmas Eve, 1950 marks the final retreat of US, UN, and ROK forces from North Korea. In reading Roman philosophy at the very end of a failed occupation, Lee confirms the insufficiency of Christian revival. Moreover, Lee is reading in Japanese, a reminder of the last occupation. Learning Japanese was one of many colonial policies, and privileged students went to Japan for their advanced studies. This small detail of translation is the only mention of the colonial period in the novel, and its presence on this of all days suggests that Americans rations may not be so different from Japanese translation—both are evidence of imperial rule. Imagined alongside Japan's occupation, the three-month-long occupation of North Korea is itself unmasked as an imperial venture.

Lee's solitary journey is framed by two American meals—the first with Shin, and the second with his copy of Aurelius—and so American sustenance nourishes his personal retreat, and Lee's individual development is an American one, free from the novel's more labored attempts at an alliance routed through Christianity. In denouncing propaganda meant to serve American interests, Lee takes on a truth-telling role which ultimately secures a deeper relation to the West. Both propaganda and Christian campaigns are, in Lee's eyes, compromised by their subservience to a "we"—whether the state, the church, or American interests. In fact, Lee more directly serves American interests in keeping the general retreat a secret, and this "grand deception" significantly serves his own interests as well. Lee closes the door on Shin because the minister stays back at his own expense—but it is through the retreat that Lee discovers an American "I."

IV

Between Shin's self-renunciation and Lee's retreat stands a minor character who appears in Pyongyang in the last days of the occupation. As the impending evacuation reorders the text, we meet Major Minn, an Army doctor who transforms Lee's headquarters into a field hospital, only to discover that his patients will be left behind in the evacuation. Minn explains his devotion to his patients: "I am not trying to be holy or brave. I am just trying to be decent" (210). Later, Minn breaks from the final convoy out of Pyongyang to return to the fallen city; turning his jeep back, he "roared back into the city" (211). Unlike Shin, who refuses to evacuate in order to minister to his people, Minn is a moral actor who turns back under the banner of decency and not religiosity: the good doctor serves the people without the deception employed by the minister.

Major Minn has a literary precedent: Albert Camus's Doctor Rieux in *The Plague* (1948), a figure of simple decency who attends to his patients in extraordinary circumstances.[16] *The Plague* provides case studies of a handful of men as they confront this unthinkable yet familiar pestilence. Kim's distillation of Camus's famous doctor in *The Martyred* reflects his admiration for Camus, to whom Kim dedicated his book: "To the memory of Albert Camus, whose insight into 'a strange form of love' overcame for me the nihilism of the trenches and bunkers of Korea." Kim cites from Camus's meditation on solidarity through rebellion, *The Rebel*, and Kim has lifted the epigraph from Camus's book for his own.[17] *The Rebel* and *The Martyred* thus share an identical epigraph, a quotation from Hölderlin's *The Death of Empedocles*:

> And openly I pledged my heart to the grave and suffering land, and often in the consecrated night, I promised to love her faithfully until death, unafraid, with her heavy burden of fatality, and never to despise a single one of her enigmas. Thus did I join myself to her with a mortal cord.

The pledge binds the speaker to the land in a nighttime ceremony. Kim's dedication to Camus is premised on a "strange form of love" which pledges the "I" to "the grave and suffering land," and the epigraph describes a marriage between the speaker and the land, joined together "with a mortal cord." In *The Martyred*, those who love the land "faithfully until death" do not survive: Chang's devotion to the state dooms him, as does Shin's devotion to the people. It is through the late introduction of Doctor Minn that we finally discover a character who can declare his love for the land without the ruses that compromise the others—but Minn, too, is lost once he turns his jeep back into the city, because the city itself has been forsaken.

By contrast, Lee is ultimately a figure of retreat: the novel begins in the northern capital and moves ever southward—Lee is wounded again outside Seoul and sent to recuperate in the southern port city of Pusan, and the novel concludes on an island off the southern coast. If we read Lee's movement against the progression of the Korean War, which saw the line of fighting move up and down the peninsula, we see that Lee never breaks from his southward drive. And for Lee, to travel south ultimately becomes a means of traveling toward the West: he turns away from the people toward an imperial power across the Pacific. Kim's protagonist thus eludes the mortal cord that would bind him to the land, and the "I" Kim discovered on his passage to America is a world away from these men who pledge themselves unto death.

The Martyred ultimately reframes a political and military failure as an act of renunciation. Kim traces religious forms into profane content, from Shin's confession of faithlessness to the abandonment of Pyongyang. The Cold War alliance between South Korea and the United States reinforces all of the ideological maneuvers within the text, whether military or religious, but what is perhaps most striking about the novel is how carefully Kim shields his protagonist from political aims while framing him within the larger political alliance. Captain Lee is a renegade who remains aloof from the novel's "plots and counterplots," and he comes into his own at the end of the three-month-long occupation: like the political calculations that renounced rollback, Lee understands that to bind himself to occupied land would be utter folly.

The Martyred won acclaim for its existential dimension: reviewing the novel for *The New York Times*, Chad Walsh claimed that Kim's "purpose here is not to tell the deeds of war but to probe the involutions and ambiguities of conscience—the meaning of suffering and of evil and holiness, the uncertain boundaries between illusion and truth." Similarly, in his *Los Angeles Times* review, Robert R. Kirsch applauded the novel for delving into a "second plane," in which "we see these men as allegorical figures, taking their meaningful and symbolic roles in a modern passion play, roles with which we who live in the modern world play as well." Rave reviews of *The Martyred* propelled it up to number five on *The New York Times* bestseller list; *The Martyred* was nominated for the National Book Award, and it occasioned a flurry of adaptations—into drama, film, and opera.

The sensational reception of *The Martyred* applauds the "I" Kim discovered in English—and marks the unfathomable distance he has traveled from the Korean "we." Kim has transcended the "deeds of war" through an inward exploration which elevates his tale of military intrigue onto a "second plane." The allegorical resonance of *The Martyred* freed the novel from its minor setting: the novel was heralded for rising above the distant skirmish of Korea to blossom into a "modern passion play." *The Martyred* was not received as a novel about Korea or its war; instead, the critics identified it as a triumph "written in the great moral and psychological tradition of Job, Dostoevsky, and Albert Camus."[18] Kim's lofty achievement was to write *The Martyred* in the language of the Self reborn in the Pacific; he transposed a faraway war into a Western key.

For a brief time, Richard Kim was hailed as "the most well-known Korean writer in the world"[19]—but his fame did not last and *The Martyred* fell into obscurity and out of print. Published in 1964, *The Martyred* preceded the ethnic nationalist movement of the late 1960s, when the term "Asian American" was born. Asian American studies has unearthed and claimed a growing canon of literary texts written before the movement, but *The Martyred* is not an obvious candidate for this body of literature. Kim's novel depicts a very different kind of Asian American from the now-familiar minority subject fashioned out of a discourse of exclusion within

the United States. Not only is *The Martyred* set in Korea, its protagonist is, at best, proto-American. Yet the novel itself is entirely
American, and its literary aspirations and existential sensibilities
were not only recognized, but celebrated, by American audiences.
By writing on an allegorical plane, Kim achieved an alliance free
from the modes of dependence that compromise the central actors
of his novel: his novel is finally not bound to a state or a religion—
instead, it installed itself within the Western tradition.

Remarkably, after decades out of print, Penguin Classics issued
a reprint of *The Martyred* in 2011. Susan Choi's foreword to the
novel recounts her own discovery of Kim's forgotten work: though
she was presented with a first edition of *The Martyred* in 1998, at a
reading of her novel *The Foreign Student* (by an elderly man whom
she falsely assured that she knew the book) it remained unopened
on her bookshelf for the next twelve years. Choi recounts her reluctance to read Kim's novel:

> All these years walking around with a Korean last name, scrib-
> bling and publishing stories—and now just as success is in
> reach, this grandfather whom no one has mentioned turns
> out to have done it all first, and is crashing the party? Richard
> E. Kim had never been discussed at the Asian American read-
> ing group, he had never appeared on the syllabus. (xiii–xiv)

Never discussed at the Asian American reading group, never on the
syllabus, yet reclaimed as a Penguin Classic: a fitting retrieval for a
book that confounds the established category of Asian American
literature. Choi's response to finally reading the novel echoes
the plaudits it garnered in 1964: "In *The Martyred* Kim forges a
drama of such devastating universality that an electrifying sense
of recognition binds us to the page" (xiv–xv). The universality that
Kim forged out of an existential alliance electrifies all these years

later—the intervening years, in which Asian American literature became a studied category, only make *The Martyred* more astonishing for its attempt to fashion a morality play steeped in the Western tradition out of a distant skirmish in the Far East.

The Martyred is a strange and elegant book. Kim tells an inner drama: he creates a protagonist embroiled in the politics of proxy war yet impatient with a proxy identity, one who at once transcends and secures political aims to strike a deeper accord with the West. In order to find his way to America, this Korean War friendly discovers a way to inhabit an unequal relation. *The Martyred* is finally a complex expression of allegiance which fashions an American consciousness out of a neocolonial relation. And Kim's high literary gestures—most evident in the dedication to Camus—map his protagonist's southern journey onto his Western one. The universality he forges is a literary resonance capable of transcending propaganda campaigns via an existential gravitas. *The Martyred*'s "devastating universality" rewrites the abandonment of rollback and the implementation of containment into grand literary terms. Kim's fevered, inward drama thus presents a defining shift in Cold War foreign policy via a native informant who charts his own way to the postwar superpower.

Captain Lee is a new kind of friendly, one elevated out of this distant battlefield of the Cold War to claim an allegorical identification with the West. Richard E. Kim's aesthetics of alliance delivers his South Korean officer to an American readership. The seeming depoliticization of Captain Lee presents a corrective to American fantasies of political betrayal by these lesser allies, and Kim's portrait of a young man disillusioned by the politics of civil war, yet capable of protecting superpower interests, remakes the friendly to serve a grander alignment. A decade after the unpopular war and years before the revolutionary creation of Asian American studies—whose literary luminaries enshrined an aesthetics of political resistance—Kim's portrait of the friendly as an ethical soldier stands as a singular and long-lost potential for alliance. Captain Lee's distaste for local propaganda campaigns purifies his character, despite his ultimate abandonment of Pyongyang. Indeed, this betrayal lies at the heart of his friendly qualifications: forsaking his people is the buried yet central condition for the friendly soldier, whose ultimate isolation is the only guarantee of his fitness for friendship.

The book closes with Lee's visit to a tent church for northern refugees on an island near Pusan, and the final paragraph ends on the shore:

> I walked away from the church, past the rows of tents where silent suffering gnawed at the hearts of people—my people—and headed toward the beach, which faced the open sea. There a group of refugees, gathered under the starry dome of the night sky, were humming in unison a song of homage to their homeland. And with a wondrous lightness of heart hitherto unknown to me, I joined them. (228)

It is in this final passage that we discover that Lee, too, claims "my people"—and yet it is the "open sea" which lures him, and once on the beach, he joins refugees separated from those suffering in the tents. Lee's "wondrous lightness of heart" is foreign to the mortal cord that binds others to the land; instead, this lightness properly belongs to the "unknown" that Kim embraced in the light of the Western sun. In singing the song of the refugees, Lee echoes his author's exile: he faces the ocean and the land on its far shore.

3

Loving Freedom in Susan Choi's
The Foreign Student

Susan Choi's 1998 novel *The Foreign Student* concludes with a homecoming:

> When he found his family in Pusan his mother shooed him away from the door, because she thought he was a beggar. He had recoiled from her rebuke, gone down the street, and sat against a wall for hours before he went and knocked again. And yet he hadn't been angry or frightened, but only relieved. His cowardice, his weakness and sickness, were all swept away. In his mother's failure to recognize him, his duty to his family was done; and the suspicion that he had, despite shame and uncertainty, secretly harbored all along—that this could not be his life, that this war would never define him—finally proved to be right. And although his mother had wept that night, endlessly, and found food to give him, and washed his clothes, and sat clinging to his hands until he simply fell asleep in front of her, and although he went the next day to the USIS offices in Pusan and got a job, and spent the next two years, until the cease-fire, translating wire—consuming it, as if it could give him a new frame for thinking, a new lexicon—he was already gone, at that moment. He was already free. (324–25)

A mother's misrecognition and rejection transforms her son; when she turns him away, he is simply "gone." He is free to live a new life, governed by "a new frame for thinking, a new lexicon."

This closing passage was, in fact, the kernel of the novel. Choi has identified this passage as a distillation from her writing toward her MFA at Cornell University, and the beggar in the scene is an imagined rendering of her father.[1] The epic resonance of this ending marks the ambition of Choi's first novel, which reveals the odyssey of her father's wartime travails and imagines his subsequent life as a "foreign student" in America. This reunion—at once bleak and serene—transforms the figure of Choi's father: he was the scion of a prominent family, broken by the war and reduced to rags, but his utter abjection frees him to pursue a new existence. The narrative structure of *The Foreign Student* layers these lives together, moving back and forth between his wartime and American careers, and in tracing these strands, Choi concludes with the originary knot between them: the moment of his freedom.

The secret unveiled in this final passage—"that this war would never define him"—is startling because *The Foreign Student* is replete with multiple tellings and retellings of the Korean War. Choi shows us the war not only through her father's eyes, but also in vivid renderings of American military history, in which Army officers come to life in the pages of her fiction. Yet Choi closes her intricate tale with this secret truth of identity, which detaches her protagonist from the war that both severed his familial ties and launched his American career. The novel's ultimate revelation presents the extraordinary challenge at its heart: Choi set out to fashion a subject created out of war, but ultimately free from it. Her protagonist is shattered by the terrible whims of war, but through a strange alchemy he transforms his abjection into a mode of freedom. [2]

Significantly, Choi's final evocation of her father's freedom both names and eludes its political context. In the hours between first being chased away and then tearfully welcomed by his mother, his "cowardice, his weakness and sickness"—references to his prior attempts to elude military conscription and his political betrayal of his best friend, elicited by physical torture—"were all swept away"; in the freedom of his mother's rejection, he has extricated himself from the war. And yet he spends the next two years immersed in the "new lexicon" created out of, and in the service of, the Korean War. In his work with the USIS (United States Information Service), Choi's father translated American wire reports into Korean, and in Choi's words, "translating wire" becomes a means of "consuming it, as if it could give him a new frame for thinking." This "new frame" is an American discourse that created the "free world," in which Western freedom was posed against the slavery of the East; the freedom proffered by the United States promised to transport allies out of abjection and into a world of prosperity. The two phrases Choi sets off in this passage are thus curiously at odds with each other: the first revelation "that this war would never define him" sits uneasily with the "new lexicon" learned from consuming American wartime propaganda. *The Foreign Student* is balanced on this fine line between abject freedom and the "free world" promise of deliverance from abjection: Choi imagines a figure who transcends the war, yet folds himself into a wartime alliance.

With the puzzle of her protagonist's complicated freedom, Choi has set her portrait apart from what scholars of US imperialism have identified as the slogan of the postcolonial subject: "We are here because you were there."[3] These voices explain their presence within the United States by indicting imperial wars; in claiming decolonizing identities, they identify often forgotten US interventions. Choi's contrasting modes of freedom are significantly untouched by the proliferating movements that stand between her father's 1950s experience and her imaginative, late-twentieth-century rendering of it: the novel simply leaps over the global decolonization movements of the 1950s and the domestic movement politics of the 1960s. In keeping her novel free from the politics of these resistance movements, she has detached her fiction from ethnic cultural movements and the Asian American literary tradition in particular. In fact, Choi writes her separation from this tradition into her novel: *The Foreign Student* features a brief episode of pan-ethnic solidarity which seems to deliver her protagonist from his isolation, but he quickly abandons this community for a romantic entanglement. Daniel Y. Kim reads this episode to demonstrate "that the literary resources provided by the Asian American tradition are ultimately inappropriate for telling the story" of Choi's protagonist (569).[4] Her subject treasures a freedom premised on isolation, an individual understanding far removed from the clamor of ethnic solidarity.

The conclusion of—and inspiration for—*The Foreign Student* ultimately offers a neocolonial alignment that miraculously preserves the subject's integrity. Choi's protagonist is unambiguously a wartime friendly: he works as a local translator for the US propaganda offices in Seoul and Pusan. It is through this contact that he reorients his own fate, and when he has taken in the new lexicon, he launches a letter-writing campaign to become a foreign student. Foreign students were newly visible in the postwar era. The 1946 Fulbright Act funded the international exchange of students and faculty to foster "international understanding and good-will through interpersonal contact,"[5] and a panoply of civic and religious organizations followed suit.[6] In the words of a 1951 report entitled *Universities and World Affairs,* published by the Carnegie Endowment for International Peace, "the university has a stake in international affairs" because "to oppose totalitarianism is to defend the essential birthright of the university," and through foreign students "the university has a vast network of international relations all its own"[7]—a statement echoed by Senator Fulbright: "Educational exchange can turn nations into people, contributing as no other form of communication can to the human-izing of international relations."[8] The exigencies of international affairs weighed heavily on these students, who were charged with maintaining alliances. A 1952 *Foreign Affairs* article entitled "The Foreign Student in America" put it plainly: as representatives of "the nations of the free world," "we wish them to be friends of the United States."[9] Enrolled within foreign policy objectives, the foreign student had to be friendly and stay foreign; the flurry of meetings and brochures devoted to welcoming the foreign student to postwar America never considered that this figure might actually become an American.

Foreign students are everywhere in Asian American literature. Though this literary canon has been defined by a second-generation, ethnic nationalist movement—which sought and claimed proletarian literary precursors—students who ventured to study abroad significantly shaped its early literary contours.[10] The two most prominent first-generation Korean American writers were foreign students: in 1937, Younghill Kang published *East Goes West*, a picaresque account of his American studies, and Richard E. Kim, decades after graduating from Middlebury in the late 1950s, was perpetually branded as a foreign student.[11] The 1952 *Foreign Affairs* article cautioned that "the foreign student does not need to be singled out for elaborate attention," explaining that "the familiar community pattern of lionizing the student for a time and then forgetting all about him is probably harmful in both phases"[12]—a pattern familiar to these pathbreaking writers, lauded for their singularity and then quickly forgotten. The particular privilege and burden of the foreign student has marked Asian American literature from its beginnings.

The American daughter of a foreign student, Susan Choi has imagined her father's wartime experience as a means of delivering him to the land of her birth. She has defined him through the category of the foreign student, which is itself fixed in the paradox of freedom that concludes her novel. The foreign student of the Cold War is the flower of a neocolonial relation: he grows out of a profoundly unequal relationship, but he is promised the marvel of intellectual freedom. Once in America, however, he is perpetually reminded of his dependence:[13] never permitted the liberty of being a mere student, he is always singled out as a foreigner. Choi both frees and binds her father through the figure of the foreign student: he liberates himself from his family to take in the new lexicon, but in America, he is overcome by the insufficiency of his study. In Choi's novel, the foreign student perpetually studies America, both in the world he has left and in a new world of alliances—and whether he can sustain this privileged yet constricting status becomes a growing concern over the course of the novel.

This chapter interrogates the figure of the foreign student as both an emblem of Cold War integration, and an utterly foreign entity. Choi's rendering of her father's wartime experience and imagined postwar union imagines a set of US-South Korean alliances that promise to free him from the war. The novel performs a series of delicate acts of alliance, in which Korea is matched to the United States in formal terms: Choi writes her protagonist into a revisionist history of the Korean War which attempts to reframe her father's service for the United States, and, having reframed the war, she undertakes to recuperate the wartime friendly within a romantic union unsullied by the strictures of Cold War integration. Yet this affair ultimately unveils how deeply the foreign student has been touched by the war, and *The Foreign Student* uncovers a searing political betrayal at the heart of its protagonist: at the end of the novel, we learn that he has literally been tortured by minions of his powerful friends—and that he has betrayed his own friend in turn. The novel's strangely happy ending thus exposes the eviscerating effects of mapping superpower conflict onto civil war.

If *The Martyred* universalized its friendly in order to render him imaginable to an American readership, *The Foreign Student* seeks to usher this wartime friendly into American arms—and both of these writerly ventures indulge in literary excesses in order to detach their protagonists from their people. Instead of the postwar modes of liberal incorporation that would have taken in such model minorities, these novels opt for the grander—and colder—comforts of literary figuration, and both protagonists burn with questions of truth and betrayal that isolate their respective fictions from the Asian American literary canon. Like Kim, Choi performs literary high-wire acts to fashion wartime subjects who exceed the Cold War politics that integrate and contain them. These novelists unleash an arsenal of literary strategies in order to rewrite the political alliances that enable these friendlies to survive the war; they shelter their protagonists within a set of isolating maneuvers that refuse political solidarity and the comforts of the ethnic enclave in favor of a set of isolating maneuvers that reopen war wounds in the service of a deeper relation. The tortuous complexity of these attempts makes these fictions singular but also significant: narrating any war is an epistemological problem,[14] and the literary effects that run through *The Foreign Student* present a set of imaginative resources for comprehending the new subjects created out of this unpopular war.

I

The novel's prologue opens in 1950, with the protagonist's prewar memory of a more distant past: his family's annual preparations for leaving sweltering Seoul for their summer house, forever lost to the 1945 division of the peninsula. This initial memory stops short, however, and we learn instead that "Now, leaving the city, he was headed south" (2). We meet the protagonist as Seoul is set to fall to the enemy for the second time during the war; he steps onto the street to make his way southward to his parents, who have already fled to Pusan. He has prepared for his departure:

> The card in his breast pocket made a stiff place in the front of his shirt . . . He had stolen everything in the office that he could lay his hands on bearing the emblem or a recognizable mark of the United States government: a regulation T-shirt, USIS letterhead, several pieces of official correspondence that were addressed to Peterfield, and a sheet of old news off the wire. At the last minute, he went back and took Peterfield's Underwood. The black case banged rhythmically against the outside of his knee. (2–3)

He has fashioned an identity for himself, cobbled together from objects left at the USIS office—a job he will take on again when he finally arrives in Pusan—and we may read the novel as a whole as an examination of his claim to the self he has crafted in this opening.

As he walks down the street clutching his US paraphernalia, he encounters a Republic of Korea Army soldier:

> "Where are you going, to study hall?" the soldier asked. He didn't answer. They watched each other expectantly. He wondered, the thought brief but terrorizing, if they could have been schoolmates. The truck's bed held two benches, both full. The floor of the bed was also full. The twin rows of boys were seated so close together that their shoulders were forced to twist to one side. They sat facing each other over the heads of those packed between their feet. The soldier said, "Can you hear me?" Balancing the butt of his rifle, he made a light jab and knocked off Chuck's glasses. (3)

We learn the name of our protagonist through this encounter: Chuck is the name given to him by Peterfield, the American who runs the Seoul USIS office. Formerly Chang, he consented to this rechristening, which was part and parcel of his service for the American office. Though few people ever call him Chuck, the novel adheres to this new name, only identifying him as Chang in the portions of the story devoted to his prior experiences; once renamed, he cannot revert to his pre-Chuck existence.

Chuck's American identity, garnered through contact with the propaganda arm of the occupying US force, aims to transcend that of the ROK soldier, who fights with and for the Americans, but remains apart from them. The soldier is attired in "American-issue boots, which were far too large, and Republic of Korea Army fatigues" (3), and the ill-fitting boots demonstrate the paucity of the military alliance. The South Korean army was, as Choi writes later in the novel, "an American-style army" made "out of the materials at hand," a force "inarguably American apart from the fact that it consisted entirely of Koreans in oversized uniforms" (67). Discounting this identity as a sham, Chuck instead seeks to fashion a civilian alliance with the United States. Yet because the US-ROK alliance is overwritten by a military endeavor, Chuck finds himself in unknown territory.

The soldier's mocking question—"Where are you going, to study hall?"—derides Chuck as an overgrown schoolboy. His glasses and the supplies he has stolen all mark him as a student—a role he will desperately vie for a few years later, when he writes to school after school in America. To the young soldier, Chuck insists that he has an official identity:

"I have ID," he said. "I work for the wire service."

"You have papers?"

"ID." He shifted the Underwood to his left hand, casually, but he did not yet reach for his card. He squinted hard at the soldier. Could they have been schoolmates?

"I translate. I have Special Status." (3)

Working as a civilian translator for the wire service merits no papers of the type that would satisfy the soldier, but Chuck has crafted his own "Special Status" for himself. The ID he wields is a carefully wrought creation, as we discover much later in the book: Chuck has taken a playing card, to which he has added a line of type and pasted on the emblem of USIS letterhead (201). Chuck's identification is a literal fabrication, but it presents a challenge to the ROK soldier, whose ill-fitting boots reveal the tenuousness of his own identity.

The repeated suggestion that Chuck and the soldier could have been schoolmates reveals a common identity: they are both students of the United States. Both young men answer to the same master, of whom each is a lesser and ultimately unconvincing version. The novel registers this similarity, but Chuck fights to detach himself from the soldier and the young conscripts in the truck. In fact, Chuck's non-military accouterments protect him from being pulled in: the soldier

> yanked the black case from Chuck's hand. Without turning the case on its side, he snapped open the clasp and the Underwood crashed to the street. The bright black carapace cracked open, spilling the carriage and throwing forward a cluster of type bars. The soldier had leaped away from the falling machine in panic, barely saving his shoes. (3–4)

The exploding typewriter becomes a weapon as it crashes to the ground, a civilian bomb that threatens the soldier's American-issue boots. Chuck first worked for the Americans in order to acquire, as he put it to General Hodge, "A guarantee. For not being enlisted" (68)—a request the general laughed off, unable to imagine the frail young man being forced to fight. In this meeting with the ROK soldier, whose truck is packed with fresh recruits, the odds and ends taken from the USIS office save him from conscription. Shunning military enlistment, Chuck insists upon a civilian alliance with the United States, and in this scene his stolen office supplies exceed the soldier's materiel. The tools of Chuck's trade in American propaganda save him—and ultimately secure his passage to America. Chuck bests his former-schoolmate-turned-soldier by being a better student.[15]

From this prologue, the first chapter of *The Foreign Student* jumps to 1955, with Chuck's arrival at the University of the South in Sewanee, Tennessee. The novel makes a beeline from Chuck's escape from military conscription to the first night of his new career as an American student. We see Chuck as a "petrified figure" who "seemed to have dropped into the pool of porch light from outer space" (6): utterly alien, he is caught in a new spotlight. In dramatic contrast to the canny operator introduced in the prologue, Chuck is frozen "with his suitcase hanging from one hand and his overcoat over one arm" (6): taking him in, the housekeeper "unclamped the hand from the suitcase's handle and unbent the arm from beneath the drape of the overcoat" (7). The stiff and awkward figure he presents to the housekeeper hardens in America, where a new light remains trained on him. This first glimpse of Chuck in America sketches the defining image of the foreign student: he is literally petrified into an eternal pose of formality and arrival, with suitcase and coat in hand.

When he is driven to his dormitory the next morning, he understands that he has finally arrived: "He knew that the warm stone façade just ahead was the end of the dream as he'd dreamed it" (11). He has a month to himself before the fall term, and in the "presemester hush" (11) he explores and embraces his new paradise in glorious isolation—but when the semester begins, the campus is suddenly "perilous" (12):

> That first day the flagstone walk had been lined with pale, tailored, spit-shined bodies completely absorbed in themselves until Chuck grew near. He seemed to be pushing a ripple of silence ahead of himself. Everyone swiveled, and smiled, and stuck out a hand, and the hysterical idea occurred to him that he was a general inspecting his troops. This idea carried him along but it wasn't able to prevent the incessant bobbing of his head and the hand he was using to shake, and the ceremony could have absorbed the rest of the day had someone not offered to show him the bicycle rack. Although he could have found that bicycle rack in his sleep, he allowed himself to be led to it, and then into the lecture hall, where he was stood up in front of the throng, and made the occasion of a speech about America's duty. (12–13)

The pool of light has become "a ripple of silence"; the hand clamped to the suitcase now shakes hand after hand. Chuck's "hysterical idea" realigns him with the military alliance that he eschewed in the book's prologue: in his procession down the flagstone walk, we see that the formal gestures of the foreign student belong to a military ceremony.

The scene's culmination in the lecture hall spells out the political dimensions of Chuck's new role: he is a living emblem of "America's duty." If the parade of greeting reminded Chuck of a military formation, his figure before the assembled throng makes manifest a political relation. This opening day sharply marks "the end of the dream"; unlike the appearance of his dormitory, this ceremony is not "as he'd dreamed it," rather, the political spotlight fixes him in the hard shell of his foreign student status. From this initial inspection, Chuck finds his niche by keeping largely to himself, but he understands his role: if he intrigues these "worldly southern young gentlemen," it is because "they had heard a rumor that Chuck worked for army intelligence during the war" (13). Hence, though Chuck's arrival at an American university is a product of his dogged insistence on a civilian alliance, on campus he is only recognized as a military product.

In Korea, Chuck fabricated a "Special Status" for himself, and once in America, he discovers that he is unable to shake off his singularity. The recognition he fought for becomes a political burden; and if he appeared too studious in Seoul, he is never a mere student in Sewanee. The foreign student of the Cold War is perpetually rendered a product of American might and benevolence; he is always smiled at on campus—and not always elsewhere, as Chuck quickly discovers—because he is an illustration of a superpower fantasy. In the United States, he learns that he has been conscripted into a far grander entity than the truck full of boys he faced in Korea, and this order of duty requires a fixed pose and a set of gestures that Chuck finds himself making over and over again.

II

Chuck must perform the role assigned to him in the lecture hall; in the words of the imperious father of a fellow Sewanee student, he is "an emissary from a distant land" (59), an identity which protects him from potential scorn and preserves his otherness. His fellowship from the Episcopal Church Council entails giving occasional lectures at churches across the South,[16] and Chuck presents the story of the war again and again to audiences of "mostly older, charity and book-circle women, and a few intent men" (50). The war, however, resists his telling:

> He always felt hopeless, called upon to deliver a clear explanation of the war. It defied explanation. Sometimes he simply skipped over causes, and began, "Korea is a shape just like Florida. Yes? The top half is a Communist state, and the bottom half are fighting for democracy!" He would groundlessly compare the parallel to the Mason-Dixon line, and see every head nod excitedly. (51)

In the labor of telling this story, we identify an extension of the work he did for the USIS in Korea: two years on, Chuck is still selling the war, but this time for an American audience.

Chuck's instinct for comparison echoes the strategy of American policymakers, who found it no less difficult to explain the war to a domestic audience: like Chuck, they relied on analogies to explain an unprecedented kind of conflict.[17] Explanations of the Korean War are always mired in the problem of its origins; the blur of geopolitics in Asia "defied explanation" to a Western imagination that had long evacuated the region of history. Chuck's reference to the Civil War suggests a revisionist reading of the war spearheaded by historian Bruce Cumings, who has made this very comparison in order to explain the Korean War as first and foremost a war fought among Koreans.[18] Yet in Chuck's telling, this analogy detaches the war from the United States, even as it provides a recognizable contour; framed as a civil war, American intervention becomes even more difficult to understand. The revisionist argument for civil war crucially exposes the imperial dimensions of US involvement—but this is not a story Chuck can tell.

Instead, Chuck skips forward, to MacArthur's Inchon landing: "He genuinely liked talking about the landing, and MacArthur.

It all made for such an exciting, simple minded, morally unambiguous story" (52). From a Civil War analogy and the legend of MacArthur, Chuck has cobbled together an uneven story meant to appeal to conservative American audiences. The two points undermine each other—one erases American intervention and the other insists upon it—and both reflect American desires back to an American audience. Yet Chuck's audience has come to learn about Korea, and they are finally rewarded in one of the final slides Chuck has prepared: "Everyone murmured with pleasure at the image of the farmers, in their year-round pajamas and inscrutable Eskimos' faces" (52). This delight is certainly an Orientalist desire, but it also reveals the failing of Chuck's propaganda: he has pandered to American self-interest—its civil war, its hero—but he has not shown them what they really wanted to see. In telling his story, Chuck says nothing about his own experience of the war; he never ventures to provide a personal testimony, and thus remains a mere emissary. His presentation is locked in the limbo between South Korean and American propaganda—and to his audience Chuck remains as inscrutable as the Eskimo faces projected on the wall beside him.

Choi's narration, however, provides an inner glimpse of her protagonist: alongside an image of the Korean landscape, Chuck tells his audience,

> "You maybe don't believe it, but Korea, the land, looks very much like Tennessee." He gestured at the picture of hills. So much, sometimes he woke in the morning and just for an instant was sure he was home. The mist coming out from the mountains. The soft shapes of hills. (53)

Like the groundless Civil War analogy, the comparison of Korean and Tennessee hills has an effect—but not on his audience. This analogy only works on Chuck, for whom the matching shapes create a sensation of homecoming. Against the stark absence of feeling in his wartime reunion with his mother, this sinuous passage reveals Chuck's true belonging: he does not belong to his mother or even to a particular landscape, but rather, to a repeating shape. He is moved by the matching of Korea to America; his very existence is the product of mapping one country onto the other.

Indeed, Choi's narration cuts into Chuck's—"The Japanese are in Korea, this is a terrible time" (50)—to launch its own explanation:

When the Japanese surrendered at the end of the war, the Soviets and the Americans split the job of overseeing the Japanese withdrawal from the Korean peninsula. A line was drawn at the thirty-eighth parallel, which split the country roughly in half. The Soviet military would administer the northern half, the Americans the southern. This was, in theory, a temporary arrangement. Provisional governments were set up on each side for the duration of Korea's reconstruction. The Soviets, on their side, enabled the return from exile of a great people's hero, a revolutionary who had fought the Japanese throughout the thirties. Chuck cut himself short. (51)

Stepping in for Chuck's more halting speech, this fluent rendering of the origins of the war in turn matches the reader to the audience in the book. Indeed, in this passage Choi shows her own hand, as she seems to be addressing us directly. Her account of the war closely accords with Cumings's revisionist history,[19] and her sketch of Kim Il Sung as "a great people's hero" violates the political core of the propaganda Chuck has consumed. It is thus not surprising that "Chuck cut himself short" at this point—the narration has revealed a political sympathy which is not only inappropriate to his presentation, but anachronistic.

Choi's intrusion lays bare the novel's own desire to explain the Korean War, as well as her own research. Chuck belongs to the adequation of Korea to America, but the novel seeks to situate his character within a critique of US military intervention. The exigencies of Choi's revisionist history lesson result in a striking melding of history and fiction most evident in the following chapter, which opens by embellishing the narration that cut into Chuck's talk at the church: "In September 1945 John Hodge arrived in Korea with the Twenty-fourth Corps, to oversee the Japanese surrender. He expected to be going home soon" (63). This story continues to unfold, to General Hodge's role as military governor of the Republic of Korea and his difficulty in maintaining order in the newly postcolonial and divided nation. Choi's revivified army general significantly interacts with her protagonist: "Hodge went to the Rhee government's new Ministry of Public Information and discovered that it was a shabby little room with peeling linoleum tiles, two desks, one typewriter, one ashtray, and three employees. . . . The third one looked, to Hodge, about fourteen years old. He could never tell how old these people were" (66). Through Hodge's eyes, we are introduced to Chang, soon to be renamed Chuck. We have already met Chuck twice—first as a scholarly fugitive on the streets of Seoul and then as an alien dropped into Tennessee—but in imagining how Chang would appear to General Hodge, Choi has inscribed her father into an American history of the Korean War.

Choi's historical perspective defines her protagonist within a logic that expands beyond her novel. She has ushered in historical actors and made them behave according to the strictures of her fiction, but these figures bring with them a determining force that necessitates elaborate acts of writing to keep her imaginative portrayals alive. Such writerly excesses are on full display in this chapter, which interweaves Chang's falling under the sway of the Americans at age fifteen with Choi's elaborate version of Korean

War history. This larger story culminates in the outbreak of hostilities on June 25, 1950: "When the fighting broke out, at four o'clock Sunday morning, the only American officer posted on the parallel was an undistinguished military adviser named Leo d'Addario who had not been granted weekend leave. D'Addario was awakened by the sound of artillery fire, but couldn't tell whose it was" (93). Choi's portrait of this hapless American officer puts her literary license on display, and it is within her revised and reanimated history that the emergent contours of Chuck's desires appear.

In his work for Peterfield in the USIS office, he comes to feel an attachment that surprises him, both for its intensity and its limitations. Chuck first signed on with the Americans for a guarantee against enlistment, but as militancy intensifies, Peterfield warns Chuck that "If they try to draft you I can't go to bat for you," adding, "I can't credential a goddamned Korean civilian" (105). Through this conversation, Chuck understands that "their friendship was over"; indeed, "Chuck recognized that Peterfield hated him" (105). Hence, the fake ID that Chuck later makes for himself—and in fact never brandishes—reveals Peterfield's inability and unwillingness to protect him. Yet from Peterfield's contempt, Chuck realizes that "his loyalty had attached itself to Peterfield like an indiscriminate, compulsive tentacle, expecting loyalty and love in return" (164). In this remarkable rendering of political loyalty as love, Chuck identifies his deepest desires—only to resolve to keep himself free:

> He regrouped, declared himself a small principality, and pledged his undivided allegiance again. The Committee for the Preservation and Welfare of Himself convened its first meeting and passed a resolution excising agitators from his heart, and these included Peterfield. (164–65)

The translation of political loyalty into love has, in turn, converted Chuck into a political entity, "a small principality." In its absurd application of bureaucratic language, this new pledge reveals how thoroughly Chuck has been overwritten by a "new lexicon." We see the strange being Chuck has become: transformed by political allegiance, he cannot imagine himself in the absence of it. In fact, his political isolation hints at the larger movement toward nonalignment in the era—but only to suggest the impossibility of such an ideal.[20] This metaphor of nonalignment provides a bare glimpse of an anti-imperialism that lies beyond Chuck's grasp—and is only just visible through Choi's lexicon.

Choi's portrait of her father's political attachment, however, refuses to make him a dupe of the Americans or to imbue him with an anachronistic political resistance; instead, she submits American history to her writerly wiles. The excesses of her narration foreground her presence: in her complement to her father's imagined presentation of the war, Choi updates his canned history and revises it. Choi ultimately provides a critique of American intervention only available to the second generation, but her revised historical frame ingeniously frees her protagonist from this critical burden while at the same time lodging him within her own "new frame for thinking." And from this context, Chuck emerges as a political entity that dreams of isolation, but nevertheless perpetually seeks out alliances.

III

Choi has constructed a literary world in which historical actors are free to interact with figments of her imagination, and she pairs her protagonist with her most fanciful figure, a lonely Southern belle. [21]

Katherine Monroe is a lovely and enigmatic young woman who lives alone in her family's summer house in Sewanee:

> She was an established figure at Sewanee, and although she was not often seen, she was of long endurance, and this was enough to ensure she was frequently mentioned. He heard that her family was rich, and that somehow she had broken with them. That their ties couldn't have been very strong in the first place, he assumed and admired. She seemed particularly American to him, not in spite of her isolation but because of it. Obligation or dependence would never have entered her realm. Brushing near her he had sensed the shape of possibility, but he didn't know what it contained. (17)

Katherine's American isolation is particularly appealing to "the small principality" of Chuck. With Peterfield, Chuck converted loyalty to love, only to be cast away for his disloyalty: the American could not stomach a "goddamned Korean civilian," a dependent subject who rejects military conscription. Chuck discovers a far more promising candidate for his affections in Katherine, whose own isolation frees her from the terms of "obligation and dependence."

The "shape of possibility" Chuck senses with Katherine is a potential alliance governed by a form and not "what it contained." For Chuck, it is the shape of things that matter and not the things themselves: the Tennessee hills offer more of a homecoming than the tears of his mother. Though Chuck notes the groundlessness of analogy in his church presentation, he understands the power of comparison, and the novel grounds its unlikely romance by establishing a series of formal parallels between Chuck and Katherine. Perhaps the strangest aspect of *The Foreign Student* is the amount of ground Choi gives to Katherine, whose story takes center stage for large portions of the text. Katherine's privileged family drama simply cannot be compared to Chuck's war-ravaged experience—and yet the novel matches them, point for point. We meet both of them as teenagers, when they fall under influences that eventually detach them from their parents, and Choi portrays Katherine as herself caught in a war within her family: as she says to Chuck, "In my family you never could move a muscle without it being a declaration of loyalty to somebody and war to somebody else" (150). Both characters are shaped by war, and both embrace an isolating abjection.

Choi carefully charts their separate lives as an overlaying geography: both are bound to summer houses north of the port towns—Pusan and New Orleans—where their parents live. Chuck and Katherine each wander up and down a peninsula, and the north-south axis they each occupy traces a matching contour that can overcome the gulf that separates them. Indeed, their movements north and south run counter to the prevailing east-west axis reinforced by both Orientalist romance and Cold War ideology. Choi's romance upends a literary tradition of Madame Butterflies; in swapping the sexes, she has overturned the standard gendering of the Orientalist division between East and West.[22] And because Chuck and Katherine are each determined by the shape of civil war, they are seemingly untouched by a Cold War Orientalism that maintains a dependent relation between East and West. In thus casting its romance on a novel axis, *The Foreign Student* extricates its lovers from an Orientalist one.

In his desire for Katherine, Chuck identifies the true orientation of his endeavors:

> His lust to master the language had never been abstract, no matter how fastidious and intellectual his approach might have seemed to observers like Peterfield. . . . It had always been utterly, ruthlessly pragmatic, driven by his faith in its power

to transport him. It had gotten him into USIS, and across the ocean to Sewanee, and then, just as he was in danger of becoming apathetic from accomplishment, it had brought her within view. Every possibility of speech had been a possibility of speaking to her. (219)

Katherine marks the culmination of the trajectory from the USIS office to Sewanee: having identified her as uniquely American in her isolation, Katherine becomes Chuck's ultimate test. If the arrival at Sewanee was "the end of the dream as he'd dreamed it," Katherine offers the foreign student a glimpse into an undreamed-of existence: of being something more than a foreign student. To be a foreign student is to be nurtured within a dependent role, but the dream of Katherine dramatically extends the freedom Chuck first experienced when his mother turned him away from her door.

Their romance proceeds in fits and starts. Though she represents the standard of American independence for Chuck, Katherine is not free: at age fourteen, she fell under the spell of Charles Addison, a Sewanee professor and family friend, and she is still bound to him in the present of the novel, when she is twenty-eight. The obstacle of the professor—who tutors Chuck—is only surmounted near the end of the novel, when Chuck surprises Katherine in New Orleans, where she is tending her dying mother. Away from Sewanee, Chuck and Katherine engage in a passionate reunion. Katherine procures a room for him at the Charles Hotel, a place where "people from around the world stay" (281). Chuck is thus safely ensconced as a foreign emissary, in a hotel whose name recalls his vanquished rival. It is worth noting that Choi's protagonist is never "Charlie," a shorthand for servile and enemy Asians;[23] and staying in luxury at the Charles, he has graduated from Chuck, the person he became through his USIS work, into someone no longer dependent on that office.

Yet this happy ending provokes a new set of questions. Chuck boarded the bus to New Orleans on a whim, and upon his arrival at the bus station he is detained by FBI agents and only released when Katherine retrieves him. The agents explain to Katherine why Chuck is being questioned:

> "This is routine questioning, miss. We have a problem with Chinese Communist agents infiltrating American harbors. Ships from Communist China are barred from every port in the U.S. except New Orleans, this is their one point of entry, for their goods and their agents. Their agents recruit in this port. Among seamen. And then you've got mutinies. Communist seamen and Communist mutinies."
>
> "But he isn't Chinese," she said.
>
> He studied her a moment. "Are you familiar with the Port Security Program?"
>
> "I'm afraid that I'm not."
>
> "Are you a Communist yourself?"
>
> "Me?" Katherine exclaimed, and then they all, even the irritable shirtsleeved man, burst out laughing, and laughed together a long time while he looked on amazed. (278)

The FBI agent traces the spreading contagion of communism: from China, to other Asiatics, and then to a sympathetic American woman. Yet when the agent extends his questioning to Katherine, the scene takes on a levity which stuns Chuck. Katherine is impervious to the threat identified by the agents; in her astonished "Me?" she simply undoes their anticommunist rationale.

Katherine thus defuses the threat posed by Chuck; she protects him within her narrative, which is free from the political allegiances that define his. Indeed, their stories belong to two different genres, and in this instance Katherine's Southern Gothic tale of family

betrayal rescues Chuck from his story of wartime political allegiances. Yet though the FBI agents merrily accede to Katherine in
this instance, their presence reveals how strangely circumscribed
her world has been. This passage marks the novel's only mention of
anticommunism within the United States; reading it, we suddenly
realize what we have been missing all along: Choi's portrait of Cold
War America is untouched by the politics that roiled the domestic front. *The Foreign Student* rigorously depoliticizes its vision of
America: Katherine's family is broken because of an illicit sexual
alliance in her past, not a political one; Charles Addison is a wayward college professor who seduces a child, but he is never suspected of being the staple bad influence of the Cold War—namely,
the closet communist. Katherine's personal trauma is set within—
and indeed creates—a nostalgic image of postwar America.

America is a pristine college campus, a world away from the
brutal political upheaval in Korea. Katherine confesses to Chuck
that "I don't know anything about the war," to which he replies,
"There is not much to know" (34); and he never elaborates because
he wants to preserve the secret divulged at the very end of the
novel, "that this war would never define him." Katherine represents "the shape of possibility" because "obligation or dependence
would never have entered her realm"; Choi keeps her heroine ignorant of a recent American war because Katherine's realm must be
detached from the unequal east-west relation integral to the Cold
War. Yet the north and south of civil war invokes an American
racial divide between black and white that insists upon Chuck's
foreignness; in polite Southern society, he must be "an emissary
from a distant land." Indeed, the analogical structure that matches
Chuck to Katherine renders them foreign to each other: each sees
the other as a potential deliverance from a long-standing dependence, but the isolation they treasure in each other does little to
foster their union.

It is, finally, the Cold War that brings them together. Though the novel carefully separates their worlds, Chuck is a product of a new world order that binds Third-World subjects to a serenely ignorant America. It is thus fitting that their long-awaited union takes place under a cloud of anticommunist suspicion: once Katherine has freed Chuck from his detainment, they run from the bus station in a torrential downpour, electrified by passion. Her power to rescue him exhilarates both Katherine and Chuck: in claiming Chuck, Katherine has exercised a power she could never wield over Charles Addison; and for Chuck, the wonder of her total political innocence—capable of disarming FBI agents—literally frees him. Hence, though the axis of the Cold War threatens the careful analogy that matches Chuck to Katherine, their romance only catches fire when he is imperiled by the anticommunist policies that expose the political undercurrents just below the surface of American placidity. We may finally read their romance as a vivid illustration of the terms of Cold War integration: the strange force of Katherine's innocence contains the potential threat of Chuck's foreignness.

IV

The Foreign Student opened with Chuck's insistence on his Special Status, and it ends by disclosing the extraordinary price he has paid for this fabricated identity. Hidden away in the Charles Hotel and sheltered in Katherine's arms, Chuck falls into a deep sleep, his first true rest since the war. From this safe distance, the novel concludes the narrative of his wartime experience begun in the prologue: having escaped military conscription in Seoul, he secures a ride to Inchon, where he catches a freighter he hopes is destined for Pusan—but instead he finds himself on Cheju Island, where he is captured by the National Police and shipped to a detention center in Pusan. Because he has eluded conscription, he is suspected of being a spy, and he is brutally tortured for information. The Special Status that saved him from military service becomes a source of excruciating punishment.

Choi describes nine days of torture in horrific detail and then shows us what remains of Chuck:

> After this there was very little left of him. He mimicked his torturers, making himself deaf to his body's cries for help. His knowledge of his body propagated in chains, telephone lines, bridges between a limb and his love for it, coursing braids of communication wire. He sliced through lines and wires, exploded bridges, excised his mouth and his groin, amputated his limbs. He no longer knew when he urinated. Cast outside the boundary of itself, his body had ceased to obey any boundary between itself and the world. He was always damp and acrid with urine, trickling out of him the way blood trickled out of his various wounds. His terror at the mangling of his fingers had evaporated, and the memory of that terror was as unrecognizable as any of his other possessions. He watched his hand being mangled from a great distance. He had already sawed it off. He had thrown away his body as if it were ballast, not to speed his death, but to survive. It was his body that would kill him. (309–10)

The language of this passage depicts the fate of the "small principality": Chuck cuts his own communication wires and detonates bridges in an effort to free himself from its structure. The boundary between his body and the world dissolves; the crumbling borders of his individual state have given way. From the outer reaches of his torment, he destroys himself: he cedes his principality, his physical integrity and detachment, in order to survive.

His punishment continues after he has forsaken his body, and in a state of utter delirium, he gives away the only information he has—the name of a Catholic priest who shelters leftist dissidents on Cheju Island—given to him by a childhood friend named Kim. The unlikely friendship between Chang and Kim charted the emergence of the civil war: in contrast to Chang's privilege and growing American allegiance, Kim, of humble origins, allied himself with the left. Stranded on Cheju, Chuck sought out the priest in the vain hope of finding his friend—but he only sees Kim again after betraying him. Days after his confession, Chuck is released, and as he stumbles past a group of captured guerrillas, he recognizes Kim: "Then he saw him. A pair of outsize eyes met his, stared" (312). Chuck's defeated principality has ensnared Kim in its ruins.

The betrayal of his best friend is the extravagant price Chuck pays for his freedom. Chuck never hears of Kim again, and even doubts having seen him, but the terrible flash of recognition has transformed him: "He wondered what had shaped him more, his guilt toward Kim, or the chance it was mistaken" (313). *The Foreign Student* is a story of matching shapes, and in this late revelation we discover the shaping force that emerges out of Chuck's broken sovereignty. Made to perform his Special Status, Chuck finds himself serving the National Police, the repressive force instituted by General Hodge, modeled on Japan's imperial apparatus. It is thus only after he has been reshaped into a special informant for American political interests that Chuck may become a foreign student. The secret of freedom on the book's final page thus holds within it his political betrayal, through which Chuck "became another to himself" (318): the sovereign self has been demolished, and the new self that emerges out of the rubble belongs to America.

These revelations are intertwined with a significant change in Chuck's standing at Sewanee. Chuck found his way to Katherine by stealing cash from a summer job procured for him by Sewanee's president, and the revelation of his theft expels him. Coaxed by a melancholy and magnanimous Charles Addison into reinstating Chuck, the college president permits him to continue his studies, but without his scholarship. Instead, Chuck must work alongside the college's kitchen staff, composed of African Americans, and live among them in a rented room in a nearby town. Chuck's desire for Katherine has demoted him from his lofty standing as foreign student: he can no longer stand before the lecture hall as an emblem of America's duty; instead, he pays his own way and belongs to a classed and raced minority. This fall from grace is a welcome change, and also an opportunity to escape his Special Status—an invented identity that exacted an actual and unthinkable toll.

Just before the closing memory of his homecoming, we regard Chuck in a moment of remarkable contentment. He has returned to his rented room after a day of work with the kitchen staff, and the sun is still shining: "He turns his face toward it. There are moments like this, rare instances of certainty and self-possession" (324). Yet this ultimate self-possession is a tenuous freedom, constructed from a series of matching shapes that insinuate a pattern of romance but never attempt to resolve or heal the pain of lost identity and betrayal. The end of Chuck's war story is matched to the end of Katherine's family drama, and both are wrapped in their romance. Yet Katherine's story is far better served by the novel's romantic denouement: she brings Chuck to her dying mother, and the three of them form a surprisingly happy family. While Katherine's narrative has been driving toward her mother, Chuck's story has, in fact, been driven by his mother's misrecognition of him—and the unfolding structure of the narrative hurtles toward the gruesome account of his torture. The graphic portrayal of Chuck's broken body overwhelms the novel; his ordeal eclipses Katherine's trauma and undermines the structure of analogy that permits their rapprochement. With the revelation of the true extent of his wartime suffering, Chuck acquires a singularity that detaches him—not only from Katherine but from the fabric of the novel.

The Foreign Student presents a historical Korea and a fictional America: a carefully researched account of the Korean War and a deeply nostalgic portrait of 1950s America. Because he is a product of the alliance between Korea and the United States, Chuck stands at the intersection of these two portraits: he interacts with an army general out of the history books and a Southern belle out of Faulkner country. In lodging her father's wartime memories within an imagined romance, Choi has built a structure of analogy around him, an American scaffolding created to support an alien figure. Yet this structure is not always commensurate with her protagonist, as Chuck notes when he describes Katherine's presence in his solitary existence as "his sense that she was watching from afar, with a constant and transforming attention, as if his life were an American movie and she were his audience. He'd felt ennobled and remade. Yet he was full of immutable stuff" (285). He feels "remade" by Katherine's gaze, but his substance cannot be reshaped.

Chuck's intense suffering is the immutable stuff that remains beyond Katherine's reach, and Choi's astonishing rendering of it transports us out of her carefully crafted narrative. The audience of Katherine transforms Chuck's existence into "an American movie"; their tempestuous reunion in New Orleans is the stuff of Hollywood, but Chuck's story drives toward what cannot be shown in the movies—Choi writes what happens after the screen goes black. This pain is what Chuck refused to share with his church audience; the terrible documenting of his torture slices through the layers of narrative shaped to make him into a figure of alliance and love. The romance with Katherine leaves untouched the devastation of war, and the unveiling of this immutable core reveals the fragility of the novel's alliances.

The foreign student is finally a delicate shape that conceals an absolute otherness; this wartime friendly preserves his integrity in the imperial center only by sheltering the horror of the war deep within—a paradoxical containment which discloses a political betrayal constitutive of the friendly. At the moment when Chuck seems to have transcended his foreign student status, the terrible truth of his suffering emerges. The role of the foreign student is liberating in one world and constraining in another, and the attempt to struggle free of it reveals a primary scene of captivity. *The Foreign Student* ends at the cusp of its protagonist's new identity, born of an alliance simultaneously detached from and underwritten by the context of the Cold War. The new lives that emerge from this alliance will themselves be touched by the war—an eventuality betrayed by the fact of the book's author, who has returned to it a generation later.

That Choi's rendering of the friendly contains a political betrayal resonates with Richard Kim's friendly soldier, and perhaps the shock of recognition that Choi attributes to the universal appeal of Kim's allegorical tale also indicates a shared problem of proxy warfare: in both cases the nightmare of civil war must be contained and disavowed in order to facilitate the rapprochement of East and West. But if Kim's Captain Lee was content to aspire to an existential register beyond the local skirmish, his solitary survival is not enough for the next generation. Chuck's evolving attachments—first to the childhood friend he will betray, then to Peterfield, and finally to Katherine—insist upon ever greater accord to transport him out of his broken family and nation, and finally into a lover's arms. These concentric desires, from the politics of civil war to the broader lexicon of Cold War integration, culminate in a structure of romance which permits a figurative pairing seemingly at the expense of political understanding—but if Katherine's ignorance of the war shelters Chuck, it also reopens the war deep within and reveals the friendly's immutably political core. The romance that is the telos of Chuck's progressively strengthening attachments ultimately exposes the insufficiency of formal containment, because their pairing in fact sets the stage for a terrifying elaboration of the war's aporia. Susan Choi's study of the Korean War—and the text in fact reads like an extravagant, self-imposed history lesson—creates the friendly as a figuration of the romance and impossibility of Cold War alliance, whom the elaborate scaffolding of political integration alternately protects and exposes.

As Cold War agents of integration, foreign students were never meant to stay in the United States. Upon completing their American training, they were to disseminate not just their learning, but also the spirit of the free world, back to their far corners of the globe. The softer strategies of cold warfare relied heavily on deputizing, and the foreign student was a figure of outsize promise—as long as she faithfully returned home. But many, like Chuck, did not, and perhaps never intended to complete their duties as foreign emissaries. Asian America, of course, has been shaped from the start by sojourners who stayed on, and this white-collar variant is no better insulated from political demonization; indeed, their significant privileges are more firmly yoked to their friendly service. That *The Foreign Student* can fabricate a romance for its friendly is a formal and generic marker of this privilege, but in thus sidestepping the standard minority Bildung, its protagonist is also incapable of development. Perhaps, then, we may understand the novel's conclusion, the way it circles back to the originary moment of Chuck's abject freedom, as revealing the hard, formal limits of the friendly, whose desires perpetually reinscribe the politics of Cold War friendship.

These limits persist in Susan Choi's 2008 novel *A Person of Interest*, whose protagonist Lee, a mathematics professor, also came to the United States as a foreign student from Korea. It tempting to read *A Person of Interest* as a sequel to *The Foreign Student*: the foreign student has gone on to graduate study and acquired a professorship at a midwestern university, but Lee remains an utter, if "princely" alien into his mid-sixties, when he is suspected of a Unabomber-type attack on a colleague.[24] Lee's graduate-student career—like Chuck's undergraduate career—was marked by an illicit affair, but in this latter case, the romance is doomed from the start and ultimately exposes Lee to charges of domestic terrorism. In the light of this later romantic entanglement, we may read *The Foreign Student*'s imagination of a Cold War love that promised freedom in exchange for political alignment as an unsustainable fiction. And yet this story requires the resources of fiction, because the impossible pairing of Chuck and Katherine insists upon an enlivened history; it is the plight of every friendly to relive her war afresh at precisely those moments when she seeks the benefits of her alignment.

4

Inhuman Alliances

Chang-rae Lee's The Surrendered

In Chang-rae Lee's 2010 novel *The Surrendered*, largely set in an orphanage in South Korea in the immediate aftermath of the war, we meet a heart-rending figure:

> Min was not the youngest but he was undersized from severe malnourishment during the war. Reverend Hong had found him sitting slumped in an alleyway of Seoul, barely conscious, near skeletal, pocked with insect stings and rat bites. (112)

Children like Min were staples of popular American coverage of the war, as in a 1953 *Collier's* portrait of a nine-year-old orphan:

> the only food Tae had eaten was what he could steal or beg or buy with the few pennies he earned. His only home was the closest shelter he could find—a dry corner in some bombed-out building, a pile of boards in an alley.[1]

In *The Surrendered*, Min was rescued by Reverend Hong, the founder of an orphanage outside of Seoul, but Tae's story features an American savior: "the stock character of a good Samaritan

American GI,"[2] an American sergeant who took Tae to a hospital when he fell ill. In popular reports, the war orphan was always an opportunity to showcase American mercy—and this friendly figure became particularly significant in an inconclusive war in which Korean allies were often deemed disappointing, cowardly, or corrupt.

In Lee's novel, however, Min is not saved by an American GI; instead, he is further damaged by a soldier's care. Hector Brennan, a GI who served in the war and stayed on at the behest of Reverend Hong to work as a handyman at the orphanage, fells a tree for firewood but then fails to notice that Min has taken up the ax: the child "slipped and lost his balance and missed and the blade came down on his foot" (114). Min loses three toes but survives because his accident coincides with the arrival of Reverend Ames Tanner, an American pediatrician-turned-clergyman who, along with his wife Sylvie, has come to take over for Reverend Hong. Min is hurt and saved under American guidance; the careless soldier leaves a weapon and the missionary flies to his aid—a miniature sketch of the fraught conditions of dependency left in the wake of the war.

Min remains a particularly endearing creature. He is the only boy in a knitting group led by Sylvie Tanner—"he told her he wanted to make a present of scarves for whoever eventually adopted him" (406)—and when Sylvie checks in on the sleeping boys, Min gives her the scarf he has knitted. Though Sylvie tries to refuse his gift, Min presses it on her: "He held out the scarf to her and she took it; she wrapped it around her neck. She bent down and hugged him and kissed him on the crown of his head and he suddenly clung to her, his bony little arms strong enough to press painfully against the back of her neck. It surprised her, how much it hurt" (408). Min is a painful attachment who possesses a surprising strength. Indeed, it is because he is the least of a desperate lot that he has such a powerful hold on the reverend's wife: the orphan's frailty is, of course, his only and astonishing force, and "like every child here he was an immeasurable mass" (408) whose need overpowers Sylvie.

In Lee's rendering, however, Min is more than merely a desperately clinging child. We also witness Min cowering in the grips of bullies at the orphanage, who torment him for the special attention he has garnered from the Tanners. Min responds to their taunts with his own: "'When you're on the streets,' Min said, now quite slowly and clearly. 'I think you will be eating your own shit'" (421). Among the children, Min reveals a canniness he keeps carefully concealed from the Americans. In his taunting rejoinder to his tormenters, we realize that Min has been jockeying for position in a vicious contest. If the "immeasurable mass" of Min represents the might of "every child" in the orphanage, the revelation of his machinations exposes those of all of the other children as well. As he settles into the orphanage, Reverend Tanner begins to see something more about these children: as he says to Sylvie, "Sometimes I think I'm not seeing who they are. They're children, yes. But they're not innocents" (402). Like every child in the orphanage, Min cannot be innocent of his role.

In the light of Min's artfulness, we realize that his gift of a scarf to Sylvie Tanner was a calculated bid: Min has understood that his damaged foot has diminished his chances of adoption and so he must campaign to be taken in by the Tanners—and he is fighting for a place with them at the expense of the other children. Min is saved from the bullies by an equally knowing orphan, the novel's protagonist June, who has been angling for her own place with the Tanners. Min identifies their shared aims: ridiculing the bullies as "dumb as oxen" (422), he tells June that the boys are failing to consider "What you and I are thinking about. What's outside of this place" (423). From this moment, Min and June, both outcasts in the orphanage, team up: they are both poor candidates for adoption, and so they must attempt to earn a permanent place with the Tanner family.

Min quickly acknowledges the unlikelihood of his campaign, but June is less willing to give up on her fantasy of being taken in by the Tanners. When Min disabuses her—"You're trouble, just like me" (439)—the two children share a night of utter disillusionment. After drinking water from a ladle, Min makes a breathtaking, freeing gesture: "Then, with a surprising indifference, he threw the ladle into the stove" (422). Once the ladle has caught fire,

> Min got up and left. When he returned he was carrying two of the small footlockers. One was his, the other June's—he had stolen into the girls' side. He opened the lid of his locker and began taking out the few items it contained, inspecting them for a moment and then tossing them into the stove. She did not say anything or try to stop him. He started with his box of pencils, and then a deck of Korean playing cards, and then he put in two special pairs of dress socks that he'd received from a church group in America. Next were some letters and greetings cards from the same people. Then he drew out the fine scarf he had made; aside from his everyday clothes, it was the last thing he had. He handed it to June to put in the fire, and after he nodded to say it was all right, she balled it up and dropped it in. It burned not quickly but rather steadily and well, the fire consuming it with its own slow savor.
>
> "You want to try?" he said. "It feels good." (422)

Min's escalating destruction, from the ladle to his most cherished possessions, is an expression of his truest feelings. The orphan longing for adoption must perpetually demonstrate, even perform, his goodness; by tossing all of the scraps of his orphan existence into the fire, Min has done what "feels good." The plea-sure of immolating the ladle propels him to burn every emblem of his hoped-for American alliance: he flings the socks, letters, and greetings cards into the flames, and then directs June to add his most precious item, his knitted scarf, to the pyre. In burn-ing away his orphan status, Min experiences an exhilarating lib-erty: freed of these props, he is no longer an orphan, but rather an independent soul.

Yet this independence is terribly short-lived. Their acts of aban-donment culminate in pitching an oil lamp into the stove, after which they hold each other closely: "'We don't need anyone,' she said softly in his ear. 'We're going to stay here now'" (444). Once they have given up their orphan roles, they "don't need anyone"—but because their needs are so great, they cannot survive in their freedom. Orphans are only ever figures of dependence, and both children understand the endpoint of their acts of renunciation: to throw off the burden of attachment is to extinguish their own lives, the very terms of their existence. Yet they are not the only casualties of their impossible freedom: when they step out of the orbit of need and charity, they threaten the orphanage itself.

The fire they start rapidly spreads to the dormitories. The other children make their way out alive—and Hector Brennan miracu-lously rescues June—but when the Tanners go in after Min, all three are consumed by the flames: "And in a flash a plumed beast of flame leaped up from the flooring to enfold the couple and child, for a moment cradling them in an almost placid repose before swallow-ing them whole" (461). This flaming tableau creates a family, finally and briefly, out of the Tanners and Min. In renouncing the emblems of his orphanhood, Min paradoxically achieves the adoption he had given up on—but only as a burning, negative image. This finale reveals both Min's ultimate inability to burn off his orphan sta-tus, and the spectacular danger his strange freedom poses to his protectors. What makes Min feel good strikes down the good reverend and his too-caring wife.

In presenting Min's brief life, Lee has imagined the war orphan's secret knowledge. Min wields his own weakness, through which he compromises all of the key characters in the novel—and finally destroys his American saviors. Min is a clinging, abject figure, but he is also dangerous; he is desperately dependent, but he possesses a deeper, exhilarating desire to be free of attachments. Lee is writing against the typology of the war orphan, popularly represented as the only true friendly of the Korean War, and his novel grants this figure a perverse agency: namely, to jettison the fantasy of goodness and innocence aimed at garnering American sympathy. Sentimental Cold War portraits of domesticity significantly featured Asian orphans folded into American homes, and, as Christina Klein notes, the framework of the family "balanced emotional unity with internally structured hierarchies of difference" which "served as a model for a 'free world' community that included Western and non-Western, developed and underdeveloped, established and newly created nations"(146). Lee's unruly orphan shatters this icon of sentimental humanitarianism,[3] and in so doing reveals a nihilism that reduces the Cold War family to ashes.

This chapter reads a series of perversions of Cold War attachments in *The Surrendered*. Hector's rescue of June from the flames is a key instantiation of the central problematic of alliance in the novel, which presents a perversion of the bond between desolate orphan and Good-Samaritan GI. No sympathy sparks their alliance, and what binds their cold pairing is an ideal of mercy represented by Sylvie: just as the reverend's wife does not resist Min's embrace, she also gives herself over to the needs of June and Hector—and she is a casualty of all of these desires. Lee has revised the wartime typologies of orphan and GI and installed a curious, mediating term between them: his orphan is all too knowing, his GI is dissolute, and the angel of mercy that both require has fallen from grace. The wayward gestures of Lee's characters revolve around a dream of alliance regularly peddled in popular publications like *Collier's*—and in writing against this sentimental standard, Lee surrenders his characters to it. June and Hector each struggle against the confines of an assigned typology only to fix its contours even more firmly; they are both locked within an idealized alliance popularly advanced to cloak the chill of Cold War.

The Surrendered is a self-consciously epic treatment of a war that has hovered at the edges of Lee's previous novels, including his breakthrough first novel, *Native Speaker* (1995), in which the Korean War is imagined as a founding crisis for a charismatic Asian American politician: "his family not mercifully sundered or refugeed but obliterated ... He stole away to America as the houseboy of a retiring two-star general" (211).[4] Lee's darkly heroic portrait of an aggressively Americanizing orphan imagines the friendly's meteoric rise, which can only be checked by the novel's protagonist, whose own friendly status as a second-order product of the war extends Cold War–era espionage into the post–Cold War era. The caricatured friendlies of *The Surrendered*—which Lee has described as the fulfillment of a longstanding desire to write his father's experience of the war[5]—are immune to the sympathies that finally undo the politician and spy, however. In contrast to the transformation and demise of the Cold War friendly glimpsed in *Native Speaker*, Lee's play with and against popular wartime typologies in *The Surrendered* seals off any possibility of transformation for its stock characters—and dooms its invented angel. In thus shackling itself to midcentury figuration while simultaneously subverting midcentury sympathy, this grandly ambitious novel is critically unable to account for a war in which proxy relations of dependency were not merely figurative but, indeed, central to it.

The Martyred longed for existential grandeur and *The Foreign Student,* a living history—and both novels are overwrought by their literary ambitions. *The Surrendered* follows in this curious genealogy with an eclipsing ambition: to fashion a war epic out of the middlebrow material of the Korean War. Lee's redeployment of stock characters applies a kind of lurid sheen to his style, which thwarts universalizing ambitions. A highly unsympathetic read of this novel in fact exposed a fundamentally middling artistry running throughout Lee's oeuvre (notably, in a *New Yorker* review which reads like high literary gatekeeping),[6] and perhaps out of this disdain we may identify the extraordinary risks of Lee's experiment with middlebrow, whose powers of incorporation can in fact swallow up even the most mannered detachment. All three of my chosen novels write against the midcentury packaging of the Korean War, and Lee's late assault on its minor mythologies lays bare an entrenched symbolic order of the Cold War that not only withstands, but actually undermines, high literary machinations. The primary difficulty, of course, is the friendly, who may flirt with enmity, but whose capitulation to it would signal her demise. The friendly thus subtends the political tensions of the Cold War—a truth and a secret known all too well by Kim's and Choi's protagonists— but entirely unknown to the deeply unsympathetic friendlies of Lee's Korean War novel.

The Surrendered opens with eleven-year-old June in the early days of the war, as she is desperately shepherding her younger twin siblings onto a train bound for Pusan. Their schoolteacher father has been falsely denounced and murdered as a communist, their older brother conscripted, and their mother and older sister killed in a flash of artillery. On their own, the three children join a stream of refugees hollowed by—and inured to—suffering. In order to survive, June wishes to steel herself: "Now, after all that had happened, she thought she could suffer seeing most anything, whatever cruelty or disaster, but the notes of a human plaint would make her wish she could exist without a heart" (8). June's story unfolds as a test of wish: her survival depends upon a heartlessness that she clings to, even after the war.

In the face of war's privations, June, "always a responsible, filial daughter" (4) before the war, now fights off "her own animal impulses": in order to care for her younger sister and brother, she must "blunt[ed] herself from ever seeing her siblings as burdens. . . . It was how she had not yet allowed herself to harden against them. To hate them" (10). Once orphaned, June begins to shed her filiality: before the war, because "she was closest in age to the twins, had looked after them for as long as she could remember" (4), but once she has lost her place in the family, her siblings threaten to become mere burdens. On the train, June loses them: precariously perched on top of a car, the two younger children fall off when the train lurches to a halt. June finds her sister dead, and as the train starts up again, she abandons her terribly wounded brother. Alone, she joins a stream of refugees all engulfed in "a tide of blood" (6). This episode is Lee's rendering of his father's experience of the war, and the hardened figure of June expresses war's unsayables—and, once inured to its horrors, she remains fixed as a stony heroine throughout the novel.

At the end of the war, June encounters an American GI—later identified as Hector Brennan—who leads her to the orphanage. June does not recognize the American as her savior; instead, she sees him "as the herald of death, finally come to embrace her" (56). She attempts to run away, only to slip and sink into treacherous mud. The American saves her:

> But then she could breathe; he'd plucked her up from the mud by her shirt, ripping a sleeve at the shoulder. She hit him in the chest and tried to scratch his eyes but in a flash he struck her back; when she came to she was lying in the shade of a rusted truck carcass that had been pushed off the road, some thirty meters from where they had been. The side of her face stung. But her shirt was still on, and her trousers were as well, and the American was sitting on the metal frame of the seats, torn out of the truck cab, chewing on a stalk of hay. She began to crawl away and was trying to get up on her feet when he rattled a yellow object in his hand; it was a pack of Chiclets. He tossed it at her feet and before she could open the end fold of the flat box, her mouth watered so fulsomely that she had to cough before she could stuff in all the pieces. Their hard shells cracked and then burst with sweetness.
>
> "Take it easy, sister," he said. (57)

This meeting between orphan and GI is a far cry from the scenes of rescue presented in popular magazines and films. The orphan strikes the Good Samaritan, who hits her back; their encounter is poised between rescue and rape.

Lee's Good Samaritan GI is no hero; though he saves June, he remains detached and dispassionate. Once the threat of rape has dissipated, both orphan and GI merely seem to be playing their parts: the GI, always portrayed as a candy dispensary, lures the orphan with a pack of gum; the orphan follows, but only reluctantly. Lee has thus staged this primal scene of wartime alliance as a wary rapprochement; but devoid of the affecting hallmarks typical of such scenes, this GI and orphan merely trudge ahead. Lee has emptied this scene of the crucial spark of charity, and so both shoulder roles that they cannot fully inhabit.

The American soldier's hailing of June as "sister" names her role: she is neither daughter nor lover, and in the novel she will not be adopted or prostituted. Instead, June is the sister who has abandoned her siblings: her character is defined by the moment of leaving her brother behind and running alone for the departing train. Her solitary run took place in the summer of 1950, in the first weeks of the war, and she encounters the American soldier on the road just after the armistice in 1953. The intervening period marks out the three years of the Korean War, which remains a curious blank in her story: we never get an account of June's existence during the years when she survived on her own, between ages eleven and fourteen. In not disclosing her wartime experience, the novel evinces its unnarratability: the war is never more than the vicious freedom that June claims at its outset. And so, in striking contrast to Choi's attempt to free her protagonist from the war, Lee's heroine is only free within that same war.

June's experience of the war that orphaned her, however, has rendered her unfit for adoption. In the orphanage, she is shunned for her strange viciousness: as Reverend Tanner says to his wife, "she's not a nice girl. She's not a kind girl. Maybe she was once, but she isn't anymore" (165). She has maintained her wartime heartlessness: during the war, June stole because "it had been a matter of survival," but "even after she was settled in the orphanage, where there was plenty of food, where there was shelter and safety, there were instances when she would steal things from the other children that could hardly benefit her, and only gave them great unhappiness." June pockets "Certain sentimental objects," notably including "a flimsy, creased photograph of a family, which she'd lifted from the back pocket of a sleeping boy" (246). This anti-sentimental behavior certainly illustrates June's wartime subject formation, but the strange excess of these small acts of cruelty also exposes the novel's desire to write itself against a sentimental standard. Fashioned as both a container for actual experiences of the war and a perversion of wartime typology, June possesses a cruelty without malice that disables psychological depth.

June is never adopted, and she makes her way to America by forging a different order of alliance: surprisingly, she marries Hector Brennan. Her character is thus positioned between two different figures of alliance wrought by war: war orphan and war bride.[7] Yet June's metamorphosis into war bride is even more mysterious than her unseen wartime hardships: in the portions of the novel devoted to her perspective, June never mentions their marriage; instead, it is Hector who recalls their brief and strange union. In his account, she is the "fierce, sharp-cornered girl he'd married for her convenience only, despite how miserable and guilty her presence made him. He brought her over to the States and they had lived together (if not as husband and wife) for five months" (94). That their marriage served "her convenience only" further undermines Hector, who cannot be recognized as either June's savior or her husband. June was married at nineteen, and the novel tells us nothing about the years between her experiences at the orphanage in 1953 and her arrival in the United States five years later.

June's character is thus marked by two key gaps: the first culminates in her arrival at the orphanage; the second, in the United States. If the novel could not present her wartime trials, it is even less capable of imagining her transformation from orphan to war bride. These two paths to America are markedly different: severed from her parents, the orphan is folded into an American family, but the war bride is the first link in a familial chain of migrations. In fact, the Korean War bride was "the pioneer of Korean migration to the United States," and "her kin make up about half of ethnic Koreans in the United States."[8] Unlike popular postwar coverage of Japanese war brides,[9] the military bride of the Korean War has been long overlooked[10]—especially by Koreans and Korean Americans, who have shunned her as little more than a prostitute.[11] *The Surrendered* delivers June to the United States as a war bride, but she never truly inhabits this role; instead, she is always an orphan. To Hector she is never more than "June, from the war" (81), and when they meet again decades later, he can only see her as "That orphan girl, carved from rock" (451).[12]

June's story oscillates between her time at the orphanage and her middle age, when we discover that she cannot locate her adult son, unknowingly fathered by Hector, and that she is suffering in the last stages of stomach cancer. When we first see this older self, aged forty-seven, June is preserved in her adolescent appearance: "She had spent her life being not so beautiful as extraordinarily youthful" (32). As she struggles with the pain of her illness, she entrenches herself within her wartime identity: "she clenched her teeth and told herself as she had throughout her life whenever she needed to persevere that it was wartime again, those days between what happened to her siblings on the train and when she met Hector on the road, when every last cell of her was besieged by hunger and fear but was utterly resolved not to flag, and never did" (363). June's character is defined by the first lacuna in her story and not by the second; she holds on to her fierce independence and survival, and simply erases her dependence on the American soldier.

June brings Hector back into her life in her final year, as she undertakes a fruitless search for their son. In their reunion, Hector recalls the bride she briefly was, and when he is forced to carry her because of her illness, they are "taken for newlyweds" (446). The end of the book describes a ritual she has planned, in which she dons funereal garments in order to enter a chapel reminiscent of the orphanage. The clothes are white, in accordance with Korean custom, but to Hector's eyes, "The shape of the papery clothing took on a boxy, formal allure, the whiteness making her look like a strange kind of bride" (466). Yet June fights to the end to hold on to her solitary freedom; the final page of the text cuts away from this strange betrothal with a "NOT YET" and then returns to the moment that defined her: "She was running for the train. . . . In defiance she leaned forward and cried out, suspending her breath, and reached for the dark edge of the door. The world fell away. Someone had pulled her up. Borne her in. She was off her feet, alive" (469). The end of the novel finally confirms June's first impression of the American soldier "as the herald of death, finally come to embrace her"; in Hector's arms, she continues to struggle against the relation that first menaced her as potential rape and then morphed into a strange and unlikely marriage. If the groom's embrace is death, the orphan's run is life; *The Surrendered* has charted the end of June's life as a return to a moment of exhilarating liberty.

Lee's portrait of a war orphan presents a child heartless enough to survive the war. June is the product of a central emptiness, and the missing account of her wartime experiences infects all of her subsequent relationships. The novel seems to test June with alliance after alliance, and she spurns multiple attachments, including that with her own son. Lee preserves June's adamantine core; indeed, the missing five years before she becomes Hector's bride suggests Lee's inability to imagine her otherwise: her alliance with the American soldier is ultimately unfathomable because she treasures her solitary run. *The Surrendered* thus portrays the unthinkable: the orphan who wants to remain orphaned. Yet the orphan who jealously guards her solitude is, finally, not an orphan; instead, she is an inhuman fantasy who continues to run, even as she lies in the arms of death.

II

It is only through Hector's eyes that we actually see the war. Bearing the name of the quintessential epic hero, Hector is a poster boy for American war efforts: as a boy in aptly named Ilion (an archaic name for ancient Troy), a small town in upstate New York, "during World War II a local committee asked him to model for a war-bonds poster that would feature a handsome family, he being the boy bursting with pride as he gazed up as his uniformed older brother," and growing up, "people would tell him he ought to be a film actor" (95). Regarding his beautiful son, his father foretells his fate and utters his single injunction: "You'll live forever, anyone with eyes can see that. Just never go to war" (60). Hector disobeys his father, and in the Korean War he discovers his father was right on both counts: he cannot shake off his immortality, which becomes a "sentence of persistence" (77), and his military service dooms him to be forever at war.

Hector cites a single wartime incident as a turning point, "a situation probably not too distinctive or unusual," but which for Hector "changed everything" (67). He frames his account within the backdrop of the war:

> After the chaotic opening to the war, the initial Communist invasion, and the headlong ROK retreat to the very southern tip of the peninsula, and then the breakneck American counteroffensive pushing back all the way north to the Yalu River, which was the border with China, both sides were now engaged in what was in essence trench warfare, if in the hills. The struggle was over any given (and supposedly) strategic section of high ground, the shifting of territory measured in hundreds of meters, each hill identified by only a number (and if bloody enough, eventually a nickname). The fighting was

mostly night attacks, with small-scale raids by American and ROK units, and then operations by the Communists, who were now almost all Chinese, regulars in the People's Army, attacking often in mass, near-suicidal, waves, their aim to intimidate and overwhelm with seemingly inexhaustible numbers. (67)

If June's story illustrated the war's "chaotic opening," Hector's is grounded in the two years of gruelling trench warfare that followed the sweeping attacks and retreats of the war's first months. Lee's description of the masses of Chinese soldiers follows popular accounts which repeatedly depicted vast "hordes,"[13] and their "seemingly inexhaustible numbers" open out into a curious depoliticization, in which the masses of enemy conscripts destabilize the war's core political divide.

From this dehumanized force, we meet a single enemy soldier, a "boy soldier" taken prisoner: "The boy was short, five foot four or so, and stalk-thin, not even a hundred pounds in his winter uniform, which had been stuffed tight with crumpled newspaper for insulation, ripped canvas tennis shoes on his sockless feet" (68). Searching the prisoner, Hector discovers a diary: "It was written in Korean, and apparently the boy contended he was a southerner, first conscripted by ROKs before being captured by Communists and reconscripted again." This revelation does not save the prisoner: "the interpreter either didn't believe him or didn't care; he was a Communist now" (71). He is discarded by the officers and left to Hector, who understands that "he should walk him back to the forward line and, at some point, shoot him. It happened all the time, and was practiced by them and the enemy alike" (71–72). In the figure of this unlucky prisoner, the different sides of the war blur together: he has been conscripted by both sides, and his fate reveals an inhuman practice employed by both as well. The boy prisoner thus undoes the distinction between friend and enemy; wretchedly used by both sides, he unveils their shared brutality.[14]

Like his evocation of Chinese waves, Lee's prisoner follows popular portrayals of woefully ill-prepared Chinese soldiers who had no inkling of the strategic or political stakes for which they had been mobilized. The combination of huge masses of humans and hapless conscripts rendered the Korean War a peculiarly unsavory conflict: the enemy was at once indomitable and pathetic. Both caricatures were advertised to demonize the enemy, but instead of indicting the viciousness of the Chinese leadership, Lee's prisoner reveals American brutality. A sadistic GI named Zelenko tortures the captured soldier; Hector pits himself against Zelenko, but he can do nothing for the prisoner, who finally kills himself. Hence, though the prisoner erases the political distinction between friends and enemies, he instigates a new division within the platoon, between humane and inhumane. In using the figure of the boy soldier as a litmus test for decency, this wartime episode clearly recalls representations of grunts in Vietnam, whose platoons always fractured along moral fault lines—but Lee's restaging of the Korean War ultimately evinces little interest in American innocence.

Instead, it is June's hollow cruelty that prevails, and when Hector muses that "Before the incident with the boy soldier he had been a willing enough soldier in their war," this commonplace devolves into the emptiness of the conflict itself: "Or maybe not their war exactly, but Mao's war, or Truman's, or someone else's; it was a war that from the beginning had been nobody's cross" (99). The boy soldier belonged to neither side, and the war belongs to nobody. Hector concludes that the war was "both too cold and too hot" (99); he can only flirt with the politics of the war, which the novel deliberately unmoors. The novel repeatedly expresses such seemingly careless renderings of Lee's evident research into the war; indeed, the narrative seems most intent on dehistoricizing the war into a kind of epic platform for its minor archetypes. The deliberately flattened history of *The Surrendered* permits its reversals, but at a considerable price.

Hector's realization that the war was "nobody's cross" turns him into the nobody who bears the war's cross.

Hector's humane treatment of the prisoner only prolongs the boy's suffering, and after the war, when he is working at the orphanage, Min's misadventure with Hector's ax provides further proof of Hector's inability to protect those in his care. In the wake of the accident, Hector drinks an entire bottle of whisky and engages in a night of vice, after which he contemplates the effects of the war:

> seeing for three long years these destitute people and their children serve as handmaidens in their own wrecked house had finally begun to vanquish him. It had not seemed a problem at first, for it was nothing compared to what he had witnessed in the war, but he sensed that he was being replaced, cell by cell, with bits of stone. Even in regard to Min his guilt was as much conception as feeling. (121)

The war's bewildering political reversals result in this moment of bitter insight, and it is the postwar discovery that these people "serve as handmaidens in their own wrecked house" that renders Hector a victim of the war: like June, he is turning to stone. In the orphanage, she is the only one who can see his true nature: "June, the girl who had followed him here from the road, could see through his surface to the potential disaster lodged in every cell of him" (130). The novel is structured by this key resonance between Hector and June, GI and orphan, and Lee's experiment is to free his orphan from servitude in a nation of handmaidens and to match them, not through neocolonial bonds, but by turning both to stone. Hector is a strangely good soldier not because of his humane instincts, but because he is paradoxically vanquished by "these destitute people." Hector's experience stands in sharp contrast to period accounts of the war's devastation, which were typically couched in swaggering or condescending tones. And Hector, like June, is burdened with representation: he is a literal poster boy for the US Army.

Decades later, when Hector is fifty-five years old and passing his nights drinking and fighting in a dismal corner of New Jersey, he is still bound to the inhumanity of the war. Hector works as a janitor in a run-down mall managed by a slovenly Korean American named Jung, who calls him "GI":

> Jung had been calling him GI since learning that Hector had been in the Korean War, or else called him Joe, or Rambo, something else Hector would have never suffered from anyone else but didn't mind from Jung. In fact he took a small pleasure in the idea that more than thirty years of tumultuous world history should presently lead to a moment like this, for him to be dressed in cheap coveralls, mop in hand, preparing to clean the toilets of a grubby Korean mall in New Jersey for this most slothful of their kind, a man who was, literally, born in a roadside ditch during the war but didn't remotely know or care a thing about it now. (102)

Fixed in his wartime role by a man born in the same wartime circumstances, Hector takes a "small pleasure" in this latest reversal brought on by the war: he is now a handmaiden in Jung's wrecked house. Hector indulges and even protects Jung because he appreciates their relationship, which he views as a kind of atonement for his failed service in Korea, both in the war and in the orphanage. His curious rectification, of course, only mires him further in the trench opened by the war.

When June reappears in Hector's life to rouse him out of the humble equilibrium he has achieved with Jung, she reinstates her claim to his service. June's unsettling revelation that they have a son only hardens the roles they forged in the war; the son is never found, and the book concludes by sacralizing the union between GI and orphan. Lee's GI finally serves his orphan—not as her savior but as a strange combination of bridegroom and manservant. In disobeying his father's injunction against war, Hector discovered a demoralized world governed by relations of servitude, and his sentence is to redress the imbalance that vanquished him in Korea. His service for Jung and ultimately for June are apologies by an ignoble American soldier—and he must fight on for eternity. In the immortal and profane figure of Hector Brennan, Lee has taken the image of the valiant American soldier and forced him into unending servitude.

III

At the heart of *The Surrendered* is the reverend's wife, Sylvie Tanner, who attends to both orphan and GI. Not long after June and Hector find their way to the orphanage, walking "in tandem but separate" (111), Reverend Tanner and his wife arrive to minister to the children. Sylvie takes a special interest in June, and the two become inseparable, "whispering to each other like thieves" (136). Hector, too, is captivated by Sylvie, who appears "as lovely to him as a bride awaking on the first dewy morning of marriage" (160). The reverend is wary of both of them: Ames Tanner considers June to be a vicious girl and Hector, a debauched soldier. He cautions his wife against them, but Sylvie allows both to play out their overwhelming desires for her, at the ultimate expense of her own life.

Long afterward, when June and Hector meet again, June acknowledges their shared wish "To being with her always" (312) and Hector recalls Sylvie's particular allure: "he loved not just her sharp wants and carnality but how tightly bound up those were with her decency and beauty and goodness" (312). Sylvie is "a mother and a lover and a kind of child" (312) to both June and Hector because Sylvie morphs to match their shifting needs: mother to both and lover to both, and always as delicate as a child. At the end of the novel, as she suffers in the last days of her illness, June expresses a simple maxim, "Every person needs the love of a good woman" (464), which reveals the necessity and banality of Sylvie: she is what Lee's orphan and GI are both missing. Indeed, her goodness is the necessary spark of the neocolonial relation between them—and its detached manifestation underscores the novel's depoliticizing operations, which must elude the unequal alliance in order to match June to Hector.

Lee delves into Sylvie's past, in which we discover that she is a product of extraordinarily selfless parents: "They were two people who over the years had honed themselves into ideal instruments of mercy "(177). Moving from mission to mission in destitute corners of the world, her parents purified themselves of every encumbrance, including religion: Sylvie notes that "they seemed to have lost all zeal for proselytizing, and her father had even begun asking the missionaries to identify him and her mother to the locals not as a minister and his wife but as teachers from the Red Cross" (183). Their sacred text is *A Memory of Solferino*, an account of the 1859 battle at Solferino by the founder of the Red Cross, and they make a pilgrimage to the church at Solferino, in which "the bones from the known mass graves were exhumed and cleaned and arrayed inside, transforming it into a sacred reliquary of the dead" (186). In the church, Sylvie is awestruck by "the unusual, lovely filigree of the walls" composed of human bones (187), and her copy of *A Memory of Solferino* becomes her constant companion—and later a source of fascination to June and Hector.

Sylvie is a willing acolyte to her parents. Unlike June and Hector, who have lost or disobeyed their parents, Sylvie is forever the figure captured in the inscription on the title page of her treasured book: "To our steadfast daughter. May you be an angel of mercy" (249). She is first and foremost a daughter: we discover that Sylvie lost her parents, but she is a world apart from the bereft orphans entrusted to her care. Indeed, the death of Sylvie's parents only deepened their influence. By inscribing her role within *A Memory of Solferino*, her parents hold Sylvie to a humanitarian standard; she proffers mercy to all, and those in greatest need collect around her shining figure. Like her parents, Sylvie is an instrument: the novel presents her not as a type akin to June and Hector but as a quality, the manifestation of a longing that neither orphan nor GI can express. Humanitarianism, of course, is a significant compensatory discourse for Korea, and even more so for Vietnam, because both wars were popularly salvaged as humanitarian victories. But, *A Memory of Solferino* is distinct from the American Christian mission that Sylvie and Reverend Tanner represent, and the circulating copy in the novel is, as an object of desire, a metonym for Sylvie.

The Surrendered recounts the death of Sylvie's parents at the hands of Japanese imperial soldiers in Manchuria in 1934. A Japanese officer forces his way into their mission in search of a Kuomintang (the nationalist opposition to Mao's Communism) operative, who is now Sylvie's Chinese tutor; upon finding him, the officer tortures the suspected agent for the names of his comrades. Unable to break him, the diabolical officer hands Sylvie's father his gun, offering to free them if her father kills the tutor. Her father objects, saying to the officer, "You are determining the moral choices here" (208), and when her father returns the gun, both Sylvie and her mother feel "a great searing rush of love" because "mercy was the only true deliverance. There was nothing more exaltedly human, more beautiful to behold" (209). Although the tutor, already beaten nearly to death and certain to be killed, nods weakly to Sylvie's father to pull the trigger, her father's moral choice is to remain merciful.

The moral choice taken by Sylvie's father is informed by his own political sympathies. During their ordeal, we discover that her father had been fully aware of the young tutor's true identity, and a fellow mission worker suspects the truth as well, saying, "it would be no big news to me if he had some involvement in that business. I wouldn't blame him. Whether he's with the Communists or Kuomintang, here's a young Chinese man with patriotic feeling, and he's going to be fine with the Japanese taking over his country? I'd think he was with the resistance, wouldn't you?" (203). In understanding the tutor's resistance, these mission workers acknowledge the politics of moral choices, which do not emerge out of a vacuum, but rather are inextricably bound up with political allegiances. Indeed, the refinement of Sylvie's parents into instruments of mercy, detached from religious affiliation, has been premised on sharpening political allegiances: "They still packed a Bible among their things but read it less and less, returning instead to their Marx and Zola and old pamphlets of Debs, for already by then they had become missionaries of action, a Socialist streak rising in them, which would ultimately draw them to northern China" (185). Their very presence in Manchuria is thus a political act, and her father's ultimate act of mercy is a manifestation of his political beliefs.

Manchuria in the 1930s was the "tinder box of Asia,"[15] and Lee's account of this traumatic incident presents a roiling political scene:

> The Japanese were becoming more and more brutal as they drove to make permanent their grip on the region. Manchukuo, as the Japanese called it, was now a reality. There were unverified accounts from peasants who had witnessed how they treated the soldiers of the Communists and the Kuomintang and the civilian resistance, rumors of how they tortured and executed their prisoners and innocent villagers. (193)

Manchukuo was "the jewel in Japan's imperial crown";[16] it was the centerpiece of Japan's imperial designs. In Lee's narrative, Japanese encroachment on the mission is evidence of the empire's absolute brutality, and in the figure of the Japanese officer, a young man with "the drawn, placid expression of a seasoned soldier" (188), Lee presents a villain who shatters bones and orders rape: the Japanese soldier is an absolute enemy.

Lee's evocation of 1930s Manchuria echoes the political analogy espoused by Truman's administration, which argued for US intervention in Korea as a preventive strike against a third World War. Yet the novel makes no effort to create parallels between these two historical moments: though we may compare Sylvie's experience in Manchuria to Hector's incident with the boy soldier—the tutor and the prisoner are both sacrificed as turning points for Sylvie and Hector—the novel offers no substantial continuity between the two wartime scenarios. In pointed contrast to the acknowledgment of "a young Chinese man with patriotic feeling" in the 1930s, political conviction simply seems to have drained away in Korea. In *The Surrendered*, Manchuria is a dangerous political arena, but Korea is an incoherent destruction; the moral choices taken by mission workers in Manchuria have no place in Korea.

Hence, in stark contrast to Sylvie's father, who serves political ends, Hector's perspective on the Korean War strips away political distinctions: whether Mao's or Truman's war, this war is a morass in which a helpless boy is conscripted by both sides and driven to suicide in American hands. Indeed, the novel's portrait of Manchuria shows us what is missing from its depiction of the Korean War: though Hector remarks that the war is "too hot and too cold," no understanding of either hot or cold war touches the story. Basic political distinctions have vanished: neither the division of Korea's civil war nor the Manichean divide of Cold War is registered by the narrative. Lee has evacuated the war of its political distinctions and as a result rendered both heroism and villainy impossible; instead, the war only orphans children and disillusions soldiers—and the boy soldier is both—to produce hardened figures incapable of making moral choices.

Rendered as a past instance of moral and political faith, a curious nostalgia pervades the Manchuria episode: though the scene culminates in the novel's most ghastly moment—the Japanese officer cuts away the tutor's eyelids—its caricatures of evil and good are reassuringly predictable. The Japanese officer is demonic and suave; Sylvie's father is merciful and valiant. Indeed, as they confront each other over the beaten tutor, the officer proclaims with dark amusement, "We must act out the remainder as best we can, according to our roles" (208). Lee has written Sylvie's sexual awakening into this episode, and the scene ends with her rescue from rape. Such melodramatic rescues are nowhere evident in Korea, whose grimness is only darkened by the bright anguish of this episode. The Manchuria material reads like a Hollywood tale, and by contrast, we see that Lee's Korean War is cast with wearied and toughened actors, in which even the smallest children know better than to pray for salvation. If Lee hews to the strictures of popular narrative in his Manchuria story, he has written his Korean War drama against type—but whether written within or against such standards, the types remain the focus.

Sylvie's goodness has been tempered by the horrors of Manchuria. Her single act of mercy in the episode was to assist the mission's reverend—whose wrist was broken by the Japanese officer—by administering a shot of morphine, and when we meet her in her mid-thirties in the orphanage, she has long been dosing herself with "the high slow horse" (212). The drug has become a mercy to Sylvie because it has taught her the beauty of surrender, but she indicts herself for perverting her parents' ideal of mercy. Sylvie laments her "ruinous clemency" (399) and admits to herself

"That she was finally as unfit to be a mother as she had been a wife, and even a mistress"; indeed, naming herself "a bleeding heart and a coward," she concludes that she is "a person unfit, it turned out, to be herself" (405). The mercy exercised by her father was part and parcel of a political awakening, but in the context of a ruined postwar Korea, mercy becomes a hollow—because depoliticized—gesture. In the absence of moral choices, Sylvie can only remain steadfast in her commitment to her parents' ideals by numbing herself.

Sylvie Tanner is an angel of mercy strangely devoid of integrity. Unmoored from religious or political conviction, she is an instrument guided only by a principle of surrender. Governed by "the compulsion to yield" (397), she strays to those most damaged in order to submit to their desires—and to June and Hector, Sylvie ultimately becomes a drug. At the very end of the novel, June and Hector retrace Sylvie's steps to Solferino, and once in the chapel, they discover that Sylvie had mysteriously willed the chapel in the orphanage to recall this haunting place. Their concluding pilgrimage echoes Sylvie's journey long ago, but their awe is different. June and Hector are not inspired by mercy; instead, they remain in desperate need of it. They cling to an empty notion of "a good woman" that sustains their strange union but empties the Korean War of humanitarian impulses. And June and Hector's arrival in the chapel only plunges them back into the war.

IV

In their search for their missing son, June and Hector revive their old roles. Conceived on the final night of their strange, brief marriage, Nicholas was raised by June in Manhattan, where she supported the two of them by dealing in antiques. She kept her son ignorant of his father's identity, but in the throes of her illness, June has determined to reunite them: with the help of a private detective, she learns that Nicholas is somewhere in Italy stealing antiques, and she discovers that Hector has wandered through a life of squalor to settle in a crumbling neighborhood in New Jersey. June's sudden appearance in Hector's life wreaks havoc on the little contentment he has found, and he finds himself accompanying his long-lost war bride to Italy to hunt down an unknown young man.

Following Nicholas's trail to Siena, Hector wonders "about this elusive, apparently criminal person whose bloodlines were drawn from a most unfortunate pairing": "Was he as diamond hard as June? Was he a misfit like Hector, some self-incarcerating soul? Or was he, like anybody else, desperately yearning to be discovered again, by any good stranger or beloved?" (300). Nicholas is all of these things: in her dreams, June sees him walking alone, self-sufficient and "perfectly needless," "a mirror of her own difficult character" (42). Growing up in her shop, he contentedly tinkered in the back, as naturally capable a handyman as Hector. Despite his "remarkable composure" (238), Nicholas betrayed that he was "desperately yearning": as a child, he cried in his sleep, and he treasured the inscription in his mother's most prized object, Sylvie's copy of *A Memory of Solferino*, longing for his own angel of mercy. Nicholas is thus an amalgam of June and Hector who is filled with the same desire that forged their "most unfortunate pairing."

As she contemplates her son, June accepts her failings as a mother: she recalls moments when "she would find herself being particularly unreasonable, sometimes squarely merciless," and she wonders "whether an objective observer would determine that on balance she had been the most damaging presence in his life" (242). Most tellingly, she remembers her responses to his nighttime fits, when, "although it would have been the simplest thing to wake and comfort him, she inexplicably stood over him in the dark, staring at his racked mouth and the tight, quivering shrug of his shoulders, and it took everything in her to renounce the thought that here was a boy she would have to carry about forever" (240). Just as she fought to keep from hating her siblings during the war, she has to struggle against seeing her son as a similar burden. As she searches for Nicholas, June determines to ask his forgiveness, but she acknowledges her "effortlessly monstrous ability" to detach herself (323). Heartless enough to orphan herself, June has, essentially, orphaned her son.

In Siena, Hector discovers that Nicholas died months earlier, and he and June have been following an imposter who has assumed Nicholas's identity. When Hector finally meets the imposter, a young, mixed-race Britisher, he recalls children from the orphanage:

> At the orphanage there had been a number of mixed-blood kids, a natural consequence of the war. They were sometimes teased or shunned by the others, but to Hector they looked like no one in creation with their wide, petaling eyes and buttery, earthen coloring. Yet despite their beauty and hybrid vigor he couldn't help but see them as being somehow vulnerable, too, doomed to their singularity, their species of one, which mirrored, strangely, how he had always felt inside. (347)

In Hector's recollection, he identifies "mixed-blood kids" as their own species, their own type. That the young man he finally corners reminds Hector of these particular orphans links this type back to the war: they are its singular products, beautiful and doomed.

Mixed-race children instigated the first wave of overseas adoptions by American families. Though *The Surrendered* presents the Tanners busily preparing adoption files for Korean children in 1953, "adoption" in the context of Asia had been a "fundraising innovation" to inspire financial sponsorship from afar by American donors,[17] and only a handful of Korean " 'waifs of war' and military 'mascots'" were adopted by American military personnel until 1955.[18] It was the plight of "GI babies"—"half-American children" abandoned by their fathers[19] and unwelcome in a society which "massively rejects the mixed-blood"[20]—that inspired a wave of adoptions which ultimately shaped the business of transnational adoption.[21] Until the early 1960s, the only children with any hope of being adopted out of Korea were these "mixed-blood kids, a natural consequence of the war."

The idea of Americans adopting these orphans was largely the product of the enterprising efforts of a single American couple.[22] Harry and Bertha Holt made news as emblems of "the Biblical Good Samaritan"[23] when they adopted eight GI babies in 1955. Pearl S. Buck describes the legend of Harry Holt: "I first heard about Harry Holt some years ago. The rumors were strange and unbelievable. An American business man, who was also a farmer, also a lumberman, was bringing Korean-American orphans to the United States for adoption" (151–52). With his wife Bertha, a vision of "old-fashioned braids, unrouged face, plain dresses, and sensible shoes,"[24] Holt revolutionized international adoption by cutting through bureaucratic red tape to bring scores of GI babies to American parents. The Holts bypassed the cumbersome process of endorsement by social service agencies through "the proxy adoption method," described by Buck as a means by which "a child could be legally adopted by American couples by proxy in Korea and could therefore enter more easily into the United States" (157).[25] This unorthodox method, as well as their fundamentalist Christian screening of prospective American parents, made the Holts controversial figures, but the efficacy of proxy adoption was remarkably fitting for a proxy war.

The Holts make an appearance in *The Surrendered* as the Stolzes, a "kindly-faced, plumpish older couple" (385) who arrive at the orphanage determined to choose six children to take home to their farm in Oregon. June is a contender for their affections, and when she is approached by "these two smiling folk dolls, their cheeks round and pink," "a tide of longing unexpectedly washed over her" (387), and June surprisingly dissolves into tears. Mrs. Stolz comforts her, promising to take her with them, but when she touches a tortoiseshell clasp in June's hair, a gift from Sylvie, June breaks away and sabotages her chance at adoption. Lee's fiction imagines an orphan with the will to refuse a long-dreamed-of opportunity; June rejects the matronly warmth of Mrs. Stolz for the angular fragility of Sylvie.

Yet in reality, the Holts would have been far more interested in a child like Nicholas, who is a GI baby figuratively orphaned by June and Hector. The GI baby was, first and foremost, evidence of alliance: the US postwar occupation of Japan also produced mixed-race children, but the GI babies of Korea marked the novelty of the US-ROK alliance, the core alliance of this first UN war. The desirability of these orphans lay in their mixture of American and Korean, and in the minds of their passionate advocates, the politics of the Cold War were never far off: such adoptions were held up as political acts. Eleana J. Kim explains that the welfare of these children was "key to an American postwar communist containment policy that sought to use humanitarian aid as a means of building good will among the Korean people" (48),[26] and, as paradigmatic friendlies, their humanitarian rescue ultimately stood in for victory in a war fought to a stalemate. This late substitution capped an echoing logic of substitution unleashed by the Korean War, a distant skirmish designed to stand in for a world war.

The GI baby insists upon the unequal political alliance that the novel's rewriting of types obscures. Lee has played against type in his portrait of orphan and GI, but the figure of Nicholas reopens a Cold War order of familial obligation: though June perversely rejects the Stolzes, the GI baby discloses the care that attends a Cold

War alliance. In reclaiming these children, good Americans remedied the profligacy of American boys, and the political ideal of Cold War integration retrieved these children from oblivion: though they were emblems of an unpopular war, their adoption back into the American fold heralded a new, benevolent alliance. The Holts matched American benevolence to American might, and their brand of mercy reframed political alliance within the supremely unequal relation of charity.

In laying bare the unequal terms of the alliance, the GI baby showcases the moral duty of a Cold War superpower. Chang-rae Lee rewrote the hallowed tableau of orphan and GI, but at a significant cost: no spark of mercy unites them, and *The Surrendered* requires a mediating angel to match its defiant orphan to its servile soldier. Sylvie Tanner's story must reach back to 1930s Manchuria to provide a political context for merciful alliance that has simply fallen away in the novel's portrayal of the Korean War—thus betraying a historicizing instinct that the novel otherwise flouts in order imagine its fiercely independent orphan and servile GI. Perhaps it is because of his perpetual articulation of Cold War alignment and substitution that Nicholas must remain lost: he is a phantom of Cold War integration with the power to bind June and Hector within the neocolonial relation that Lee's novel struggles to elude. In the absence of their GI baby, the book concludes with June and Hector suspended within their reversed roles: the GI serves his recalcitrant orphan, and both remain mired in a war without sides or end.

Chang-rae Lee's rendering of the Korean War zeroes in on the war orphan in order to free this friendly from political dependence. June is perversely independent, and she treasures a freedom that is simply unthinkable in the context of the Cold War, in which freedom is always an attachment to the dictates of the free world. Lee's hardened orphan requires an equally perverse GI, as well as an angel of mercy contrived to bind them together. These imagined reversals render incoherent the politics of the war, and *The Surrendered* is finally uninterested in the Cold War. The present of the novel, when June and Hector set out in search of their lost son, is an emphatically post–Cold War narrative. True political alliances belong to the 1930s, in Sylvie's backstory, and the novel evinces a preference for the anticolonial politics of that era over the proxy warfare of Korea's civil war. Lee is not the only Korean American to bypass the Korean War in favor of this earlier period, and *The Surrendered* is not the only instance he has done so in his career: his 1999 novel *A Gesture Life* tapped into a then-contemporary movement for political redress for the Korean comfort women of this period—to far greater acclaim.[27]

The Surrendered spins a perverse war fable, in which intertwined actors persist in an atomistic detachment. Unlike *The Martyred*, which rewrites Cold War alliance as existential discovery, and *The Foreign Student*, which can only spark its romance by remembering the politics of Cold War alliance, *The Surrendered* daringly attempts to undo this alliance. Richard E. Kim and Susan Choi employ writerly wiles to free their protagonists from the shame of political dependence, but Lee's orphan simply does not register this feeling. Yet June's missing feeling is precisely what is required of the friendly, and June's inhumanity detaches her from the war, even as she is doomed to relive it.

Chang-rae Lee has notably explained that *The Surrendered* isn't historical fiction: "I don't think this is a book about the Korean War. It observed what went on in the war, but it's much more interested in the private, singular expression and consequences of war in general."[28] This literary investment in singularity and epic resonance— Iliadic ambition is everywhere evident in this novel—cuts away the political middle between these ends. And yet, of course, this is indeed a book about the Korean War—not only because the war

conditions the paired protagonists, but because the displaced longing for mercy that overwhelms the narrative itself performs a version
of the humanitarian substitution that became a hallmark of Cold
War logic, in which merciful acts were made to replace and reinstate less satisfying political ones. It is Lee's innovation to pitch this
humanitarian impulse into the past, and *The Surrendered*'s return
to occupied Manchuria reveals a nostalgia for an era of isomorphic
political and humanitarian aims—which would be upended by a
Cold War logic that reveled in often wildly incommensurate substitutions. In the aftermath of the Korean War, it fell to the orphan to
justify a new era of militarized alliance—an ill-fitting burden that
Lee has attempted to foil, but at the peril of forgetting the Korean
War all over again.

REVIVING THE WAR
IN VIETNAM

PART II

REVIVING THE WAR
IN VIETNAM

5

Losing Friends

If the Korean War consolidated the military armature of the Cold War's midcentury consensus, the Vietnam War shattered it. And if that first hot war taught us how to make war disappear, we cannot seem to shake off the second: we still seem to be fighting the Vietnam War, whether as a military caution, a political syndrome, or as continuing grist for a cultural mill that continues to churn out pastiches of grunts and unseen enemies in the jungle. Korea was the distant release valve that enabled the transformation of peacetime into a glacial war, and Vietnam was meant to be another Korea—only to overrun every aspect of limited warfare to become a strategic and ethical morass. Indeed, the 1963 US-backed assassination of South Vietnam's first president—formerly America's premier friendly—seemed to mark the grisly end of the politics of friendship that defined Korea. And yet Vietnam teemed with friendlies, whose plight after the war's loss laid bare the perils of alliance—and also offered a late, humanitarian salve.

Writings on and representations of the war in Vietnam have not slackened in pace from the early phase of US interest in the 1950s all the way to the early twenty-first century. A vast and multifarious corpus spans Eisenhower's dominoes, the massive escalation of the war and its concomitant protests in the 1960s, 1970s accounts of homecoming amid military loss, the right-wing 1980s recuperation of a "noble cause"—and so on, to our ongoing reliving of this same trajectory from neocolonial arrogance to chagrin, transplanted to the Near East. Over the course of our long reckoning,[1] "virtually the only story that has been told by Americans about the Vietnam War," as Katherine Kinney put it in her 2000 study *Friendly Fire*, is the "idea that we fought ourselves" (4). The tale of "friendly fire" significantly occluded the friendlies themselves: in the closed loop of friendly fire, the Vietnamese—whether friend or foe—were rendered immaterial; they only served to awaken a waiting darkness in the American heart. And yet, after the war, the friendly would be marshaled to salvage a tarnished American reputation. Recuperated as late evidence of Cold War promises kept, this friendly has been made to prop up a narrative of rescue.

Significant recent scholarship offers a long-overdue focus on Vietnamese actors, and, critically, the war's refugees[2]—a turn which notably reattaches Vietnam to the Cold War logic militarized and instituted in Korea. Mimi Thi Nguyen's *The Gift of Freedom*, a study of the burdens imposed by "an empire of liberty" (6), tellingly turns to Truman's 1949 inaugural address to spell out the neocolonial transaction that saddles the Vietnamese refugee with an unending debt. Nguyen cites Truman's pivot away from "The old imperialism" to "envisage a program of development based on the concept of democratic fair-dealing" capable of "weaving a world fabric of international and growing prosperity"; and she reads this key "clustering of the concepts and targets that underwrite the gift of freedom" in order to elaborate how "such ambitions to sovereignty and virtue" are "realized through the alibi of the wanting other, the negative image" (13). Friendlies are alibis for superpower ambition, and as debt-ridden specters locked within a perpetual desire for the Cold War's "free world," they are freighted with the extraordinary burden of containing the quagmire of Vietnam within the very political consensus ostensibly overthrown by it.

The particular and revealing belatedness of this application of Cold War integration recuperates the war's refugees as friendlies—despite the fact that their friendly claims had been systematically disabled over the course of the war. Indeed, we may read the progress of the American war as the increasing foreclosure of the Vietnamese friendly. The conflict that mired Americans obliterated Vietnamese well beyond the battlefield, executing not only noncombatants but also the very idea of the friendly. American brass tallied success by body counts, and every Vietnamese body counted, thus undoing the scant niceties of servile alliance that championed Korean soldiers and orphans. Further, in contrast to Korea's friendlies, South Vietnamese soldiers offered little faith—indeed, Buddhist protest inspired the antiwar opposition—and attempts to rescue Vietnamese orphans were met with cynicism and marred by tragedy.

After all that we have read and seen about Vietnam, the friendly's disappearance may seem like a commonplace, and yet it was an ideal of Cold War integration and proxy warfare learned in Korea that led American advisors into Vietnam in the first place—and in the war's aftermath, discarded wartime friendlies would be made to revive these ill-fitting roles. To trace a continuity between Korea and Vietnam is thus to provide a Cold War political genealogy for the Vietnamese refugee, who is ultimately "deployed to 'rescue' the Vietnam War for Americans," as Yen Le Espiritu so cogently expresses in her landmark study *Body Counts*, which proceeds from the key assertion that "Vietnamese refugees thus constitute a *solution*, rather than a *problem*, for the United States, as often argued" (2). The incommensurability of this application of Cold War logic betrays a longing for a midcentury sympathy eviscerated by popular accounts of the war—and further burdens the long-forgotten friendly with an anachronistic feeling and a fealty that no one else could muster—least of all the GI, who notoriously lost his innocence in the jungle.

The epic proportions of Vietnam fashioned its own genre, almost entirely governed by the American combat veteran. To seek out the Vietnamese friendly in this oeuvre, of course, is to misunderstand its very premise: she simply does not belong to these scenes of existential despair, even though she serves as a necessary prop. And yet so many of the now-canonical imaginative texts of Vietnam revolve around a particular military figure whose explicit charge was to create friendlies: the American special agent. Initially imagined as an idealistic and anti-imperialist operative who forged alliances, this figure became the quintessential antihero of Vietnam as the war expanded. Tracing the metamorphosis from young American genius to primeval foe in major renderings of the American exploit in Vietnam, this chapter tracks the disappearing friendly at the mercy of this increasingly imperious American. My readings begin at the cusp between the French loss and a new American way with Graham Greene's Alden Pyle, to follow quiet Americans all the way to Rambo, who rose out of the ashes of Vietnam to practice a dark magic all too evident today, in our present reverence for Special Forces.

Graham Greene's *The Quiet American* (1956) famously pitted imperial desire against Cold War logic in Vietnam. The novel stages a changing world order—a fading imperial hold on a colony subject to a new security interest—as a love triangle between an aging Britisher, a young American, and the Vietnamese woman they both desire. Vacillating between imperial subject and Cold War friendly, the novel's impassive and alluring Vietnamese lays bare the political shift from imperial desire to Cold War integration. Thomas Fowler, the middle-aged British reporter who narrates the story, is

not "*engagé*" in the manner of the French colons, [3] but his appreciation of Vietnam is deeply colored by an old colonial wisdom: when
Fowler regards the French in battle, he registers a familiar picture,
"fixed like a panorama of the Boer War in an old *Illustrated London
News*" (46). By contrast, the American Alden Pyle is, as Fowler
describes him, "a soldier of democracy": he is a CIA agent operating under the cover of an "American Economic Mission" who has
come to Vietnam to enact democratic reforms pitched against both
colonial and communist aims. Fowler derides Pyle's determination
"to do good, not to any individual but to a country, a continent, a
world" (18), wearily adding, "God save us always from the innocent
and the good" (20)—and feebly attempts to protect his Vietnamese
beloved from these qualities as well.

Phuong, the young Vietnamese woman who binds the dissolute
Britisher to the ambitious American, is at once the heart of the tale
and its delicate backdrop: though she inspires acts of heroism and
futility, she is little more than the "girl waiting in the doorway" (11)
we see at the opening of the novel, likened to a fragile, twittering
bird. For Fowler, she is an addiction, like the opium pipes she pre-
pares for him; for Pyle, she is a dependent to rescue—he offers to
whisk her away to America in the security of marriage. Her single
act of volition takes place when she refuses Pyle's advances, opt-
ing instead to stay with Fowler, but when Fowler falters in keeping
her, she submits to the American. Abandoned by Phuong, Fowler
puzzles over the relationship between his rival and his former mistress: "I wondered what they talked about together. Pyle was very
earnest and I had suffered from his lectures on the Far East, which
he had known for as many months as I had years. Democracy was
another subject of his—he had pronounced and aggravating views
on what the United States was doing for the world. Phuong on the
other hand was wonderfully ignorant" (12). Beyond her single "no"
to Pyle, her desires are unfathomable; indeed, the two men conduct

their contest for her largely in her absence. Repeatedly likened to Vietnam itself, Phuong is an object defined by the eye of her beholder: for the Englishman, she is a treasure; for the American, she is a mission.

Yet small hints suggest that Phuong may not be entirely ignorant. At the beginning of the text, when she waits with Fowler for Pyle on the night that, unbeknownst to her, the American would be murdered with Fowler's assistance, Phuong asks, "Did he go to see General Thé?" (14), revealing a political knowledge that Fowler uncovers more slowly, over several chapters. Much later in the text, we, along with Fowler, discover that Pyle has been supplying Thé with plastic explosives for use against the communists. Phuong thus reveals her knowledge of a secret political alignment that Fowler discovered only with considerable effort. Not only does Phuong betray her knowledge of Pyle's covert world, but she also identifies him: " 'He's quiet,' she said, and the adjective which she was the first to use stuck like a schoolboy name" (37). Phuong's "quiet" names Pyle's schoolboy seriousness and resolve—as well as his fate. In thus naming the American and his covert actions, [4] Phuong sees what Fowler sees—indeed, she sees more than he can—and she also knows what Pyle does.

On the long night of Pyle's absence, Fowler records Phuong's reaction to the eventual news of Pyle's death: "There was no scene, no tears, just thought—the long private thought of somebody who has to alter a whole course of life" (22). The subject of seductive and powerful interests, she preserves her thoughts, which comprehend both imperial perception and American political aims. In fact, every Vietnamese character in the novel, from the clinging girl in the brothel to the man languishing in a squalid alley, is burdened by such long private thoughts. In his investigation of Pyle, Fowler discovers an unseen, private world of Vietnamese military and political operatives relayed to him by his assistant, "an Indian called Domingues," whose intelligence-gathering skills Fowler attributes to the "fact that he was an Asiatic" (122). Fowler's attraction to Phuong, of course, is premised on her mystery: his colonial intimacy preserves her remoteness. The shared impenetrability of all of the novel's Asiatics reveals not only how little Fowler—or any colonial or neocolonial outsider—can know, but also the comfort he takes in his own distance from an order of intelligence that Phuong, for all of her ignorance, must know.

The American publication of *The Quiet American* was met with furious criticism,[5] and Hollywood presented its rebuke in Joseph L. Mankiewicz's 1958 film version, which rewrote the novel to absolve Pyle of his destructive acts. In the movie, it is Fowler who is unveiled as the dangerously naive interloper, and the American is recast as a hero.[6] If Fowler was understood—and attacked—as a mouthpiece for Greene's own critique of American intervention, the film excoriates Fowler for misunderstanding his own accusations, and when he attempts to shrug off his responsibility by asking "What difference does it make?" he is sternly lectured by the film's Vigot, the French investigator of Pyle's murder: "If this were a work of fiction, or entertainment, there would be none, but you have applied it to a very real historic disaster."

Neither work was intended or taken as mere fiction or entertainment. Greene's dedication in the novel states "This is a story and not a piece of history," but his note scrupulously separates fact from fiction to isolate a key history figure: General Thé, the maverick military leader responsible for a bomb that killed civilians;[7] and in the film, Pyle advertises to Fowler his acquaintance with "a very prominent Vietnamese living in exile in New Jersey" to whom the film is dedicated in its closing frame: "To the people of the Republic of Vietnam—to their chosen President." The film thus concludes by declaring itself a gift to the people of South Vietnam and its leader Ngo Dinh Diem, then the darling of the American political scene[8]—a burdensome gift indeed. Between Thế and Diem, we may mark out the competing ambitions of the two works: the novel indicts American intervention for its alliance with a dangerous thug; the film ultimately celebrates American intervention as a benevolent partnership. Hence, to Greene's denunciation of befriending a mercenary general, Hollywood responded by enshrining a Cold War friendly—though Diem would become a major liability, and his friendship with the United States would come to a murderous end. [9]

Greene's novel persists as a prophecy of American involvement in Vietnam.[10] *The Quiet American* launched a fierce debate about American political motives that came to define representations of American intervention in Southeast Asia, and the ongoing debate sparked by Greene's novel transported Alden Pyle into the twenty-first century, as evidenced in the 2002 film remake, which splits the difference between Greene's novel and the 1958 film: both Fowler and Pyle have softened their stances, and each seems to understand the other. The 2002 version concludes with a montage of Fowler's newspaper stories, through which we trace the French defeat in 1954, Ho Chi Minh's formal entry into the war in 1959, the massive American airstrikes and major ground operations of 1965, and finally the 1966 count of 495,000 soldiers in Vietnam, accompanied by a photograph of a bandaged GI. The closing shot of the film tracks into this photograph, but the picture is curiously unremarkable—particularly in light of the now-iconic images of the American war in Vietnam.[11] Against the haunting memory of burning monks, terrified children, desperate men shot, and whole families cut down, this bandaged American soldier marks the circumscribed terms of the debate instigated by Greene's novel.[12] The single American body displaces countless Vietnamese bodies; the question of American innocence blots out the multitudes destroyed by the war.

II

If *The Quiet American* launched the debate over American intervention in Vietnam, *The Ugly American* (1958) was a primer on how to succeed where Alden Pyle failed. Penned by two former naval officers,[13] *The Ugly American* took direct aim at Graham Greene's critique of American naiveté to expound the virtues of American bonhomie and know-how. *The Ugly American* advertised itself as an exposé of bloated and ineffectual foreign service—and, in a series of satirical political fables, prescribed a cure for languishing American policies abroad. Remarkably, the American establishment took heed: *The Ugly American* "became 'an affair of state' when Senators John F. Kennedy, Clair Engle, and others presented every member of the U.S. Senate with a copy and when President Eisenhower read it and appointed a committee to investigate the entire aid program."[14] The extraordinary political influence of *The Ugly American*—Richard Slotkin dubbed it "the *Uncle Tom's Cabin* of counterinsurgency"[15]—resulted in a transformation of US foreign policy.

The Ugly American lambasted the isolation and elitism of American foreign servants abroad by highlighting instead those Americans who worked their way into native hearts and minds. Lederer and Burdick created a template for effective American intervention through the figure of Air Force Colonel Edwin B. Hillandale, a thinly fictionalized account of Air Force Colonel Edward G. Lansdale, a former advertising executive and CIA operative credited with shepherding the Philippines into independence after World War II.[16] Lansdale was no stranger to fictionalization: he was widely thought to have been the basis for Alden Pyle, a contention Lansdale himself promoted despite Greene's assertions to the contrary. Lansdale was not a quiet American, and in *The Ugly American*, he is positively rambunctious: "Colonel

Hillandale became Manila's own private character. The politicians and the eggheads fondly called him Don Edwin; the taxi drivers and the *balut* vendors and the waiters called him the *Americano Illustrado*; and the musicians referred to him as the Ragtime Kid. The counsellor up at the American Embassy always spoke of him as 'that crazy bastard'" (110–11). The portrait concludes with the key point that "within six months the crazy bastard was eating breakfast with" the future head of state, to whom he would soon become an "unofficial advisor" (111). Hillandale's outlandish character insinuates himself into all strata of Manila society because he understands that his job is, first and foremost, to make friends. Indeed, friendship is posed as the corrective to the unattractive imperial model of colonizer and colonized: against France's failed recolonization of Indochina, Americans—as Lederer and Burdick would have it—succeeded in decolonizing the Philippines through the power of friendship.[17]

Hence, while *The Quiet American* punished its characters for local attachments—Pyle's dangerous alliance with General Thé, Fowler's collaboration with the communist agent, as well as their competing attachments to Phuong—every story in *The Ugly American* preaches the necessity of native friendship. *The Quiet American* revealed the dangers of its fresh-faced American youth; in pointed contrast, the title story of *The Ugly American* presents Homer Atkins, a retired "practical engineer" who made millions with "his ugly strong hands" (206). Free from the naive idealism that blinded Alden Pyle, the ugly American is a hard-headed man who refuses political niceties: his ugliness is an index of his capability—and he makes equally competent friends.

Sent to Vietnam in an advisory role, Atkins scorns "the princes of bureaucracy" (205) and proposes grassroots development instead. His ideas captivate Gilbert MacWhite, the newly named American ambassador to fictional Sarkhan—the laboratory for

Lederer's and Burdick's policy solutions—and MacWhite invites Atkins to his new post, where Atkins initiates an ambitious project to pump water into the hills. He seeks out a local counterpart, and discovers Jeepo, so named for his ability to repair jeeps. Atkins assesses the native mechanic:

> Jeepo looked like a craftsman. His fingernails were as dirty as Atkins', and his hands were also covered with dozens of little scars. Jeepo looked back steadily at Atkins without humility or apology, and Atkins felt that in the mechanic's world of bolts and nuts, pistons and leathers, and good black grease he and Jeepo would understand each other.
>
> And Jeepo was ugly. He was ugly in a rowdy, bruised, carefree way that pleased Atkins. The two men smiled at one another. (220)

The steady gaze between the two men establishes them as equals, and their matching ugliness seals their friendship.

"The Ugly American" thus does not depict the bombastic American abroad we have come to associate with the phrase: instead, the ugliness of the two men protects their friendship from an ugly history. In *The Quiet American*, Phuong's beauty only prolonged fading colonial relations, but this ugliness is a guard against unequal relations—and a guarantee of true alliance. Ugliness is not confined to these characters; indeed, the book itself is "ugly in a rowdy, bruised, carefree way": brash and awkward, its uneven tales unfold with a rough intensity. *The Ugly American* has often been paired with *The Quiet American*, but there is obviously no comparison between the tumbling episodes thrown together by Lederer and Burdick and Greene's formal control. The American policy that followed from *The Ugly American* was no more lovely: in fitful attempts to make friends, vast numbers of American advisors stumbled into Vietnam armed with "practical" ideas—only to be replaced by heavily armed soldiers.

The 1963 film of *The Ugly American* gutted the book to present a single US-Sarkhanese friendship that goes terribly awry. Stewart Stern's screenplay, a product of his travels in the region,[18] explores the friendship between Ambassador MacWhite and Deong, the popular native leader of Sarkhan. MacWhite and Deong were comrades-in-arms during the Japanese occupation of Sarkhan: together they conducted "sabotage activities behind enemy lines."[19] The drama of the film is a test of this friendship in the postwar era, in which MacWhite has become an American suit and Deong has risen to become a fiery Sarkhanese nationalist. When the two friends reunite in Sarkhan, they engage in a long night of talk and drink that begins warmly but nearly comes to blows: when Deong denounces US imperialist intervention, MacWhite labels his old friend a communist.

The fervor of Deong's criticisms against America is striking: in Deong's voice, screenwriter Stern expressed the myriad concerns of Third World nationalists in a new security era.[20] Deong assails MacWhite: "Your democracy's a fraud. It's for white people only. If we have to die again, we will die again. If we have to kill you, we will kill you, but we won't let the Yankee imperialist bastards tell us what to do."[21] In furious response, MacWhite extends the hotly contested development of Freedom Road—against the counsel of moderate American and Sarkhanese advisors—in an outright imperialist move which mires Sarkhan in war. The film version of *The Ugly American* thus exposes the impossibility of the friendship advocated by Lederer and Burdick. Indeed, during the long night of their soured friendship, Deong exposes the profound inequality of their relationship, saying to MacWhite, "And who do you think I am? Your little brown brother?" While the book held up Hillandale's friendships in the Philippines, with Deong's phrase "little brown brother"—popularized when the United States took possession of the Philippines—the film reveals the imperial condescension at the heart of US-Filipino friendship. MacWhite's friendly has turned against him.

By the film's end, when Sarkhan has descended into chaos, MacWhite and Deong both realize that they have become, as MacWhite puts it, "a couple of political cartoons." Perhaps we may read this line as a critique of the book, which is a series of such cartoons: Deong and MacWhite are both political dupes who find themselves advancing communist and imperialist propaganda at the expense of not only their friendship, but Sarkhan itself. In 1958, *The Ugly American* drove changes in Cold War foreign policy; the film version expresses a trenchant critique of political solutions sketched in caricature a mere five years later—the very year of the American-backed coup in Vietnam. Diem and his brother were murdered in the back of a truck as they fled to the Catholic mission: Diem's devout Catholicism had been instrumental in securing powerful American friends in the mid-1950s, but these friendships, of course, did not last. The nightmarish cartoon of the end of Diem's regime and the political turmoil that followed—twelve different regimes seized power between 1963 and 1965—marked the end of the political vision sparked by *The Ugly American*.

III

The quiet and the ugly American were both civilian agents, and neither imagined large-scale American military intervention. Between the high-minded civilians of these early theoretical texts and the heavily stylized tales of military grunts in the jungle that have come to define the war, we may identify a critical hinge: the militarized special agent. Special Forces first came into existence in

1952—the year of Alden Pyle's arrival in Saigon—as an unconventional military unit designed to work behind enemy lines in Eastern Europe, and by 1965, with the publication of Robin Moore's best-selling *The Green Berets*, these small military detachments ("A-teams") became a fixture in American popular culture. *The Green Berets* remains the most widely read text of the American war in Vietnam; the book spawned a ballad, a comic strip, and a John Wayne movie. Under its influence, volunteers reportedly swelled the ranks of the military draft.[22]

The Green Berets is a collection of short stories that recount various Special Forces exploits. Moore, a journalist, was permitted to tag along with the Green Berets, but only on the condition that he complete Special Forces training: three weeks in airborne school—which culminates in a parachute jump—followed by a three-month guerrilla exercise course. Touted as "one of the first true 'embedded' journalists,"[23] Moore expresses starry-eyed reverence for Special Forces officers. The Green Berets were the heroes of the war as the first wave of regular American troops arrived in Danang in 1965: this elite force combined the wiles and nerve of "ugly Americans" with military know-how. These "brilliant, young, great physical specimens in their green berets," as one sardonic reporter put it, could speak "six languages, including Chinese and Russian . . . had Ph.D.'s in history and literature, and ate snake meat at night."[24]

The mystique of the Green Berets did not endear them to the military leadership. Moore made a drama out of the leery regular Army commander and his highly unconventional Special Forces officer in "A Green Beret—All the Way," the first story in the collection. The Green Beret is Captain Sven Kornie, whose creative tactics—especially his use of Cambodian mercenaries to attack the enemy across the border—incite the ire of Lieutenant Colonel Train, the regular Army officer in charge. Special Forces camps were typically positioned along Vietnam's borders, and their primary task was to train and deploy paramilitary troops[25]—a covert operation that presents a pointed contrast to Van Fleet's regimented "service corps" in Korea. Kornie's mercenary transaction reveals the vicious edge of these assignments: knowing that the small band of Cambodian fighters will likely be decimated by the much larger enemy force, he arranges payment after the mission, to a handful of ragged survivors. Apprised of this maneuver, Train is aghast:

> "Kornie, you know you can't go off attacking across borders, hiring bandits, acting like"—he sputtered—"like the CIA. We're part of the United States Army." He picked up the green beret on the table beside him. "Do you think this hat gives you some kind of special license to go off on your own, conduct operations that may endanger the peace of the world?" (49–50)

The hat, of course, did precisely that. President Kennedy approved their distinctive headgear over the objections of the military brass, and the beret became a potent symbol of an allegiance that eclipsed regular military to serve at the behest of the Commander in Chief. The actions of the Special Forces were often indistinguishable from those of the "Agency"—in fact, they were often contracted to CIA operations. The green beret is a "special license": its wearer can flout every rule because his devotion to fighting transcends military and political regulations.

In Moore's tale, Colonel Train urges a promising young officer to return to a conventional assignment: "You have the makings of a fine career. But none of us can afford to do more than two tours at most in Special Forces. After six years your thinking gets unorthodox. After nine years you're typed. You'll be lucky to retire a bird colonel" (52). The Army cut off Special Forces from its career track by capping promotions,[26] but the young lieutenant is unswayed: "I know staying in Special Forces has slowed up a lot of careers . . . but wars are changing. We'll either be fighting against guerrillas like we are here, or we'll be guerrillas—maybe in Cuba or Eastern Europe, probably pretty soon now in North Vietnam" (52–53). This fluid understanding of a new conception of warfare matches guerrilla to guerrilla, and we may read this young Special Forces lieutenant as the heir to Alden Pyle: both are idealists who argue for a new kind of force. Impatient with ossified conventions, they operate through covert alliances.

When the ill-defended camp is attacked by "ferocious, suicidal Communists" (61), Kornie's unconventional tactics predictably save the day. Train heartily approves of his heretical captain, and he thanks him: "I am grateful to you for helping me understand this special unit of ours" (66). Yet understanding this unit is not always a gratifying exercise; as Christian Appy notes, "*The Green Berets* provide the material for a very effective antiwar manifesto" (127)—most notably in "Home to Nanette," which recounts the tale of a Green Beret who has been assigned to Laos by the CIA to train "hardy Meo tribesmen" "to stand up against the Pathet Lao and North Vietnamese Viet Cong troops" (164–65).[27] Over the course of the year, Major Bernard Arklin, a family man with two children, becomes "one with the Meo": when he is picked up at the end of his tour, he has "shucked his fatigues and was wearing a Meo loincloth. His skin had been burned almost as dark as theirs and only the graying stubble of beard on his chin outwardly identified him as Caucasian" (207–208). A regular army colonel regards him with distaste: "You Special Forces people always go native or something" (210).

The most damning evidence of Arklin's degeneration is his Meo wife, a girl chosen for him by the chief. She is a peculiar creature: "One of the girls was much lighter colored than the others, smaller breasted and more delicately boned," and the chief explains, "She is half French ... Her father came to this mountain in the early days of the war against the Viet Minh for the same reason you are here now" (171). Nanette—the name given by her French father—is a visible link between French and American efforts in the region.[28] Both her lineage and youth lend an incestuous air to their relationship: Arklin tells her, "My own daughter is only two years younger than you, Nanette" (173), but his "resolution to keep his relationship platonic proved no match for Nanette's efforts to make him treat her as the loving wife she knew herself to be" (174). Her Western features and youth are at once troubling and alluring; when she dons a sweater mysteriously delivered to Arklin, Nanette is transformed: "Wearing the Angora sweater she could have been a suntanned teenager" (181). His tribal wife thus appears as the disturbing product of their union: a manifestation of imperial intimacy, Nanette collapses generations to meld one imperial power onto another.

"Home to Nanette" is a frametale which begins with Arklin in a bar in Saigon, after a year in the field. Moore describes the major: "He was a lean, almost cadaverous-looking man when I met him, just out of the Laos mountains. There was an unmistakably bitter twist at the corners of his mouth" (164). In dramatic contrast to Moore's gleeful fighting machines, this Green Beret is a melancholy figure who admits, by the end of the story, that he still longs for Nanette. Sven Kornie ably manipulated his allies, but Bernard Arklin has formed a disturbing attachment: Kornie was "the ideal Special Forces officer" (23) because he crafted cold-blooded alliances, yet Arklin's assignment reveals the other side of the Green Beret, who operates through intimate attachments. The Green Beret free of attachments is monstrous—Kornie, the "blue-eyed Nordic giant" (22), despises the Vietnamese, and he displays exceptional skill in exterminating them—but the Green Beret consumed by them is a hollowed, bitter figure: Arklin is no hero, and after his primitive descent, he can never truly go home again.

Quiet and ugly Americans engendered the Green Berets, and in popular representations of the Special Forces lay the seeds of the nightmare that would come to grip the American imagination in the years after the 1975 defeat. Moore's pulp fiction reveled in brutality and primitivism: the license of the Green Beret is to descend into darkness, and the celebrated and controversial narratives that appeared in the late 1970s installed the Green Beret as the chaotic heart of the American war in Vietnam.[29]

IV

After the war, Special Forces fell out of favor,[30] and the lawless soldier came to represent not the heroism, but rather the horror, of Vietnam. The unconventional military officer took center stage in Francis Ford Coppola's *Apocalypse Now* (1979), the cinematic event—alongside *The Deer Hunter* (1978), which also featured a Green Beret[31]—that transformed the war into an epic frame for metaphysical rumination. *Apocalypse Now* famously presented the war in Vietnam as a fevered hallucination, but amid its excesses the film traces a single mission to Colonel Kurtz, a Special Forces officer who has crossed the border to become the irretrievable dark soul of the war. A pensive Army general presents the problem of Kurtz:

> Walter Kurtz was one of the most outstanding officers this
> country has ever produced. He was brilliant; he was outstand
> ing in every way. And he was a good man, too. A humanitarian
> man. A man of wit and humor. He joined the Special Forces,
> and after that his ideas, methods, became unsound. Unsound.

A member of the general's staff elaborates on these unsound methods: "Now he's crossed into Cambodia with this Montagnard army of his that worship the man like a god and follow his every order, however ridiculous." In his distaste for Special Forces tactics—and in particular their intimacy with mountain tribes—the general echoes Moore's skeptical regular army commander. Indeed, Kurtz is an amalgam of Kornie and Arklin from *The Green Berets*: he is brilliantly unorthodox, and he has attached himself completely to the natives. Further, if we consider Coppola's Green Beret against Alden Pyle's covert operations, Colonel Kurtz has mastered Pyle's tactics—but in Coppola's antihero, *The Quiet American*'s distinction between imperial and American intervention collapses. Transposed from Joseph Conrad's modernist classic, Kurtz is the dark heart of empire, and as the film approaches Kurtz, the war itself falls away to reveal a primeval core.[32] In Coppola's mad colonel, we witness the descent of the Green Beret. As Moore's bright young lieutenant predicted, guerrilla tactics have turned them into guerrillas; the avant-garde soldiers of the New Frontier have become the enemy.

Captain Willard, the soldier assigned to kill Kurtz, has been chosen for the job because of his own unorthodox methods: in his last assignment, he worked for the CIA on a mission to assassinate a Vietnamese government official. If we recall Diem's fate, we see that the time for making friendlies has long since passed into a phase of chastisement and punishment, in which former friends are ultimately eliminated. The film's famous opening presents Willard broken after this covert operation, and the remainder of the film traces his growing attraction to his latest target, who has embraced what Willard fears. From the general's briefing, the film metes out bits of Kurtz's dossier across the film's episodes: we follow Kurtz's developing profile, from his promising beginnings (his CV includes a Harvard MA thesis entitled "The Philippine Insurrection: American Foreign Policy in Southeast Asia,

1898–1905," thus demonstrating his understanding of American imperial policy) to his first tour in Vietnam in 1964 and his enrollment in Special Forces training two years later, at the advanced age of thirty-eight, after being rejected twice. Willard marvels over Kurtz's audacity: "If he joined the Green Berets, there was no way you would ever get above colonel. Kurtz knew what he was giving up." Willard takes in this choice: "He could have gone for general, but he went for himself instead." Rejecting the career track was a virtue in *The Green Berets*, but in Kurtz, the devotion to unorthodox tactics has become merely a means to self-gratification.

Kurtz marks out the nightmare trajectory of unconventional warfare. First promoted in the service of political aims, this strategy evolves to create a new kind of killer. The atrocities born out of adopting enemy tactics lay bare the structural risks of counterinsurgency, in which the quiet American—and ideal Special Forces officer—becomes an enemy to be terminated. Unorthodox tactics require unorthodox responses—a lesson already learned in *The Quiet American*, with Fowler's dark engagement to eliminate Pyle—and in *Apocalypse Now* we confront a dizzying reflection of killer and prey. Kurtz was seduced by the purity of the enemy and the brilliance of his tactics, and he in turn seduces Willard with his own strange discipline. Indeed, Willard's assassination of Kurtz—famously intercut with a ritual killing of an ox—is only a submission to Kurtz's primitive fantasy. And in Kurtz's realm, Willard discovers that he is not the only soldier drawn to him: a late addendum to Kurtz's dossier revealed that another soldier had previously been charged with Willard's assignment, and Willard identifies Colonel Colby, the preceding mercenary who failed the mission and instead became an acolyte. We see Colby in a green beret, flanked by native girls and children—a tableau that vividly recalls Arklin's predicament in "Home to Nanette." The Green Beret who has gone native has a faraway look and inhabits a dream world: he is a figure of

Apocalypse Now's ultimate hallucination, brought on not by drugs or violence but by simply crossing over, into enemy terrain.

Of course, the Green Beret came back from the brink of metaphysical despair to become an action hero: the most popular incarnation of the Special Forces soldier is John Rambo. In the first cinematic installment of the blockbuster series, this killing machine returns home from the war, his rage unabated. Sylvia Shin Huey Chong's study of the "phantasmatic space of imagined racial relations" (16) created out of Vietnam—an American unconscious fueled by images of the war—opens and closes with Rambo, a 1972 fictional creation by David Morrell, a literature professor who imagined "what might happen if 'the Vietnam war literally came home to America'" (38). Numerous narratives of return extended the time and place of the war;[33] in the extraordinary afterlife of the war in Vietnam, the disaffected veteran bred nightmares at home. The American boys who fought in Vietnam were astonishingly young and disproportionately impoverished, and they returned home to a stigma they struggled to comprehend.[34] Their plight inspired fantasies of annihilation, in which men deranged by the war attack at home.

In *First Blood*, Rambo lays waste to small town America: a hostile sheriff expels the ragged outsider from his town, only to provoke a major assault by this wounded killer. Rambo is a master of enemy tactics: in the American wilderness, he fashions traps learned from the enemy and finds shelter in a network of underground tunnels—remnants of a former mine that recall the extensive tunnels burrowed by North Vietnamese soldiers. With his men under siege, the sheriff muses aloud, "What possessed god in heaven to make a man like Rambo?," to which a green-beret-clad man materializes to reply that "God didn't make Rambo. I made him." Identifying himself as Colonel Trautman, he explains, "I recruited him, I trained him, I commanded him in Vietnam for three years. And I didn't come here to rescue Rambo from you; I came here to rescue you from him." If Kurtz became a primitive god, Rambo is a slave, an automaton programmed to kill. *Apocalypse Now* and *Rambo* occupy the far ends of the genre: on one side, a grandiose epic aimed to transcend the politics of the war; on the other, a b-movie intent on fashioning a right-wing hero. The 1985 sequel that made Rambo a household name begins where *First Blood* left off: Rambo reunites with Colonel Trautman to famously ask, "Sir, do we get to win this time?" And so, ten years after the war, the Green Beret returns to Vietnam to retrieve POWs. Hollywood was astonishingly receptive to the POW/MIA myth:[35] Rambo was matched by the pulpier *Missing in Action* series, and Hollywood's fascination with such rescues notably included an ill-conceived POW rescue effort funded by celebrities.[36]

But the real POWs of Vietnam[37] were the South Vietnamese allies left behind in communist Vietnam, where they faced terrifying reprisals. Fleeing these conditions, legions resettled in the US, where they found themselves corralled back into a friendly status long deemed a liability. From the enshrined portrait of Diem that closed Hollywood's *Quiet American* to the dangers of "going native," Cold War friendships morphed into betrayal and diabolically ensnared America's best and brightest. In tracing the fate of the American counterinsurgency agent in Vietnam, this chapter has marked out the narrowing political contours available to the Vietnamese friendly. The chapters that follow in Part II explore the "long private thought" Greene could not divine in his portrayal of Phuong, the unknowable yet knowing heart of Vietnam. Turning to Vietnamese American testimonies, the following readings examine professions of friendship that ultimately reframe the war.

6

Goddess of Reconciliation
Le Ly Hayslip's Memoirs

In his *New York Times* review of Le Ly Hayslip's 1989 memoir *When Heaven and Earth Changed Places*, David K. Shipler, the paper's former Saigon correspondent, expressed a wish that came partially true: "If Hollywood has the courage to turn this book into a movie, then we Americans might finally have a chance to come to terms with the tragedy of Vietnam." Oliver Stone, Hollywood's most celebrated veteran of the war, optioned Hayslip's story to complete his war trilogy: the first installment, *Platoon* (1986), featured the metaphysical plight of the grunt in the jungle; the second, *Born on the Fourth of July* (1989), the melodrama of a battered soldier's return; and the finale, *Heaven and Earth* (1993), was a streamlined version of Hayslip's life story taken from her 1989 memoir and its 1993 sequel, *Child of War, Woman of Peace*. The first published Vietnamese American testimonies of the war, Hayslip's paired books trace her tumultuous life, from her birth in rural Vietnam through a series of devastating removals that ultimately land her in the United States. Stone's use of this material was shot through with Shipler's lofty ambitions for Hayslip's story—though the film itself was met with critical scorn and poor ticket sales.

Stone's tale of his plucky heroine is riddled with fortuitous and pernicious alliances, and the film notably synthesizes Hayslip's American lovers into the single character of Steve Butler, a middle-aged American soldier who rescues her from the war, but cannot retrieve himself from its nightmare. *Heaven and Earth* ultimately dispatches with the tormented American vet: the prior films in Stone's trilogy illustrated the calamitous effects of the war on once-innocent American heroes, but Steve Butler is already a weary soldier at the opening of the film, and his death frees his young wife. The damaged veteran is a lost cause; the story instead belongs to the Vietnamese American woman, whose powers of reconciliation transcend the veteran's anguish.[1]

In the culminating scene of Butler's distress, he threatens both Le Ly's life and his own. Speaking in a trance-like state, he reveals that he is unable to free himself from the war:

> I'm a killer, baby. I killed so many over there. I got so good at it they assigned me on the projects, you know, black ops . . . Psy ops, baby. Knives. Rip a man's guts out, take a bite out of his liver, drop it on his chest so he don't get into Buddha heaven. Leave him laying on the road. Cut his nuts off. Stuff them in his mouth . . . The more I killed, the more they gave me to kill. One day they cut me off and one day I found you and it all changed, I thought. But baby, nothing ever changes.

Special Forces is the secret of Butler's torment, and his "black ops" lore provides a fitting conclusion for Oliver Stone's American soldier, who discovered the play between good and evil in *Platoon* only to lose himself to the dark side in *Heaven and Earth*. The first film of the trilogy famously concluded by saying "we fought ourselves" in the jungle, and by the third, the American soldier has become a tormented soul who cannot free himself from the war.

Butler's confession belongs to a strange figure in *Child of War, Woman of Peace*: the enigmatic Cliff Parry, who, after sweeping Hayslip off her feet, tearfully reveals his career as a military assassin contracted to the CIA: "The CIA was into a lot of bad shit in those days—drugs, gun-running, white slavery, you name it" (291). After unveiling this dark past, Parry expresses his devotion to Hayslip as a way "to put things right" (292), but when he disappears after their engagement, she discovers a disturbing truth about her lost fiancé: "It seems Cliff Parry was a professional swindler—a pathological liar and a con man—with a long list of aliases" (296). When Hayslip inquires as to whether Cliff ever served in Vietnam, she is met with an uncertainty ("Who knows? He's a very accomplished liar") that she paradoxically welcomes: "I felt myself uncoil inside. Cliff, or whatever his real name was, might have a lot to regret in his life, but slaughtering my people may not have been one of them. I could only hope and pray that his war stories, too, were a lie—but who could be sure?" (296). For Hayslip, Parry is, curiously, saved by his lies, and her fervent hope that he never engaged in "slaughtering my people" offers a strange absolution. She does not punish Parry for manufacturing this fiction, but instead prays that he does not feel what she knows firsthand, because unlike Parry, she is not privy to the luxury of the war as a fiction. Hayslip's knowledge thus affords her not only a remarkably sanguine response to a devastating heartbreak, but a poise and even authority derived from her experience of the war.

Cliff Parry's lies, however, become the dark truth of Steve Butler in Stone's movie, whose soldier is a through-and-through fiction—not only because he is a fictional amalgam who enshrines a dubious confession, but because his "black ops" fantasies are so patently a product of the Special Forces fantasies of Hollywood's nightmares of Vietnam. Covert operations licensed and unleashed proliferating fictions that traveled from Hollywood to a common swindler.

Special Forces fictions, however, shield a deeper untruth: as the title of a provocative 1966 *Ramparts* article put it, " 'The Whole Thing Was a Lie!': Memoirs of a Special Forces Hero." In the article, former Special Forces officer Donald Duncan recounts his increasing disenchantment with the organization, from its racist recruitment efforts to its utter "contempt of the Vietnamese" (15). Concluding that "The more troops and money we poured in, the more people hated us," Duncan indicts the American enterprise: "The whole thing was a lie. We weren't preserving freedom in South Vietnam . . . We aren't the freedom fighters. We are the Russian tanks blasting the hopes of an Asian Hungary" (23).[2] The lie that Duncan exposes resonates with Hayslip's curious instinct to rescue Parry: both know the truth about American intervention in Vietnam, which was never about "preserving freedom" and only resulted in "slaughtering my people."

Cliff Parry is a striking outcome of the lie of counterinsurgency in Vietnam that Donald Duncan exposed during the heyday of Special Forces lore. Duncan's furious exposé returns to the founding Special Forces mandate, "that reliable support can be gained only through friendship and trust" (21), and the lie of the American effort is a racist contempt that violently thwarts popular will. In praying for the lie of Parry, Hayslip seeks to protect him from the lie that haunts Duncan—and in so doing, performs a late gesture of friendship that is at once futile and revealing: though she is the wronged party, she seeks to shield Parry from the evil of "slaughtering my people." Hayslip's best-selling memoirs are shot through with such friendly instincts, through which she reached legions of readers—and also helped a famous Hollywood auteur "come to terms" with his own Vietnam tragedy. It is thus strangely fitting that Stone's recycling of Parry's hackneyed lies leads to the demise of his American soldier, who moves from existential crisis (*Platoon*) to wounded disillusionment (*Born on the Fourth of July*) and, finally, into the background. This latest damaged soldier sinks into the shadows to facilitate the emergence of a new heroine.

Stone uncharacteristically consigned himself to the background with this film, which, in the words of Janet Maslin's *New York Times* review, is a mismatch between his typically "volatile, angry and muscular" direction and the story of "a resilient, long-suffering victim." In his defense of the film, Stone insisted on the authenticity of the film's casting and locations, particularly emphasizing Hayslip's tenure as technical advisor.[3] In Thailand, Stone recreated her village—all the way to planting rice paddies, with Hayslip herself leading the way in raising and harvesting the crop. In the midst of their collaboration, Hayslip converted Stone to Buddhism: their alliance thus transformed one very famous Vietnam vet. Hence, though the film was deemed a failure for Stone, his conversion behind the scenes marks Hayslip's success: as she writes in her second memoir, "Like so many veterans I had worked with, he still held in a lot of anger about the war. But he also had the god-given soul of an artist, which allowed him to appreciate his feelings and transform them into compelling, and ultimately healing, images on film. I saw in Oliver a kindred spirit who could help my story touch a much bigger audience that only movies can reach" (359). Hayslip's extraordinary power lies in claiming a spiritual advance over the American veteran, who is still mired in the war. In relegating the Hollywood auteur to "so many veterans," she casts him within her experience and turns him out of the spotlight: through her alliance with Stone, she conscripts him into advancing her own story as a mode of healing.

Hayslip's achievement is thus to offer the soldier recovery, but at the price of his centrality. Indeed, he must convert himself to her cause. Her sense of Stone's "kindred spirit" presents an alliance in the service of the formerly lesser partner, whose recuperation comes at the expense of the American soldier. This late application of the politics of friendship lends Hayslip a benevolence with material outcomes—and mires the soldier in a spiritual debt. If Hollywood's Vietnam eliminated the wartime friendly, Hayslip more than revives this figure: she has bequeathed herself healing powers that empty the American soldier of his terrible force.

This chapter reads Le Ly Hayslip's work of reconciliation as a mode of alliance that unmasks the lie of American intervention. In reading Hayslip both within and against the foreclosure of friendship in Vietnam, I consider her writings within a genealogy of spiritual attachment that returns to Thich Nhat Hanh's Buddhist politics of peace, born out of the war. This philosophical resource, however, requires material support: Hayslip's memoirs chart a political education that reincorporates the wounded GI within a healing collaboration that not only undoes, but indeed critically indicts, Cold War divisions. It is my aim to take seriously Hayslip's politics of friendship as an enlivening force against the deadening frame of war. Her work sidelines the American agent in Vietnam—who is revealed to embody a pack of lies—in favor of reclaiming the Cold War friendly for her own ends.

The prologue to *When Heaven and Earth Changed Places* speaks directly to the American veteran of the war in Vietnam:

> If you were an American GI, I ask you to read this book and look into the heart of one you once called enemy. I have witnessed, firsthand, all that you went through. I will try to tell you who your enemy was and why almost everyone in the country you tried to help resented, feared, and misunderstood you. It was not your fault. It could not have been otherwise. Long before

you arrived, my country had yielded to the terrible logic of war. What for you was normal—a life of peace and plenty—was for us a hazy dream known only in our legends. Because we had to appease the allied forces by day and were terrorized by the Viet Cong at night, we slept as little as you did. We obeyed both sides and wound up pleasing neither. We were the people in the middle. We were what the war was all about. (xiv–xv)

Hayslip not only offers empathy, she goes so far as to grant absolution, writing, "It was not your fault." Her pardon claims an authority earned by firsthand witness that not only shares in the plight of the GI, but ultimately replaces him with "the people in the middle," the ones subjected to a Cold War logic that divided the day into two opposing political spheres. In thus speaking to the terrified GI, she explains to him, gently and firmly, that his story is not the story of the war. In this extravagant frame, Hayslip fashions a prophetic self that promises to heal the war's deep wounds: "If you have not yet found peace at the end of your war, I hope you will find it here. We have important new roles to play" (xv). Hayslip's memoirs present her growth into the "important new role" she fully inhabits in this prologue, which situates the story of a peasant girl as the true heart of Vietnam.

A critical turning point in her first memoir occurs at age fourteen, when she has already been wretchedly abused by both sides. Asking "I might be arrested again by the Viet Cong, or perhaps by the Republicans—but what did it matter?" Hayslip presents her political philosophy: "From now on, I promised myself, I would only flow with the strongest current and drift with the steadiest wind—and not resist. To resist, you have to believe in something" (97). This resolution against resistance establishes attachment as the primary means of Hayslip's subject formation, and her decision to "flow with the strongest current" directs her into the arms of the

Americans. She charts a continuing course to "drift with the steadiest wind" which ultimately takes her to the United States. This strategy has not enamored Hayslip's writings to Asian American critics, who have dismissed her efforts as collaborationist and presently ignore them altogether, despite their groundbreaking popularity and burgeoning scholarly interest in Vietnamese American cultural studies.[4] More charitable readers, too, found fault with this philosophy of attachment, as in Lynne Bundeson's *Los Angeles Times* review, which championed Hayslip as an "Anywoman" but lamented that "Hayslip looks on any man as a helpmeet. Hopeful about men I can understand. But romantic I cannot grasp."

This romance of attachment renders Hayslip suspect. Wartime political alliances are so often underwritten by sexual ones, and Hayslip, a victim of rape at the hands of comrades and abuse by lovers, endures attachments that demonstrate the difficulties of alliance, which, of course, is no less perilous than resistance. The philosophy Hayslip developed at age fourteen is not a license to profligacy; rather, it is a political coming-of-age learned from the hard lessons of a roiling context in which innocence, whether political or sexual, was never possible—"a hazy dream known only in our legends." In Hayslip's understanding, resistance is akin to a fantasy of purity that neither Hayslip nor any of the people who suffer alongside her can claim. The possibility of political resistance belongs to the GI's Manichean logic: "For you, it was a simple thing: democracy against communism. For us, that was not our fight at all. How could it be? We knew little of democracy and even less of communism. For most of us it was a fight for independence—like the American revolution" (*Heaven* xv). Hayslip's canny gesture of linking Vietnam's anticolonial struggle to America's layers together independence movements to suggest a philosophical and ultimately spiritual mode of alliance that transcends the Cold War.

Hayslip presents this critical attachment as the fulfillment of the wishes of her beloved father. Long before he was broken by the war (believing his family to be lost, he committed suicide), her father imparted the essential lesson of her life: when, as a child she proclaims that she will become a "woman warrior," her father corrects her, saying, "Your job is to stay alive—to keep an eye on things and keep the village safe. To find a husband and have babies and tell the story of what you've seen to your children and anyone else who'll listen. Most of all, it is to live in peace and tend the shrine of our ancestors" (*Heaven* 32–33). *When Heaven and Earth Changed Places* charts the difficulty of heeding these words: staying alive is hard enough, and, once disgraced and in exile, the task of continuing the family—into both the future and the past—becomes a Herculean one. Indeed, this lesson demonstrates the shattering consequences of the war: for a child assaulted and banished from her village, the simple ideal of finding a husband and tending the ancestral shrine becomes a near-unattainable goal.

Decades later, after having buried her first husband and borne three sons, Hayslip follows her father's directive to "tell the story of what you've seen." With only a third-grade education and a heavily perused Vietnamese-American dictionary, Hayslip resolves to write her story "to try to explain to Americans what it was like to grow up in a village and what the war meant to ordinary people in the countryside" (*Child* 163). She must work on her manuscript in secret, hidden from the vicious judgment of her second husband Dennis Hayslip, who warns her: "I'll tell you this: you start talking about the VC and the Commies over there and they'll take away your kids" (*Child* 163). In the chaos of her deteriorating marriage, her writing offers solace—"It became a lifeline to my past and, I also realized, to my future as well" (*Child* 163)—but "the memories brought cold sweats, cramps, and tears, like a mother's hard labor" (*Child* 209). Her "job" to "live in peace" requires a writerly birthing, whose labors demonstrate the difficulties of attachment and the tortures of reliving and, indeed, living—as evidenced by her husband's reprimand. And so, though Hayslip "began to doubt my will to finish" the manuscript, "I persevered. How could I not? I had a million lost souls behind me: pushing, wailing, singing a joyful chorus at every completed page" (*Child* 209). Though her writing threatens her individual existence, it bears a driving, representative force that expresses a much larger set of attachments to her people. The foundational shift from warrior to survivor of war, as exhorted by her father, thus necessitates an enlarged frame. From the start, Hayslip directed her story at an American readership, and as she struggles on, she imagines her story as a voice for a vast and disregarded population.

In tracing her life from rural Vietnam to eventual prosperity in the United States, Hayslip's story wanders and circles, perpetually returning to an ideal of peace and harmony never fully attained in her experience. Her narratives are governed by an arc of return that seeks to undo the imposed logic of the war, a formal labor elaborated in *When Heaven and Earth* as an alternation between a chronological account of her life and the story of her 1986 return to Vietnam.[5] In collapsing temporal and spatial distances, the narrative's oscillation between these two strands offers a formal means of heeding her father's call to grow her family while tending the ancestral shrine. The 1986 narration quiveringly anticipates a family reunion which insists upon continuities in a life of almost unthinkable ruptures, and the strategy of juxtaposition bridges past and present, United States and Vietnam. The structure of her first memoir thus creates a formal counterpart to her insistence on attachment as the means of completing "our fight." Indeed, Hayslip's extraordinary ambition is to effect a face-to-face encounter between the embittered GI and the "million lost souls" of the war—and she offers herself as a reconciling spirit.[6]

The memoirs detail the price of this hubris, however: she remains at the mercy of men like Dennis Hayslip and Cliff Parry, who exploit Hayslip's readiness for attachment. But each of these men finds himself consigned to the edges of her story—as even Oliver Stone did, for a moment. Hayslip's major effort—namely, to reinstate the war's proper subjects—thus critically relies on American conduits that are at once threatening and enabling. The curious mixture of romance and hard-headed pragmatism that sweeps through her memoirs echoes her father's wish—and ultimately enshrines Hayslip herself within "an important new role" in the war's wake.

II

Hayslip's perseverance in writing her story is fortified by her discovery of an "unusual little store" called the Philosophical Library, in which, "Instead of shouting best-sellers and coffee-table books of warplanes and bikini-girl calendars, the walls were adorned with spiritual posters. . . . Instead of shelves lined with dust-dry books by dead European authors, there were lively volumes on Taoism, Confucianism, Buddhism, Hinduism, and both amateur and professional guides to astrology—most written by people with Oriental surnames"(*Child* 210). Hayslip presents the wonders of the Philosophical Library as a series of replacements, in which Oriental wisdom replaces the worst of American culture: mystical images take the place of warplanes and scantily clad girls—both American exports whose deadly and corrupting influences Hayslip experienced firsthand in Vietnam. Hayslip explains that what "was an introduction to a 'new age' in Western thinking" was, for her, "like meeting old friends and family. Best of all, this discovery came at a time when I needed it most, when my spirit was almost drained dry by the confrontation with my own war memories" (*Child* 210). This "new age" discovery critically shapes her writing:

> Before, I didn't believe Americans could care about the spiritual life of my people. Now, after seeing America's new awareness firsthand, I decided that to tell the story of a Vietnamese family without its soul would be like giving stillbirth to a baby: a lifeless imitation of what god and nature intended to be vital and complete. As I studied, I went back to my self-appointed task with new energy and hope. (*Child* 210)

The decision to tell the story of Vietnamese souls breathes new life into her work and transforms her autobiography: more than an account of an untold experience of the war—already a tall order, with wailing and joyful voices at her back—her redefined "self-appointed task" aims to provide spiritual elevation.

That Hayslip pitches her books as spiritual guides is most evident in their framing pages, which, as we have seen, express her desire to attain and share enlightenment. Hayslip's narratives evince her interest in everything the Philosophical Library has to offer—village shamans and California mystics alike—but their spiritual flights are anchored by a sense of karmic destiny. Like the vast majority of the Vietnamese peasantry, Hayslip was raised in the tradition of Pure Land Buddhism, a Vietnamese variant of Mahayana,[7] and her story repeatedly gestures toward the completion of a Buddhist cycle of return. In presenting the fulfillment of a daughter's duty to her father, who has urged her to seek peace, she authorizes herself to serve as a shaman to an American readership, whom she claims the power to forgive—a paradoxical elevation through duty familiar to religious autobiographies, in which spiritual strengths arise from abasement.

Hayslip's spiritual and generic claims for this "new age" provide a crucial context for her work: the Buddhist call for peace that powerfully emerged during the American war in Vietnam. The monks who sacrificed their lives—whether in flames or in the crossfire—refused to accept Cold War divisions and sacrificed themselves as symbols of peace. Vietnamese spiritual leader Thich Nhat Hanh emerged from this crisis to become a major voice in the West: exiled for his social and religious activities, he educated Western audiences in the spiritual and political history of Vietnam. In his "explosive little book"[8] *Vietnam: Lotus in a Sea of Fire* (1967), Nhat wrote against "the widely propagated calumny that Vietnamese Buddhism is not a force in itself but is a mere tool of the Communists or the National Liberation Front" (47). Tracing the history of Buddhism in Vietnam to emphasize its significant social impact, Nhat presented a "third possibility" (81)—neither communist nor anticommunist—to resolve the war: a ceasefire for peace. To that end, he crafted a formal proposal: "The creation of a temporary interim government that would represent the religious and political groupings now existing in South Vietnam, particularly the religious groups since these are almost the only remaining centers of loyalty of the population" (83). Against great power politics, Thich Nhat Hanh advocated a series of local alliances in the form of a coalition government (84).[9]

In his foreword to *Vietnam: Lotus in a Sea of Fire,* Thomas Merton introduced Thich Nhat Hanh as an important voice "for a renewed and 'engaged' Buddhism" (vii). Nhat's "engaged Buddhism" critically bridged a division between the work of enlightenment and that of social work,[10] resulting in a significant political movement for peace. In advocating Nhat's work, Merton's foreword points to the skewed perceptions that result from Cold War logic: "Our political and military activities in Asia are perhaps too often dictated by puerile fantasies. Fantasies of good guys and bad guys, clean-cut clear-eyed Americans with appropriate subservient Asian friends, and sinister slant-eyed Asian Communists" (viii). Against such "puerile" political fantasies, which feed racist stereotypes, the Buddhist monk is neither good nor bad; he does not belong to the Cold War's dualistic scheme. Instead, Thich Nhat Hanh counters Western mythology with a philosophy of engaged spiritual practice that speaks to what the people of Vietnam "universally yearn for": peace (85). This Buddhist refusal of dualist assumptions and its active advocacy for a politics of peace unyoked to superpower alignment presents a significant resonance for Hayslip's diagnosis of the simplicity of the GI's comprehension, as well as her claim to speak for the whole of her people.

Thich Nhat Hanh transposed his scholarly points into the warm and direct voice of his more popular books. In *Being Peace* (1987), he explains his wartime stance:

During the war in Vietnam we young Buddhists organized ourselves to help victims of the war rebuild villages that had been destroyed by the bombs. Many of us died during the service, not only because of the bombs and the bullets, but because of the people who suspected us of being on the other side. We were able to understand the suffering of both sides, the Communists and the anti-Communists. We tried to be open to both, to understand this side and to understand that side, to be one with them. That is why we did not take a side, even though the whole world took sides. We tried to tell people our perception of the situation: that we wanted to stop the fighting, but the bombs were so loud. Sometimes we had to burn ourselves alive to get the message across, but even then the world could not hear us. They thought we were supporting a kind of political act. They didn't know that it was a purely human action to be heard, to be understood. We wanted reconciliation, we did not want a victory. (69)

This principled decision not to take a side is pointedly not an effort of alignment or even nonalignment; instead, it is attachment to both sides. The "human action" Nhat advocates is a call for reconciliation that offers a wholly different perception of the politics of the war. Hayslip's peculiar drive and benevolence become newly legible within this context, which offers a means of comprehending reconciliation. Indeed, this reframing exposes the thorough penetration of Cold War politics in conceptions of peace, which can only imagine an end to fighting as a one-sided victory.

Being Peace concludes with the Fourteen Precepts of the "Order of Interbeing," the school of engaged Buddhism Thich Nhat Hanh founded in Vietnam. The first directly addresses the political division of the war: "Do not be idolatrous or bound to any doctrine, theory, or ideology, even Buddhist ones. All systems of thought are guiding means; they are not absolute truth." In order to explicate its importance, Nhat spells out the danger of ideological orthodoxy: "If you have a gun, you can shoot one, two, three, five people; but if you have an ideology and stick to it, thinking it is the absolute truth, you can kill millions" (89). A fixed ideology is war's most deadly weapon, and the Order of Interbeing offers a wholly different order of politics, one based on alliances in the service of peace. Thich Nhat Hanh's closest acolyte, Sister Chan Khong—a member of the first group of Buddhist novitiates he ordained—explains the distinction between "two kinds of politics": "partisan politics to gain power and fame for ourselves, and the politics of reconciliation to bring peace and happiness to the country" (89). Against a murderous politics created out of blind adherence to a divisive ideology, Buddhist activists offer a politics of reconciliation.

Hayslip acknowledges Thich Nhat Hanh's guidance in the 2003 edition of *When Heaven and Earth Changed Places* (377), and to read Hayslip within the context of Nhat's spiritual advocacy for peace is to take seriously what the Philosophical Library has to offer. Hayslip's belief in a "new age" insists upon human action which is not mere depoliticization or, worse, a cover for extending neocolonial alignment. Hayslip's memoirs, in fact, force her readers to wade into the difficulties of thinking beyond a Manichean division: her spiritual plea for peace belongs to a politics of reconciliation which comprehends, but resoundingly rejects, partisanship. That our "concept of the political," as crystallized by Schmitt, is founded on partisanship—and that the politics of friendship embeds partisan distinctions—poses a philosophical problem that may only be resolved in the stacks of the Philosophical Library. Hardheaded readers, of course, keep well clear of such collections, but Hayslip's pitch offers a heartfelt challenge to Cold War logic, routed through a Buddhist order pitched against the war's brutality.

III

Thich Nhat Hanh's Buddhist order has been particularly welcoming to American veterans of the war. The experience of Claude Anshin Thomas, an especially troubled veteran who became a Zen monk,[11] testifies to the power of Vietnamese Buddhism to reach the damaged warrior. Thomas describes first seeing the spiritual leader: "The first night of the retreat, Thich Nhat Hanh talked to us. The moment he walked into the room and I looked into his face, I began to cry. I realized for the first time that I didn't know the Vietnamese in any other way than as my enemy, and this man wasn't my enemy" (40). Nhat's arrival launches an interior exploration that would result in a dramatic metamorphosis: the former

soldier, now tonsured and in robes, wanders the globe as a mendi-
cant monk. Rehabilitating the veteran, of course, was a widespread
concern in the aftermath of the war, and what is particularly notable
about Hayslip's politics of peace is her attachment to these wounded
souls. Indeed, launching her first memoir as a means of healing the
GI was elemental to establishing her "important new role," one
grounded in spiritual alliance.

Well-known efforts to heal these battered American warriors included psychologist Robert Jay Lifton's famous 1970s "rap
groups," which brought veterans together to work through a transformation from war to peace.[12] Lifton identified a collective problem in the psyche of the American soldier: a "gook syndrome," in
which the Vietnamese—whether women, children, or allies—are
"seen as symbolically death-tainted" so that they "can be more
readily killed" (198). Against this deadening, Lifton exhorts former soldiers to make a critical shift from "gooks to men: from the
gooks they had created to the Vietnamese men and women they
were beginning to experience, and from the gook in themselves
(the numbed and brutalized portions of their psyches) responsible
for this victimization to the men they were struggling to become"
(193). Lifton's healing process critically binds American soldiers
to the Vietnamese: to rehabilitate the soldier is to rehumanize the
Vietnamese. Indeed, Lifton fits his therapy within a much broader
opposition to the "war system in general" (15), and the weighty
symbols of his work with veterans belong to a larger project of "psy-
chohistorical investigation, to developing new theory and method
for applying psychological principles to historical events" (15).
Hayslip's project is no less grand: to Lifton's psychological principles, Hayslip offers Buddhist ideals—and both work toward a collective transformation.

Hayslip explains her attachment to American veterans of the
war: "encountering a Vietnam vet (soldier or civilian, it didn't

matter), whether he hated, respected, or just tolerated me, was like finding a long-lost cousin. A distant cousin may dislike you, but you are united by a bond of blood. For many Vietnamese and Americans alike, the blood bond of battle was stronger than the blood tie of birth. We were all orphans of the same shattered dream" (*Child* 32). This special relation trumps wartime political allegiances, and the notion of a shared orphanhood rebalances Lifton's rehabilitation efforts, which humanized the Vietnamese in order to heal the American vet. In Hayslip's version, the GI's healing is predicated on a political and spiritual education which sidelines him: to learn the true story of the war is to comprehend his political ignorance and to embrace a spirit of reconciliation that not only enlivens the "gook," but concedes to her powers of perception.

Hayslip finds herself conducting her own "rap groups": after the death of Dennis Hayslip—increasingly violent and unstable, he commits suicide—she opens a restaurant that gradually attracts "regulars" captivated by her stories of wartime experience and her interest in "spiritual matters" (*Child* 225). Hayslip plays at fortune-telling to discover that she may be a "conduit for some very interesting insights" (*Child* 225), and her growing popularity draws in a group of men with "the furtive, uncertain glance I had come to associate with angry soldiers." "One of the men said they were all Vietnam veterans who were curious about 'the other side,'" and with these men Hayslip exchanges her "impressions as a stranger in America" for "their experiences in 'Nam'" (*Child* 226). Such encounters multiply: "Word spread and more and more veterans sought me out for information, comfort, companionship, and solace" (*Child* 227). Not all of these meetings are happy ones, and Hayslip endures angry, lashing confrontations: "To these bloodied and worn-out souls, I could only offer my father's advice: *Lay thu lam ban, an oan xoa ngay*—Turn enemies into friends and your hate will yield to joy. Forgive yourself, forget the sins of others, and get on with your life" (*Child* 227). Hayslip's brand of rehumanization presents a simple but wholesale political transformation.

Hayslip details one particularly frightening encounter with an angry veteran who makes a scene at the restaurant: "He stalked off and some of the staff worried that he would come back with a gun but I didn't think so. He wore his hatred like a suit of armor and armor is defensive—it protects what's weak and does not threaten the strong" (*Child* 228). His weakness girds her strength, and Hayslip intuits her role: "The best defense, I felt, was not to be steel, but sponge—to soak up whatever bile he threw out and ask for more ... We had both suffered much in the war and now he, too, realized that was a kind of bond" (*Child* 228–29). Hayslip thus derives strength from her decision to be "sponge" because taking in his anger enforces their bond—and catapults her into a near-mystical role. Her power is a product of their relation, and her calm is itself an assessment of the soldier's recognition of this bond. Hence, while the soldier only weakens himself by raging against the "blood bond of battle," she becomes serene in her absorption of it.

Hayslip has thus marshaled healing powers to follow her father's advice to "live in peace," a corrective to her mistaken instinct to become a warrior. The woman warrior, of course, is the foundational heroine of Asian America, the titular creation of Maxine Hong Kingston's groundbreaking 1975 memoir. In fact, Hayslip's disavowal of this figure resonates with Kingston's late work, which engages with American veterans. In Kingston's 2003 book *The Fifth Book of Peace*, she recalls her chagrin at discovering that *The Woman Warrior* "is being used as a text at the United States Air Force Academy," saying, "I have to make up for that" (49). *The Fifth Book of Peace* retells the legend at the heart of *The Woman Warrior*: "I have told her story as a women's liberation story, and as a war story.

But now I understand, it is a homecoming story. Fa Mook Lan leads her army home from war" (390). In Kingston's evolving understanding, the woman warrior has morphed from an instrument of vengeance into a guiding angel who leads her soldiers home—a late transformation that echoes Hayslip's father's exhortation to replace war with peace.

The Fifth Book of Peace presents a series of meditations on peace, and at the heart of the project is an intertwined understanding of peace and writing: "Peace begins in thought. Thoughts enworded go from mind to mind, and mind makes the world" (54). Meandering through various genres and materials in order to write out this "logic of peace" (54), Kingston describes the writing workshops for veterans she led in Berkeley in the wake of a 1991 fire that incinerated her house (and the manuscript of her fourth book).[13] Kingston's workshops were inspired by Thich Nhat Hanh's retreats, to which she contributed "writing meditation" alongside Nhat's foundational meditations on breathing and walking. In her opening remarks to her own workshop, Kingston holds up a sheet of blank paper, saying, "Write things out, and you won't need to carry memories in your body as pain. The paper will carry your stories. We, your readers, will help you carry your stories. See how light paper is?" (266). Kingston offers the veterans a means of transferring the burden of war memories; the page will bear their crippling weight, as will Kingston: "I feel a vow coming on—that I will be the writing teacher of veterans for my whole life. I will help them write until the stories full of explosions become quiet" (314). Kingston's vow echoes the precepts of Thich Nhat Hanh's Zen order, which derives from two basic vows of compassion and understanding[14]—and her "new role" echoes the tone of compassionate guidance that frames Hayslip's memoirs.

As the workshop progresses, Kingston notes "that there are many Asian women among the veterans" (324). Wondering why, she contemplates her own interest:

> And we have our own motives. America's wars with Asian countries. Our wanting the people of our several nations to love one another. They can start by learning to love us. We're here to be loved . . . We're here to give them mercy. We look like the goddess Kuan Yin, and provide images of her. Veterans who've been to Asia recognize her . . . We're reminders of her. She is everywhere, and all will be well. (324–25)

These tangled motives sacralize Asian women as goddesses of mercy and present a strange evolution from the woman warrior's feminist empowerment, to an agency that is at once divine and passive. In vowing to bring veterans home through writing meditation, Kingston has remade herself into a reconciling force. Like Hayslip, Kingston reroutes her desires through a Zen-inflected Buddhism and a love that purifies and ritualizes sexual relations between American soldiers and Asian women, ultimately fashioning herself as a late apotheosis of the wartime friendly.

Kingston's vision of women as sanctuary from war[15]—a significant portion of *The Fifth Book of Peace* is devoted to a fictionalized account of her participation in the Sanctuary movement in Hawaii during Vietnam, in which peace activists sheltered AWOL soldiers—marks an anti-ideological turn deeply marked by Thich Nhat Hanh's political philosophy. Vince, a new participant to her writing workshop, insists that "Vet writers should have an ideology" (329) and lambasts their stories because they "have no ideology. No political consciousness. No sense or vision of how or why we came to be there and whether our being there was right or wrong" (330). He is met with silence: "Nobody debates him. Nobody argues. In the silence, Vince repeats, 'No ideology. Where's the ideology?' Nobody answers" (330). Their silence registers their meditative refusal, and Kingston congratulates their resistance to this weapon of war: "Good for us, I think, we don't have an ideology" (330). It is this seeming lack of political consciousness that has cast suspicion on Hayslip's work—or nullified it as naiveté. But reading Hayslip alongside Kingston, we may register the peculiar force and logic of the politics of reconciliation that they share, which refuses, and finally empties out, ideologies of war. A near-perverse rigor attends their political silences, which are not indications of resistance but modes of attachment and, more grandly, love.

Hayslip shares Kingston's insight that this order of attachment does not humble the loving Asian woman but instead magnifies and concentrates her strength. Within Cold War logic, this effort reads as nonsensical—but both women apply standpoints that are only available to them after the war. Their late espousal of new age variants of Thich Nhat Hanh's philosophy proceeds from a post–Cold War sensibility which is less a direct response to the war—as was Nhat's Buddhist order—than a product of the popular obsession with GI trauma that flooded the American scene after the war. Hayslip and Kingston have carved out new roles for themselves as healers, and Hayslip's highly strategic positioning of herself as goddess of mercy pivots away from the GI even as she reaches out to comfort him. And if Kingston's evocation of the Asian goddess presents a partner for the American GI, Hayslip enshrines herself when she dons this mantle. She has seized upon the wounded American veteran to offer healing on her terms—and in the service of a new set of political projects.

IV

The framing portions of her books not only spell out Hayslip's spiritual ambitions; they also enlist support for her humanitarian endeavors.[16] She concludes her first memoir with the foundation she created:

> In the name of my father and all the other victims of the war, I founded an agency in 1987 to help my brothers and sisters in Vietnam while helping my brothers and sisters in the United States come back from their wartime experience. The East Meets West Foundation seeks support from the U.S. Government, Vietnamese Government, the American and Vietnamese people, corporations, charitable groups, religious organizations, and individual benefactors of all nations to heal the wounds of war and break the circle of vengeance that perpetrates suffering in the name of justice around the world. (367)

Hayslip's agency is a friendly exercise par excellence: the parallel constructions in the above sentences exemplify her belief in rapprochement between East and West as the means toward healing. This extraordinary undertaking requires a new political education that facilitates Hayslip's return to Vietnam in an era when, as she explains, "Few people except diplomats, lawmakers, or military men had ventured into the country" (*Child* 220). Hayslip's narrative of return is thus crucially enabled by a humanitarian venture that pitches her spiritual reconciliation within the context of large-scale political negotiations.[17]

In seeking a way back to a country closed off by the US, Hayslip decides "to start at the top" (*Child* 220): she writes a letter to Reagan, in which she explains that "I had to go back to Vietnam. I wanted

President Reagan to understand that the Vietnamese people—almost all Asians—feel strong bonds with their families overseas . . . I didn't care about politics. I didn't know anything about communism or democracy and never had. I felt sorry for everyone who had been harmed by the war, on either side" (*Child* 220). Hayslip emphatically separates her pilgrimage from Cold War logic, and this latest profession of political ignorance distinctly resonates with Kingston's self-congratulatory lack of ideology in her work as healer. Replacing politics with feeling, Hayslip foregrounds her first person, appealing to the president as a "little Vietnamese woman" (*Child* 221). Shelving Cold War politics, of course, is a calculated necessity for advancing her humanitarian ambitions—and we may in fact read her two memoirs as an account of her growing political awareness.

Child of War, Woman of Peace—the title itself charts her development—elaborates her self-styled education in navigating government bureaucracies: her first letter to Reagan is the start of a proliferating correspondence with politicians and organizations that results not only her visit to Vietnam, but ultimately the opening of a rural health clinic. Hayslip displays a striking canniness in her humanitarian efforts: for example, in her first return, she allies herself with a solicitous gentleman who turns out to be "a Norwegian emissary to the UN's technology training mission to Vietnam" (*Heaven* 58). This agent facilitates her smooth entry into Vietnam, and Hayslip presents him as a fatherly figure who layers a diplomatic veneer onto her father's wishes.

Yet this assistance later becomes a source of suspicion: upon her return to the United States, a State Department official alarms Hayslip by inquiring after "a gentleman from Norway" (*Child* 259). Indeed, Cold War politics present a recurring stumbling block to Hayslip's mission. After her first trip to Vietnam, in which she was constantly "supervised"—as she writes, "I expected nothing less

from a war-worn, paranoid, totalitarian government" (*Child* 249)—
once "back in the 'land of liberty'" (*Child* 249), Hayslip is astonished to find herself facing an FBI agent at her door. Confronted
with official rebuke by both sides, Hayslip's politics of peace and
reconciliation decry Cold War political divisions as outmoded and
vicious. In the epilogue to her first book, she indicts US foreign
policy:

> Some observers estimate that between six and seven million
> Vietnamese men, women, and children are dying slowly of
> starvation, malnutrition, and disease because food and other
> necessities cannot be produced or imported in sufficient quan-
> tities from Western countries, some of which, like the United
> States, continue a wartime embargo. The circle of vengeance
> persists. (366)

The US embargo against Vietnam continued the American war "by
other means";[18] ongoing Cold War politics perpetuate wartime mis-
ery. This significant framing of US policy as an element within the
Buddhist concept of a "circle of vengeance" connects Hayslip's critique to the politics of peace elaborated by Thich Nhat Hanh. In the
epilogue to her second book, Hayslip notes political progress, both
within Vietnam through its 1986 policy of "*doi moi*, or economic
renovation" (*Child* 364) and by the United States: "For America's
longest war, the circle of vengeance appears to be breaking. The U.S.
State Department has devised a four-phase plan for normalization of
political and economic relations with Vietnam, beginning with the
March 1992 lifting of its ban on organized travel to the country and
a grant of $4 million for humanitarian assistance" (*Child* 364). This
economic reopening of Vietnam to the United States may certainly
be read as a belated capitalist victory,[19] but Hayslip's Buddhist lens
insists on a politics of reconciliation that has superseded Cold War

distinctions. For Hayslip, this political rapprochement marks the true end of the war's political divisions—and not the late triumph of the other side. This perhaps willful misrecognition of the politics of American "normalization" elaborates the subtlety of her own friendly position, whose spiritual edifice in part shields her conduct from the charge of neoliberalism.

Further, in transposing her critique and approval of US foreign policy into her spiritual worldview, Hayslip permits individual action to resonate on a global political stage. As she explains in her first epilogue, "We have time in abundance—an eternity, in fact—to repeat our mistakes. We only need to correct them once, however—to learn our lesson and hear the song of enlightenment—to break the chain of vengeance forever" (366). The personal nature of her politics comes home in her negotiations within her family upon her homecoming, because her eldest brother Bon Nghe is a Communist functionary in Vietnam, and her reunion with him requires a series of delicate negotiations: government permits and witnesses, agreed-upon meeting places. Hayslip's fragile reunion with her brother reveals how thoroughly the family has been imbricated within warring political systems (both his stiff reserve and her overwhelming effusiveness have been conditioned by the two political systems they represent), yet their rapprochement is a human reconciliation that forges a new kind of political alliance. As the youngest in the family, she saw and knew little of the eldest, but their adult reconciliation is built on a shared humanitarian interest. It is to Bon Nghe that she first divulges her humanitarian ambitions—"Perhaps we'll build a clinic for the poor people of Danang" (*Heaven* 311)—and his enthusiastic reply warms the chill between them: "'If you can bring the Americans,' Bon Nghe said, 'we'll find a place to build their clinic!'" (*Heaven* 311).

What Hayslip initially discounts as "brave and heady talk" (*Heaven* 311) ultimately materializes into a health clinic in

Vietnam, for which Hayslip notably enlists the assistance of American veterans groups that have been conducting return visits to Vietnam and gradually incorporating medical assistance.[20] Her trips to Vietnam multiply, and her second memoir concludes with the emotional grand opening of her "Mother's Love Health Clinic"—a name that emblazons the purified love Kingston championed. The epilogue to *Child of War, Woman of Peace* depicts her clinic's "first patient":

> a former soldier who had carried pieces of a fragmentation grenade in his hand for the last twenty years. Government doctors who had last examined him thought the operation was too minor to consume their valuable time, so the patient was advised to "grin and bear it." Until today, that's just what he did. (363)

The local doctors remove these painful traces of the war: "they presented three jagged fragments to the soldier as a souvenir, his last from the war" (363). It is with considerable surprise, however, that we discover the identity of this patient: "Louis Block, U.S. Viet Nam Veteran from Plummer, ID, USA; On tour-of-duty mission with East Meets West Foundation, Oct. 22, 1989; Da Nang, Quang Nam Province, Viet Nam" (363–64). The first patient is not Vietnamese, but rather an American veteran who is literally healed by his enlistment in a humanitarian mission. The clinic's first order of business addresses American wounds; the goddess of mercy heals the GI's lacerated hand.

The perversity of this first act complicates a highly available reading of Hayslip's humanitarian mission as an instance of neoliberal extension. Randall Williams offers a piercing critique of human rights discourse as "a convenient cover for the extension of capitalist-democratic uneven relations of power by reinforcing imperialist hegemonic control"—which he launches against "optimistic formulations" of humanitarianism as "an answer" whereby "contemporary globalization is understood as having created new, objective conditions for progressive, even radical opportunities" (xv). Hayslip's efforts, of course, require this rosier view, in which political normalization creates the conditions for breaking "the chain of vengeance." Humanitarianism as answer, of course, is particularly vexed for Vietnamese Americans: Yen Le Espiritu and Mimi Thi Nguyen have exposed both the alibi and debt of humanitarianism. Their critical accounts attend to the plight of the war's refugee, who is made to take on this burden—to which Hayslip's welcome shouldering of American military trauma layers a complex possibility. Hayslip understands that to absorb the war's bile is in fact to reclaim it, and her wild optimism assumes a miraculous end to the politics of the war.

Perhaps we may understand her success by returning to the simple reversal advocated by her father: "Turn enemies into friends and your hate will yield to joy." At the heart of Hayslip's humanitarianism is a joyful redirection of wartime political alignments, not political neutrality. This distinction in part explains Hayslip's contrarian decision to make the American GI the first recipient of her "Mother's Love"—her efforts require a perpetual attachment that does not transcend or ignore the war's divisions, but rather absorbs them. Hence, in healing the American soldier's long-neglected wound, she indicts American "Government doctors," and not Vietnam's medical establishment—and, more broadly, her humanitarian efforts have been squarely directed against the American embargo. We may thus read Hayslip as having coopted an imperialist humanitarianism in the service of a set of ongoing reversals which expose American enmity and, indeed, require a healing prophet who is able to see past the war's divisions but also, critically, to dwell within them.

The bracing experience of Vietnam has been foundational to a contemporary humanitarian ethic—devised out of working through the crisis of the war's refugees—that Neda Atanasoski has identified as "the consolidation of postsocialist imperial and humanitarian fantasies of the 1990s and beyond" (74): the shocking exposure of wartime atrocities in Vietnam "became linked to the possibility of national transfiguration and resurrection rather than deterioration" (75). Atanasoski reads the popular sacralization of the war's horrors as a means toward an American assumption of "older racialized frames of human redemption" (77). Hayslip's humanitarianism flirts openly with this order of fantasy, and indeed even harnesses it when she forgives the GI; her good works are founded on the exceptionalist sacralization that awakened a triumphalist American narrative that could then skip back, from neocolonial to outright colonial benevolence. But the true brutality she uncovers does not belong to the grunt in the jungle but rather to governmental policies of vengeance; her spiritual awakening permits an individual intervention into a larger political cycle.

That her enlivening of Vietnamese suffering heals the GI and enshrines herself are not merely byproducts of her humanitarian vision, but rather that vision's very conditions of possibility. The romance and grandeur that have cast doubt on Le Ly Hayslip's humanitarianism paradoxically distinguish her efforts from those that would mire the refugee in a psychic and ethical debt that she can never repay: her devotion to healing the wounded GI indicts American vengeance and her willing assumption of his psychic burden relegates him to the peripheries of her perception of the war—and positions Hayslip herself in the center of the frame. This complicated dance is thus not entirely complicit with a neoliberal or imperial humanitarianism, but it is certainly not readily reproducible—and perhaps not even desirable. This vision reintroduces the friendly long after she has been eliminated, in a singular formulation that supersedes the Cold War logic that she must perpetually recapitulate in order to play her "important new role."

Hayslip's overarching and convoluted ethics presents a significant contrast to the universalizing efforts of the friendly in Richard Kim's existential order, in which high literary endeavors of truth-seeking preserved US interests in Korea. If the secret of Kim's novel was a nonbelief that seemed to offer a shelter away from US alliances but only deepened the friendly's betrayal of his people, Hayslip's story presents a friendly urged on by her people and even welcomed back. Hayslip's friendly is remarkably impervious to the betrayal that Kim's cold warrior must not acknowledge, but her success is premised on attachments that ultimately keep her within the circle of vengeance even as she breaks through it—and consign her own books to the shelves of the Philosophical Library.

7

Fabricating Friends in Lan Cao's
Monkey Bridge

Lan Cao's 1997 novel *Monkey Bridge* constructs a coming-of-age tale around a family secret. Mai Nguyen and her mother, Thanh, escaped Vietnam in 1975 to settle in Falls Church, Virginia, but Mai's grandfather Baba Quan—the only other living member of their family—has been lost, left behind in enemy territory. Four years later, mother and daughter are both tormented by the missing Baba Quan: after a debilitating stroke, Thanh calls out to her father, "his name coming out of her throat as a long infernal moan" (4); and seventeen-year-old Mai desperately longs for her grandfather's support, as she notes that Baba Quan "was the buffer I needed to help me make it through the continuing gravity of our family's emergency. He could step in and take care of her, and I could leave home for college with the reassurance that she would not be—would not feel—abandoned" (17). Mai's perspective governs *Monkey Bridge*, and her drive to find her grandfather ultimately reveals both her mother's tragic past, and the divisive politics of the Vietnam War.

Mai has been told that although her mother and grandfather were to have departed Vietnam together, a "mishap" left her grandfather "without the means to leave Saigon. For some unknown reason, they had missed each other at their place of rendezvous on the 30th of April, 1975, and the preapproved car that was supposed to take both of them, along with a few other Vietnamese, to an American plane, had had to leave without him" (4). The date of April 30, 1975 lends a political significance to this purported meeting, which failed to take place on the day Saigon fell. As Mai worries over her grandfather's fate, she concocts imaginary scenarios of her grandfather as "a frail figure pacing the cement sidewalk" (164) desperately looking for his daughter. The fact of Baba Quan's absence leads Mai to return to this date repeatedly and obsessively—and this date, we discover by the novel's end, is a clue to his true whereabouts. Baba Quan was not lost in the chaos of that fateful day; instead, as Thanh finally reveals in a letter to Mai at the very end of the novel, "he was in fact part of a conquering army whose tanks blasted through the barricades and stormed down Saigon's boulevards with predatory fury on April 30, 1975" (228). Baba Quan remained behind because he was a part of the enemy force.

Mai is shielded from this truth and instead fed invented tales of Baba Quan's exemplary devotion and spectacular bravery. Alone in the apartment while her mother recovers in the hospital, Mai burrows into her mother's private papers to discover a diary—which we later learn was fabricated by Thanh for Mai to find—in which Thanh paints a loving portrait of her father as a virtuous farmer in the Mekong Delta. The truth, we later learn, is that Baba Quan was a failed farmer and a vindictive drunk, and the novel contains several strategically placed hints about his true allegiance. Early on in the novel, Mai recalls his "hushed refrain" when recounting Vietnam's legendary repulsion of Mongol invaders: "The moment the first American soldiers set foot on Vietnamese soil, they should have been told the story of how Vietnam had conquered the Mongols" (18). And later, in her mother's planted diary, she reads his political sentiments converted into village wisdom: "And for those like my father who did not own the land, it was further understood that tending the fields through flood and drought was in itself a worthy discipline, for ownership was not a prerequisite to tilling the land with pride. 'The land isn't ours, any of ours, to own, in any event,' my father used to say philosophically" (184). Packaged as the wise words of a village sage, Baba Quan's rural virtues are actually an alibi for political resistance.

Baba Quan's mysterious plight reveals complex political machinations well beyond the orbit of their family. Mai expresses her frustration at her inability to contact her grandfather:

> My grandfather might as well have walked through the hum of our orbit into a stillborn space where all tangible residues could simply be made to disappear. It was an accruing mystery, but that, in effect, was what an American trade embargo could do, make an entire country vanish like an electronic blip from the living pulses of the world's radar screen. Mail service to Vietnam was not reliable. Packages of monetary significance could not be sent. And telephone connections transmitted from the United States were simply prohibited. There was no getting around the distance of miles and the implacability of an embargo, the fate, it appeared, for countries unlucky enough to defeat the United States in war. (196–97)

Mai's indictment of the US trade embargo marks a rare critique of the new world she has otherwise eagerly embraced. Hence, in addition to the politics of Third-World nationalism submerged within Baba Quan's folk wisdom, his disappearance uncovers the continuing US aggression against its former foe.

Monkey Bridge contains the political critique enabled by Baba Quan's disappearance, however, by locking him within a family melodrama. When, in her final letter, Thanh unveils his true nature, she converts his political resistance into "wholly personal" desires: her letter exposes the "inexhaustible passion that he managed to hide behind the cold, calculating doctrine of class warfare between landlord and peasant" (234). A significant aspect of the mystery of Baba Quan is his relationship to a rich landlord, Uncle Khan, whom we discover is Thanh's true father—a secret which drives toward a lurid scene between the two men:

> Through the faint streams of light cast by a kerosene lantern, I could make out the red-smeared face of Baba Quan. While another man pinned Uncle Khan to the ground, Baba Quan plunged a knife through Uncle Khan's throat. Right there, on sacred earth, our village burial ground, a murder was being committed before my eyes, a slow-burning rage that had begun years before, finally released with the deadly precision of a knife's edge.
>
> "Don't you have something to tell him?" a man's voice asked as Baba Quan dug his knife into a tangle of veins. "Let him know. Crimes against the people cannot go unpunished. Land to the Landless."
>
> "Believe me, he knows, comrade, he knows the way he knows the beat of his own lustful heart exactly why he is being punished," Baba Quan sobbed. Here was the man, he must have thought, whose hands had once touched his wife's naked body. (249–50)

Shifting from crimes against the people to private lust, Baba Quan's resistance is emptied of political significance. Thanh's final letter bluntly states "that Baba Quan, the man I call Father, is a Vietcong from whom I am still trying to escape" (227), and in burying this "Vietcong" in the family, the novel submerges and vacates his political identity.

Michiko Kakutani's otherwise glowing review of *Monkey Bridge* in *The New York Times* concedes that "Ms. Cao's orchestration of these melodramatic revelations is far from fluent,"[1] and Cao's authorial hand is all too visible in the fantastic scene of murder. Yet this "orchestration" embellishes a fairly unremarkable truth: that villagers supported the National Liberation Front (NLF) is no revelation. Indeed, what is extraordinary about Baba Quan's character are the writerly lengths taken to conceal, and then to reveal, his enmity. In the vicious arena of imperial and civil war, contrasting political loyalties often divided families, and Cao's own family was no exception: her uncle joined the NLF, and, as an interviewer explains, "It was this uncle who regaled Cao with Vietnamese nationalist myths and stories and who was the model for the character of the grandfather in *Monkey Bridge*."[2] The novel's formal excess thus fixes a fluid political position within melodramatic modes of betrayal.

The ultimate disclosure of Baba Quan's villainy dooms Thanh and utterly detaches Mai: Thanh's revelatory final letter is a suicide note which frees Mai to begin a new life. Indeed, Baba Quan finally does do what Mai has longed for: given that Thanh's letter frames her suicide as an inevitable consequence of her father's sins, Baba Quan has released Mai from the burden of caring for Thanh, and so she can leave for college. Mai's search for her grandfather uncovered the language of Third-World nationalism and a critique of the continuing US embargo; his figure reveals "political realities" that threaten to destabilize Mai's place in the US, but with his fantastic demonization, these realities become obscured by Cao's fiction. The lurid scene of murder transforms Third-World revolution into a personal vendetta: his character twists political realities into impossible tales, and the fiction of Baba Quan ultimately provides a safe mode of critique that protects Mai and ensures her own status as an American friend.

This chapter reads fictionalized enemies and friends in *Monkey Bridge*. From demonizing the American enemy through Baba Quan, Cao dispenses with a notoriously bad friend of the war, represented by Thanh: Madame Nhu, the much-maligned "Dragon Lady" of the South Vietnamese leadership. To Mai's shame, Thanh is a visible reminder of what America would like to forget, and the novel ultimately replaces Mai's ailing and threatening mother with Mai's truest friend: Uncle Michael, a Green Beret whose real-life counterpart was a beloved father figure for Cao herself. Against Hollywood's dark fantasies of Special Forces gone awry, the novel restores the Green Beret to his primary role in making friendlies, through the knowing gaze of the friendly herself. *Monkey Bridge* imagines all-too-perfect American friends: embodiments of loyalty and devotion who ultimately transport Mai away from her refugee community and into an American family.

In fabricating enemies and purifying friends, Cao's novel layers an ordering fiction onto her own story: Mai's story closely matches Cao's own biography, from the conditions of her entry into the United States, to her settlement in Falls Church, and finally her matriculation at Mount Holyoke College. The novel's imaginative overlay, however, is vital to restoring the political alliances that disintegrated over the years of US intervention in Vietnam. If Hayslip's testimony sought to heal America's nightmare of the war in order to stake a claim for her place within an East-West romance, Cao's fiction constructs and then exposes family secrets in order to uncover true friendship—and cast away her Vietnamese family.

The Vietnamese family returns armed with history in Cao's second novel, *The Lotus and the Storm* (2014), which revolves around an elegiac portrait of her father. While *Monkey Bridge* turns away from a damaged mother, *The Lotus and the Storm* imagines the war recollections of Cao's father, a former general in the South Vietnamese army. In the first novel, the father is a secondary figure—he dies suddenly in Vietnam—but the second novel enshrines his figure as the true friendly of the war. In *The Lotus and the Storm*, he retells the war's history as a set of missed opportunities for friendly triumph. Lan Cao's rendition of her father's story requires an order of historicizing reminiscent of Susan Choi's efforts at enlivening and freeing her own father within a revisionist history of the Korean War—and Cao's late history lesson revises by incorporating the perspective of the South Vietnamese military leadership. The daughter of the bad mother and good father in these novels abandons the bad friend and lovingly cares for the good—and both protagonists are tellingly named Mai, thus creating a continuity between the two novels. But while the Mai of *Monkey Bridge* frees herself from a depressive mother who represents a lost country, the Mai of *The Lotus and the Storm* herself suffers psychological ailments directly tied to the war. Both of these fictions are tantalizing in their strategic nondisclosures, which play with a readerly desire for wartime testimony by offering idealized friendly perspectives of the war—which ultimately reveal themselves to be unreliable on multiple fronts.

I

Thanh's figure lies at the heart of *Monkey Bridge*. Repeatedly identified with Vietnam—Mai likens her mother's silhouette to Vietnam's "long twisted peninsula" (150)—Thanh's body represents both the land and the war. We first met Thanh in her hospital bed, after she has suffered the stroke: "She lay with one arm diagonally shielding her face, breathing hard. I avoided looking too closely at it, her red blotchy face that had been burned by a kitchen fire years ago" (3). Like her face, her body has been ravaged: "Her body had become a battlefield, she a war wound fastened to a bed in a suburban hospital" (7). Thanh's metaphorical identification with the war becomes literal by the novel's end, when we discover that her facial burn was in fact the result of a napalm attack in a free-fire zone in the

Mekong Delta: her battered body thus presents a searing reminder of the war.[3]

Thanh persists in living a wartime existence: as Mai remarks, "Danger lurked everywhere, every day, for my mother" (20). When they first move into an apartment in Falls Church, Thanh forces Mai to confront the rental manager over an imagined threat: "'You tell him we refuse to live in a place that's been hexed with a curse,' she screamed and pointed a stern chin at the giant antenna on the building across from our apartment. In the gleaming darkness, the big metallic rod threw a menacing shadow across our window" (20–21). Mai links her mother's fear directly back to the war:

> The antenna's counterpart, in my mother's mind, must have been the colossal black statue of several South Vietnamese soldiers cemented directly opposite the National Assembly in Saigon. On the attack, their brutal guns had pointed straight into the building, the heart and brain of the legislature of the South Vietnamese government itself. "What kind of a way is that to fight a war?" my mother often complained. "Who needs enemies when your own guns are pointed at your head?" (23)

Connecting the antenna in Falls Church to the statue in Saigon, Mai creates a political context for her mother's fears. These menacing symbols both prefigure self-destruction: we later learn that a South Vietnamese colonel "had shot himself in front of the war memorial my mother believed to be a bad omen. Minutes before the South's surrender, the colonel, dressed in full uniform and decked in medals, had walked up the steps leading to the black statue, faced the National Assembly, saluted, and shot himself" (43)—a terrible fate for a wartime friend that foretells Thanh's eventual suicide.

Though Mai is impatient with her mother's superstition, the connection she makes to the war memorial lends a dark weight to this shadow in the window. In the scene that follows, we discover that American perceptions of Mai and her mother are no less defined by the war.[4] Their reception by the rental manager demonstrates how thoroughly the politics of the war have conditioned his imagination as well:

> The manager peered uneasily from beneath a baseball cap, red with "Orioles" stitched in yellow, with curiosity, fascination, and suspicion in his eyes. "Well? C'mon. I haven't got all day." A pair of veins ran along the sides of his prizefighter's neck like electrical wires. "What's Madame Nhu here saying?" he smirked, popping his knuckles and winking at a woman in tight black jeans sitting by his side. (21)

The bare threat of brutality undergirds the manager's "curiosity, fascination, and suspicion": "popping his knuckles," he is spoiling for a fight. His smirking identification of Mai's mother as Madame Nhu is especially telling: he links Thanh to a despised American ally, the emblem of all that was wrong with the South Vietnamese regime, a draconian leadership sustained by US support.

Ngo Dinh Diem, the US-backed leader of the southern regime, ruled by tyranny and nepotism. As the war continued, he increasingly relied on the counsel and support of his brother Ngo Dinh Nhu—the "regime's Rasputin," who controlled the secret police and expounded an obscure political philosophy which merged Confucianism with Catholicism[5]—and Nhu's notorious wife, Madame Nhu.[6] Because Diem was a life-long bachelor, his sister-in-law became the de facto first lady of the regime. Madame Nhu spearheaded controversial legislation and created her own all-woman militia to match her husband's cadres. "Surpassingly beautiful, with lacquered fingernails, form-fitting décolleté gowns, and stiletto-heeled shoes," Madame Nhu was regarded by American reporters as the "Dragon Lady"[7] personified, and her notoriety grew with her increasingly strident critiques of the regime's detractors—and Diem's inability to control his brother and silence his sister-in-law instigated the US-backed coup that toppled the ruling family in 1963. While Madame Nhu was concluding an ill-fated speaking tour of the United States—her vocal attacks against insufficient American support resulted in an approval rating below 8 percent[8]—South Vietnamese military leaders overthrew her family's regime and brutally murdered Diem and Nhu. From Los Angeles, where she learned of her husband's death, Madame Nhu fled to Rome with her children, where she led a reclusive life until her 2011 death, which occasioned a flurry of obituaries that recalled her singularly arresting figure.

A decade before his assassination, Ngo Dinh Diem had been feted in the American press as "The Tough Miracle Man of Asia,"[9] but he failed to unite the newly created political entity of South Vietnam—and by the early 1960s, he was struggling to manage growing popular unrest. In 1963, when the Buddhist monks who set themselves on fire in protest against the Diem regime made worldwide headlines, Madame Nhu's furious response made the news as well: she infamously derided the Buddhist self-immolations as "barbecues." In an August 14, 1963 letter to *The New York Times*, Madame Nhu denounced the Buddhist actions as a Communist ploy and ridiculed the paper in her inimitable fashion:

I may shock some by saying "I would beat such provocateurs ten times more if they wore monks' robes," and "I would clap hands at seeing another monk barbecue show, for one cannot be responsible for the madness of others."

But what else is there to say when the world, under a mad spell about the so-called "Buddhist affair"—and much thanks to the good offices of papers like yours—needs an electro-shock

to resume its senses and come better to understand the reality
of the situation?[10]

Laden with the language of the torture chamber, Madame Nhu's
defense of the regime only confirms its reported atrocities, and the
bitter humor of the suggested "electro-shock" exhibits a sadistic
touch. Yet she concludes her letter by reaching out to her American
readers: "Because of the alliance between your country and mine,
I urge that you make an effort to understand friends and allies
before rushing headlong into the trap of enemies common to both."
This jarring evocation of alliance weakened her claim: *The New York
Times*'s editorial response to her letter argues that "It is precisely
because this country is allied with South Vietnam in the latter's
anti-Communist struggle that we condemn Mrs. Nhu's callous and
self-defeating desire to apply the scourge to those who legitimately
protest injustices in Saigon." The editorial goes on to encourage
Diem toward a "more moderate approach," but the American leadership went much further: they approved the coup. Madame Nhu
railed against the Americans for their complicity in the assassinations, and as she left the United States for Rome, she spelled out the
problem with American friends: "Whoever has the Americans as
allies does not need any enemies."[11]

Madame Nhu's indictment of American friendship resonates
with sentiments expressed by Mai's mother: "Who needs enemies
when your own guns are pointed at your head?" (23). A vicious cir-
cularity governed the Buddhist crisis and its repercussions for the
southern regime: the spectacle of self-immolation led to a coup executed by friends. At the mercy of her allies, Thanh is no less trauma-
tized by the difficulty of friendship: "Danger lurked everywhere"
because she understands the curse of alliance. The Vietnamese refugee finds herself in the land of her allies, only to be despised, and
the rental manager's derisory naming of Thanh as Madame Nhu

recalls the fraught nature of the alliance, in which friends rightly suspected friends of murder. The deeply troubled political alliance of the war thus lends a material heft to the "menacing shadow" that looms in the window.

Overcome by the dangers of her existence in America, Thanh herself becomes a menace to her daughter. While Mai seeks out an American future, Thanh recalls the troublesome alliances of the past: she is an unsightly reminder of the war, and to her daughter, she is a burden. Thanh, however, makes a futile attempt to offer Mai a family history unmarked by the war. The diary she concocted for Mai falsely recounted her past as an especially beloved daughter, but Thanh's suicide shatters her illusory fable: in her final letter to Mai, she explains that her diary entries were attempts "to extinguish the imprints of my life and create alternate versions that suit my imagination and heal my soul. The new world that I tried to create is the world I left in a drawer for you to find, the world I wished I could have handed to you as the unhidden truth of a mother's life" (227).[12] The letter presents a rationalization of her suicide:

In 1963, in an act that stunned the world, an elderly Buddhist monk stepped calmly from a car into the street, crossed his legs in a serene lotus position, meditated himself into a contemplative state, and watched in silence as a group of monks and nuns encircled him, dousing him with gasoline and lighting him on fire. As passersby threw themselves reverentially on the ground, the monk performed the ultimate act of sacrifice and pressed his palms in prayer, a sermon of fire, his body in an erect, uncollapsible lotus position, while flames, burning, burning, orange and ocher, the color of his saffron robe, enveloped and consumed the flesh he offered as an act of supreme devotion.

> I'm already a dying person, Mai. This soil is as poisonous
> to my soul as the poison that once turned our village into dead
> earth. (253)

The reverential description of the burning monk frames Thanh's suicide as "an act of supreme devotion," but the evocation of poisonous soil is a political indictment: the "dead earth" of her village is a product of the US military campaign of defoliation, and American soil is equally inhospitable. This final letter brings Mai no closer to her mother; instead, Thanh is ultimately presented as a late casualty of the war.

In contrast to her false diary entries, which imagined a past expurgated of the war, Thanh's last letter reads like an especially passionate history lesson which covers the tragedy of Vietnam from the French occupation to the American devastation. Indeed, her letter insists that we reread Thanh's childhood through the frame of war: through her experience, we witness the history of America's war, from the first arrival of military advisors in Vietnamese villages in the 1950s, to the dramatic escalation of the American effort in the 1960s, which decimated these same villages. In thus retrofitting her life into the shape of the war, the letter uncovers an imperial history that undoes her fiction. It is worth noting, too, the distance between Madame Nhu's scorn and Thanh's reverence for Buddhist self-immolation. What for Madame Nhu is a cover for political enmity is, for Mai's mother, an aestheticized detachment from superpower alignment.

Yet this truth-telling document also deepens the family melodrama: Thanh's final letter contains her father's wrath within an affair of the heart. Her dramatic narration of his vengeance—the bloody scene of Baba Quan murdering his rival—exposes a generic mismatch at the heart of the novel, in which the most fanciful edge of Cao's tale meets the weight of history. Thanh and Baba Quan stand in for the two sides of the war: if Baba Quan simplifies the complex—and necessarily impure—enmity of civil war, Thanh is made to represent the war's bad friend. The novel seems to enliven both of these key figures in order to extinguish them, but in opposing modes. The melodrama kills off the enemy who comes to life through the revelation of his political intrigues; but the bad friend who attempts to explain away her failures cannot bear the weight of her true history. And Mai disavows both in favor of a true hero, whose alliance frees her from these ugly pasts.

II

Monkey Bridge prominently features an American special agent who steps in to save Mai. An army officer stationed in Vietnam for six years, Colonel Michael MacMahon is a close family friend who spirited Mai out of the country in 1975, six months before her mother's separate arrival in the United States. In the acknowledgments to *Monkey Bridge*, Cao names the real-life counterpart to Uncle Michael: General John Fritz Freund, Cao's own "Papa Fritz."[13] If the enemy grandfather is a necessary fiction, Uncle Michael is a pointedly real character—and against Baba Quan's caricature of evil, the American officer represents the standard of benevolence.

Strikingly, the novel retells Mai's initial encounter with Uncle Michael three times, each presenting a different facet of their bond. In the first rendition, Mai explains that she was a seven-year-old "occasional student volunteer" at the American Third Field Hospital: "When I first saw him, a few months after the Tet New Year in 1968, he had been strapped to a stretcher, curled like a newborn, viscous and pink and covered from head to toe in placenta" (72). Mai dates Uncle Michael's first appearance to the Tet Offensive— he was wounded "on a routine Tet patrol on the outskirts of Saigon when his tank was hit with several grenades fired from a Vietcong launcher" (72)—and she presents him as an infant reborn from the skirmish. The Tet Offensive of 1968 is now seen as marking a critical point when, in the wake of a costly and largely unsuccessful North Vietnamese push, popular American opinion turned against the war. Introduced in the wake of this struggle, Uncle Michael is a defenseless new babe.

A few pages later, Mai rewrites this first memory of Uncle Michael: "The first time I saw Uncle Michael, he was strapped to a bed, with a drainage tube up his nose and a thermometer in his mouth. He gave me a funny cockeyed wink that I tried to reciprocate but couldn't, prompting him to show off by blinking both eyes in rapid succession. We became friends over the course of his month-long recovery" (76). In this version, the previously infantilized Uncle Michael has been modified into a friend: though he remains immobile and mute, he nevertheless communicates his jovial nature. Mai's third return to this scene, however, complicates her winking portrait: "Uncle Michael on a metal bed, cocooned in a fold of army blanket under mosquito netting, drawing ragged breaths. His hands over his head, he was pulling the steel headrest, his breath making a low-pitched moaning sound" (80). In this final incarnation, Uncle Michael has been reduced to a wounded soldier. This third vision, which flashes before Mai's eyes when she is in the MacMahon home, reveals what his wife, Aunt Mary, can never know about Uncle Michael: as Mai explains, "Some things cannot be shared, like the way I was seeing her husband that very moment, next to dying flesh and unbathed bodies swaddled in cotton gauze" (89). This ultimate image lays bare the bond between Mai and Uncle Michael: theirs is a friendship forged out of war. In having attended his birth and witnessed his keen suffering, Mai possesses a claim on Uncle Michael which frames the more recognizable friendship between American soldier and Vietnamese child, sealed with a "funny cockeyed wink." This last version significantly casts Uncle Michael and not Mai as its war waif, thus balancing their otherwise highly unequal relation.

Four years after the war, in the safety of suburban Connecticut, Uncle Michael and Mai hold fast to their bond: "He was now a retired colonel in Farmington, with six unprootable years in Vietnam—now a soldier without a war—and I an immigrant from Saigon. Vietnam remained like an implant in both our brains" (91). Vietnam is "unprootable" for the career officer and his young charge, and the war forms a lasting bond for less lucky survivors as well: American military grunts and fleeing Vietnamese villagers. Mai depicts the popular Mrs. Bay, a refugee who gathers GIs around her in the Vietnamese grocery store where Thanh works. Mrs. Bay "sensed a continuing connection with the American soldiers who visited the store, for the simple reason that a common base, she believed, existed to connect us exiles, on one point, to these lost men"; to Mrs. Bay, soldiers and refugees "were in fact parts of a shared experience" (209)—a sentiment that echoes Le Ly Hayslip's attachments. The relation between Uncle Michael and Mai sweetens this inexorable bond between GI and refugee, premised upon a terrible, shared knowledge. And both carefully convert their common "implant" into an avuncular relation.

Mai fastens upon the good soldier as kindly uncle, and she revels in an image of Uncle Michael making his way through the war as a convivial spirit. We discover that he "outdid the meanest Montagnard from the Pleiku hills" (76): Uncle Michael was a Green Beret who marshaled native support for the Civilian Irregular Defense Group—the organization much touted by Special Forces advocates and typically cited as a rare success story in forging alliances in Vietnam.[14] Uncle Michael regales the young Mai with tales of his adventures with these "mountain people" (76) from his hospital bed, and Mai imagines him striding into this remote terrain: "That was how I liked to picture him, in his polished-brass belt buckles and spit-shined boots, entering the bamboo-spiked gate to the Montagnards' camp as casually as if he were crossing the threshold of his own house" (77). Cao's recuperated Green Beret parades the success of organizing paramilitary forces among mountain tribespeople, the mission which threatened to seduce American soldiers into "going native": redeemed as a Cold War operation, the dangers of imperial contact have fallen away. Indeed, Mai reinforces her childhood image of a jaunty imperial soldier with an adult perspective on Uncle Michael's ambitions:

> Uncle Michael was the kind of man who believed he owned as far as he could see. A graduate of West Point, he had certain inherited notions of American benevolence which his own experience as a World War II soldier had reinforced. Possibilities, that was what America represented to him. That was his modest wish for Vietnam. (78)

Mai tempers Uncle Michael's sense of ownership with his "modest wish," softening colonial designs with a wistful edge. Mai identifies his ideals as a throwback to a grander age, yet "what America represented to him" is ultimately what America represents to Mai: Uncle Michael is her image of American benevolence.

Lan Cao's "Papa Fritz" was one of a handful of American military officers who actively worked to improve US-South Vietnamese relations. In 1965, General John Fritz Freund served as acting director of the Office of Field Services for the Joint United States Public Affairs Office (JUSPAO), "the civilian-led agency created in 1965 to guide American PSYOP [psychological operations] in Vietnam." One of "only six of the one hundred and thirty-two Americans the JUSPAO employed [who] spoke functional Vietnamese," Freund spearheaded a campaign "of publicizing Vietnamese historical heroes to promote nationalism"—despite opposition within the JUSPAO, which refused official support. Within months, "the campaign's success compelled the JUSPAO to implement the hero concept in television broadcasts nationwide." Upon completing his assignment to the JUSPAO, Freund issued a blistering report which underscored "the JUSPAO's reluctance to incorporate Vietnamese perspectives into its campaigns. He called the relationship between American and Vietnamese JUSPAO personnel 'an area of major deficiency.'"[15] Freund's largely unheeded calls for improving US-Vietnamese relations distinguished him from the vast majority of the US military leadership, and *Monkey Bridge* presents Uncle Michael as a truly exceptional individual: fluent in Vietnamese and French, he is a paragon of cultural sensitivity.

Yet General Freund's PSYOP background sheds a new light on Uncle Michael's tales: Freund utilized Vietnamese myth and history in order to advance military objectives, and Uncle Michael's stories are similarly spun. His tales serve to protect Mai: during a screening of *The Deer Hunter*, in response to the film's infamous scenes of Russian roulette, Uncle Michael tells Mai that "I was in Vietnam for six years and I've never seen or heard of anyone doing this before" (100). After the movie, when Mai seizes on the opportunity to question Uncle Michael about his conduct during the war, he recounts a tragic story of a dying boy and his puppy, a narrative with all of the trappings of Hollywood.[16] Uncle Michael spins his war experiences to counteract the film's version of the war: he engages in a personal PSYOP campaign to reassure Mai of America's good intentions.

Uncle Michael's most important story features Baba Quan on the novel's titular monkey bridge. When Mai prods Uncle Michael for information on her missing grandfather, she is told a fantastic story of Baba Quan's valor, in which he saves Uncle Michael's Special Forces unit. In Uncle Michael's story, Baba Quan is an apparition in the mist who guides the unit safely through a mine field. Michael explains that Baba Quan navigates them from atop a monkey bridge, "a thin pole of bamboo no wider than a grown man's foot, roped together by vines and mangrove roots" (109), from which he appears "like a scene out of a movie" (111). The tale initially strikes Mai as suspect—she retorts, "It sounds almost like storybook story. You know, like it's almost too good to be true" (114)—and Thanh's final letter reveals that Baba Quan in fact laid the mines; he led Uncle Michael through his own deadly maze. Uncle Michael's tale thus shields Mai from her grandfather's political betrayal by spinning the enemy as a hero—a maneuver straight out of General Freund's heroism campaign. Cao shrouds the enemy's political campaign in melodrama, but the friend is no less animated by political ambitions. And if Baba Quan reduces the enemy's political designs to mere fiction, Uncle Michael offers a corrective truth backed by the valor of General John Fritz Freund.

After her mother's funeral, Mai discovers that "It was as if everything had been negotiated years before, planned ahead of time, just in case. My adoption papers, handing me over to Uncle Michael, had been signed years before, before I left Saigon on the Pan Am flight . . . The adoption, Mrs. Bay told me, had never been revoked, even after my mother arrived" (258). *Monkey Bridge* extricates Mai from her kin to transport her out of the war. The novel's strangely happy ending reveals that Mai had long been a war orphan; and the fact that her mother left her adoption untouched demonstrates Thanh's powerlessness before the wartime alliance Cao has crafted. In reviving the figure of the Cold War orphan—an attempt also made by US policymakers—Cao rehabilitates both the Vietnamese refugee and the American Special Forces officer: in her hands, the refugee who is never permitted political innocence and the Green Beret who has become the repository of America's political nightmares both reclaim their early Cold War relation, to become a trusting child and her Good Samaritan.

Yet *Monkey Bridge* has given us a glimpse of Uncle Michael unvarnished by his campaigns in the image of his suffering on the stretcher, which recalls Thanh's own battered body on the hospital bed. In their war wounds, the historical agent and the figure brutalized by history, too, become matched. In Mrs. Bay's elucidation of American soldiers and Vietnamese exiles as "parts of a shared experience," the narrative expands upon her sentiments to conclude, "We were like two distinctly different shapes that would come together to form an amalgamation of common and at the same time competing truths" (209). The momentarily overlapping shapes of Thanh and Uncle Michael trace the dark acts of the war: Thanh's suicide marks her total submission to its horrors, but Uncle Michael soldiers on in his campaign to make friendlies—which culminates in his adoption of Mai. Uncle Michael can replace Thanh so cleanly because he has healed while she languished—and, crucially, he never has to retract his fictions. Though Thanh is compelled to tell the truth, Uncle Michael is never susceptible to a similar suicidal drive toward confession—even though he is just as guilty of lying to Mai. Not only is he free from the history of the war; it was, in fact, his job to obfuscate it—a task he continues after the war in order to secure Mai's future.

III

The novel concludes with Mai finally safely removed from the traumas of her war-torn family, and properly ensconced within an American one. In its final pages, we see Mai in her bedroom in Uncle Michael's house, on the eve of beginning her undergraduate career at Mount Holyoke: "Across the room, on my desk, a glossy color brochure promised us incoming students the openness of an unexplored future and the safety of its sanctuary. 'A college for women, the challenge to excel'" (260). The brochure proffers a new sanctuary from war, and, like her protagonist, Cao left Little Saigon behind. In a 2005 interview, she discusses her uneasiness with "the Vietnamese community in Northern Virginia," explaining that "if you are forever community defined, I find it to be intolerable, and so I like the idea of creating one's own community"—an ideal clearly enshrined in Mount Holyoke's promotional literature.[17]

Cao's stated detachment from the Vietnamese community is evident throughout *Monkey Bridge*. Mai knows all too well that her community is perceived as "a ragtag accumulation of unwanted, an awkward reminder of the war the whole country was trying to forget" (15)—and she adopts this inhospitable and detached gaze to assess her community:

> On certain occasions, I could adopt the anthropologist's eye and develop an academic interest in the familiar. I could step back and watch with a degree of detachment the habits and manners of Little Saigon.
>
> Detached, I could see this community as a riot of adolescents, obstreperous, awkward, out of sync with the subscribed norms of American life, and beyond the reach of my authority. I could feel for them, their sad shuffles and anachronistic modes of behavior, the peculiar and timid way they held their bodies and occupied the physical space, the unfailing well-manneredness with which they conducted themselves in public—their foreigners' ragged edges. (146)

Mai claims a maturity secured by combining outsider perceptions of the group with her intimate knowledge of it. In her condescension, Mai aligns herself with "the subscribed norms of American life," which reduces these others to a series of pathetic gestures.

By contrast, Mai's authority rests on her extraordinary ability to remake herself.

Mai scorns those refugees who mistakenly "continued to present themselves as reproductions from the tropics": "Every summer, they ventured into the streets with their usual paraphernalia, umbrellas and towels wrapped impertinently around their heads . . . Once this headgear had been worn by peasants who worked the rice fields, and by old women in black pajamas whom GIs called 'VC mamas' on late-night movies" (146). Her distaste thus unveils a political danger: these "reproductions from the tropics" look like the wartime enemy. In recalling the war, their foreign manners may be rescripted into a threat. As Mai contemplates these figures, her bemused detachment shifts into a prescriptive formula for managing difference:

> "If you have to be different, you have to be acceptably different," I would think to myself. Stereotypes aren't my enemy, as long as we tinker with them in a way that strikes an American chord. Instead of drabby cotton towels, I could picture parrot-gold umbrellas opening against the midafternoon sun. I could imagine tight kimonos, vulnerable shuffles, and decorative combs. They would still be different, but they would be American-palatable and exotic. (147)

To resemble the enemy is unpalatable, but stereotypes "aren't my enemy": Mai recommends eluding the danger of political enmity by refashioning foreignness into known forms. Strikingly, her examples of "American-palatable" difference invoke the dress and manners of Japan, whose exemplary postwar transformation from enemy to friend underwrites this proposed radical makeover from drab to exotic. Mai advocates a stylistic resignification that is inseparable from political realignment: her style tips offer a way of rehabilitating the dark enemy into a bright friend.

Although Mai seeks an "American chord," the refugees she regards dream of returning home to Vietnam. The novel is set in 1979, and the border skirmishes that broke out between Vietnam and China in the late 1970s are the subject of intense speculation in the refugee community, which scours the news for hints of an opening, a break in the new regime through which they may return home. Mai rejects these hopes as adolescent fantasy, and from her scholarly perch, she explains them away:

> I wondered to myself: Did they know that Hanoi had one of the largest armies in the world, behind only the United States, the Soviet Union, and China? Did they know that they would not be able to count on American intervention to provide aid to the ragtag army of South Vietnamese guerrillas poised along Thailand's border, ready to infiltrate the swamps and jungles of the countryside? (151–52)

Like the refugee community in northern Virginia, the South Vietnamese guerrillas in Thailand are a "ragtag" assortment. Mai's assessment of Hanoi's military strength demonstrates her superior knowledge, and together with her scholarly detachment and style authority, she squarely enunciates the hard facts of Vietnam's postwar state.

Mai's knowing tone echoes the form of another book author Lan Cao cowrote with Himilce Novas, *Everything You Need To Know about Asian American History*, which was published in 1996, one year before the publication of *Monkey Bridge*. *Everything You Need To Know about Asian American History* introduces the history of Asian migration to the United States through a novel format: "We have organized this book for 'interactive reading,' meaning that the information between the covers is encapsulated in a modular, question-and-answer format" (ix).[18] A promotional page at the very opening of the book presents the volume as a hodgepodge of information, with fun facts presented alongside weightier information: "Do you know: Why chopsticks are used to eat Chinese food? What the final Supreme Court decision about the internment of Japanese Americans during World War II was?" Cao is a law professor who specializes in international law, and her answers provide a detailed account of the legal history of Asian exclusion and immigration within the geopolitical context of US-Asian relations. In fact, Cao's legal publications focus on the impact of culture on international law;[19] her scholarship argues for bringing together the two strands of information—cultural and legal—on display in *Everything You Need To Know about Asian American History*.

The knowing consciousness that presides over *Monkey Bridge* belongs to the well-schooled author of *Everything You Need To Know about Asian American History*.[20] Though Mai feels the constraints of her political identity as a refugee, she wields a learned authority that seeks to diagnose the weaknesses and failures of the refugee community. Mai's story is in fact overwritten by the dictates of this authoritative voice, which both introduces and advises Vietnamese refugees in the US. Indeed, we may read *Monkey Bridge* as an extended response to a question in *Everything You Need To Know about Asian American History*: "How have the Vietnamese adjusted to life in the United States?" (211). The answer in *Everything You Need To Know about Asian American History* explains that "The Vietnamese have adapted to life in America with various degrees of success . . . The first wave of Vietnamese refugees, from the educated upper and middle classes, has assimilated more easily than subsequent waves," which "tended to be much less educated and less skilled, and thus less employable, than the earlier arrivals" (211). Mai belongs to the first wave of refugees, and she provides critical instruction on how to attain "the norms of American life." Her successful assimilation separates her from the plight of those refugees who "remain trapped in low-paying jobs, and isolated from the mainstream by language and cultural barriers" (212).

The "riot of adolescents" in the community Mai presents show-cases the second wave of refugees from Vietnam, notably represented by "a young man in ill-fitting jeans":

> He was one of the thousands of boat people being resettled by a Presbyterian church in the area. His was a particularly tragic story, with a sad but not altogether extraordinary ending—the death of a mother, a father who might have drowned but whose fate was not known with certainty, and the rape of a sister by pirates on the South China Sea. (155)

It is striking that this heartrending story is not extraordinary—and by offering this singular tragedy as a representative example, Mai has detached herself from the thousands that his story invokes. Indeed, in the refugee framework provided by this emblematic figure, it is Mai who emerges as the extraordinary one. Cao's class stratification of the refugee community girds Mai's knowing separation of herself from her community, which ultimately transports her exceptional figure out of the community.

The evil grandfather who conceals the politics of the enemy, the sick mother doomed to play the role of the bad friend, and the good, paternal American—all serve to position Mai as the friendly child in the middle. In thus sketching out her place at the center of this constellation, however, Mai refuses to be helpless: not only does she wield a knowledge born from the war that locks in her bond with Uncle Michael; she assumes a learned authority derived from Cao herself. It is finally Lan Cao who rescues her protagonist: her superior knowledge arms Mai with nonsynchronous and extradiegetic resources that intertwine author and narrator. The complexity of this construction reveals all over again the formidable difficulty of Vietnam's friendly: she must replace faith with a complicating knowledge that undermines her innocence while ensuring the alliance.

IV

The Lotus and the Storm presents an intriguing complement to *Monkey Bridge*: seventeen years later, we seem to meet Mai again, as a reclusive adult—having graduated from college and law school, she is employed as a librarian in a law firm—who cares for her elderly father in Falls Church. This time, Mai's mother does not make it to the United States (as we discover late in the novel, she perished in the crossing), but in dramatic contrast to the difficult mother-daughter relationship of *Monkey Bridge*, Mai lovingly tends her father in *The Lotus and the Storm*. An odd similarity binds these very different single parents, however: in *Monkey Bridge*, Mai and her best friend Bobbie devised a funny name for Thanh—"'B-o-b' was a nickname we had recently picked for my mother, a short-hand reference to the 'bag of bones' she carried in her frail body. It allowed us to discuss her even when we were in her immediate vicinity" (144)—which reappears early in *The Lotus and the Storm*. Mai's father puzzles over this nickname: "One American neighbor in this building sometimes calls me Bob ... Neither my first nor my last name starts with a *B*. So I know Bob is not a pun on my real name. Of course I eventually figure it out. Bag of bones. He means it affectionately, I think" (17). The only way to "figure it out," of course, is from Cao's first novel, which in this small instance offers a curious key to the second. Her father thus intuits what her mother could not—namely, how others perceive them—and he then assumes an affection that the more suspicious Thanh never does.

Cao's novels lavish attention on Mai's parents in turn, and *The Lotus and the Storm*, like the first, is deeply informed by Cao's own story. Yet while Thanh spun an elaborate fiction to be deflated by the war's actual and cruel history, the telling of which marks the end of her troubled life, "Mr. Minh"—the moniker that identifies her father's chapters—is valorized by this history. The second novel rewrites the war with a highly researched verve that flirts with the historical reanimation featured in Choi's *The Foreign Student*:[21] Mr. Minh, a former ARVN (Army of the Republic of Vietnam) officer, can "almost see the scene as it might have unfolded half a world away. Kissinger opposite Nixon in an office far away in Washington, D.C., as they leaned back in their chairs and let the rising cold from an overworked air conditioner cool the sweat off their faces" (223). Retelling the war from the perspective of a loyal ally, Mr. Minh's chapters narrate its major flashpoints: the coup that overthrew Diem, the US escalation, the Tet Offensive, and the decline and fall of Saigon. At every point, the ARVN officer laments the failure of friendly potential, as in his defense of Diem: "Yes, blunders had been made and had been left uncorrected. But President Diem had also managed a series of reassuring accomplishments" (32). Indeed, as Mr. Minh elaborates, "it was his character that touched me. He was frugal and uncorrupted. I understood him. He was an unmarried man drawn to a spartan lifestyle and uninterested in the accumulation of personal wealth. His sin was an overinflated sense of loyalty to his family" (33). This portrait offers a reflection of Mr. Minh's own quiet heroism, which is as bound to a complicated family (his lost wife's family includes a "Vietcong" brother) yet remains "frugal and uncorrupted." His integrity preserves him through shifting political winds that corrupt his closest contemporaries, notably including his two best friends, one Vietnamese and the other American, both of whom vie for his beautiful, doomed wife.

Mai's father is a fictional elaboration of Cao's father, Cao Van Vien, a "four-star general, chief of the South Vietnam Joint General Staff, chief military advisor to President Nguyen Van Thieu, and Edward Lansdale confidant."[22] As historian Andrew Friedman explains, "It would be almost impossible to overstate the power and centrality Cao Van Vien held in the American-shadowed South Vietnamese military effort" (188). Friedman notes, too, Cao Van Vien's intimate friendship with John Fritz Freund, under whose auspices the Cao family was granted "one of the smoothest evacuations and best jobs granted any of the refugees—with a position in the heart of the Pentagon" (194). It is safe to say that Cao Van Vien was a preeminent friendly of the American war in Vietnam, and we may read his absence from *Monkey Bridge* as a critical condition of Thanh's despair. Against the plight of that bad friend, who hid and finally extinguished herself in the imperial center, the good friend of *The Lotus and the Storm* offers a very different history. If the history of the war destroyed the mother, the father revises history to prove his friendly conduct. In returning to the critical junctures of America's war, Mr. Minh demonstrates again and again his innocence in the face of American political machinations. His story ultimately serves to elaborate, as he puts it, "the calamity of being this country's ally" (23).

In thus demonstrating his political innocence, this good ally can dispense with the valiant American, who becomes suspect. Mr. Minh's passionate self-defense complicates the unwavering portrait of America embodied in *Monkey Bridge*'s Uncle Michael. Freund's counterpart in the second novel remains in the background, and his conduct maps closely onto the novel's portrait of America as "the country that both betrays and redeems" (249). Cao has added darker shadows to the benevolent America of *Monkey Bridge*, and the largely unexplained motives of John Clifford, the Freund stand-in of *The Lotus and the Storm*, consigns him to the edges of the narrative. Though "Cliff" becomes an intimate, his proximity threatens the family—and Cao corrupts him with a lust for Mai's mother that insists upon her father's rightful place, not only within the family, but also in the larger political alliance.

This tempering of American goodness, however, has complicating effects on Mai, who is well past the saving grace of adoption and so cannot free herself from the war through the methods applied in *Monkey Bridge*. This Mai is a literally tormented soul, who suffers from a "multiple personality disorder" (236) brought on by the war: as her father explains, "To understand Mai, you have to understand Tet" (192). Mai's traumatic experience of that turning point in the war unleashes multiple selves, most notably Bao— Mai's embodied shadow—who continues to batter Mai long after the war. As the dark other to Mai, Bao is figured as a Vietnamese self who sneers at Mai's American assimilation and blocks her personal and professional development. And yet Bao is also Mr. Minh's confidante: it was he who named Mai's other self, and he preserves her even as he worries about her violent attacks against the more fragile Mai.

Mai's fractured self has a curious counterpart in *Monkey Bridge*. In the first novel, Bobbie, an extraordinarily faithful friend, serves as a key agent of Mai's assimilation: "It was Bobbie who opened up America for me, steadied its quick inscrutable heartbeat for my sake. For the most part, Bobbie blended in and blended me in with her" (27). Though Mai is tormented by bloody memories of Vietnam, "Bobbie had no subverted interior and would never see the things I saw" (2). To subvert is to overthrow a political regime, and this diction suggests a politicized difference that Bobbie contains: as a refugee from a lost war, Mai is a potential threat who must be buffered by American friendship. All we really know about Bobbie is her remarkable loyalty to Mai—unlike Mai, she seems to have no interior at all—and her unimpeachable goodness ultimately renders her unlikely. Indeed, if we return to the strange nickname of "Bob," the secret name for both mother and father in Cao's novels, the similarity of "Bobbie" casts doubt on her existence as well. And if Bob is a measure of frailty for these parents, Bobbie could be a manifestation of the daughter's successful self-transformation. As an imaginary friend, Bobbie's miraculous constancy is a consoling fiction of American friendship.

The violent presence of Bao offers a mirror image to Bobbie. Bao is not a friend, but rather an internal enemy who thwarts Mai's ambitions—and lashes out at Mai, who is bruised by Bao's blows. The novel's surprising presentation of self-harm clearly figures the trauma of civil war; and so, in dramatic contrast to *Monkey Bridge, The Lotus and the Storm* binds Mai to the war. This Mai is significantly closer to Thanh, whose suicide was the only possible outcome of her history; indeed, the valorization of her father as the ultimate friendly in *The Lotus and the Storm* turns Mai out of the friendly position she knowingly secured in the first novel. Hence, the same history lesson that exonerates the father shackles the daughter to the past. She becomes an accessory to his revisionist history, which secures his integrity—at the significant expense of the fantasy of American friendship that saves Mai in the first novel.

The final movement of *The Lotus and the Storm* returns Mai to Vietnam after her father's death. Once she has returned, she discovers Bao's utility—"To truly discover myself here, I must hang on to Bao" (356)—and, improbably, reconnects with an American soldier she had befriended as a child and long presumed to be dead. Their late coupling offers a strange resolution by returning Mai to her pre-divided state: "she stands before someone who sees her as she was. Innocent. Perfect. Child" (367). Oddly, it is Bao who approves of this restored vision, which in fact preempts her altogether. If we return to Bobbie, we see that she vanished once she completed her function—Mai abandons her along with the refugee community when she leaves for Mount Holyoke—and once Mai is reunited with her American soldier, Bao inadvertently heralds her own demise: "When we return to Virginia, she will get the help we need to heal" (386). The unlikely reunion of this final episode promises to undo the history that created Bao in order to offer Mai a late emancipation from this past. The sexual alliance between Mai and her American soldier, only possible after her father's demise, is a very late attempt at rekindling a friendship that unsettles her father's meticulous history.

In the novel's final scene, Mai drives out to the countryside in Vietnam "Toward a still point. That point in the present that carries a scent from the past but is not afraid of it and so welcomes the future without fear," which she finds when she realizes "why the fields are so familiar":

> We are surrounded by green, like the interminable white of a Virginia snowstorm. Despite the elemental difference, this vast green is but an alternate version of the wintry white expanse when harsh lines and edges are muffled and softened. Its beauty too sinks right into your skin. Boundaries are erased here, contours blurred and diffused. (385)

This vision of a Virginia snowstorm returns us again to *Monkey Bridge* and to Bobbie: during her first winter in Virginia, while her mother sits "huddled in our apartment in front of the wide-open oven activated to a full 450 degrees to approximate the tropics," Bobbie takes Mai to the park "where we both stood with our faces up and watched the snow fall" (27). This reflection of the wonder of falling snow in Vietnam celebrates diffuse properties antithetical to the careful distinctions elaborated by her father—and, further, registers a shift in Mai's vision, from the beauty of the snow as a promise of assimilation, to this "muffled and softened" peace. Mai can only survive by blurring the past, and, finally, romancing it.

The haze of this conclusion marks a considerable distance from Mai's stern advance in *Monkey Bridge*, shot through with a longing for an earlier phase of Cold War integration that would enable the friendly to fold herself into an American family. *The Lotus and the Storm*'s loving portrait of Mai's father, the true friendly of the war, undoes this former ambition and forecloses Mai's adoption fantasy. Having been shut out of this mode of integration, Mai comes to resemble Thanh, the bad friend whose war wounds are all too visible. If Mai masked her divided self in *Monkey Bridge* through the very safe figure of Bobbie, in *The Lotus and the Storm* Mai cannot contain the splintering effects of civil war. The respective war heroes of Lan Cao's novels offer a particularly telling contrast: Uncle Michael shepherds Mai to safety, but her father understands and even accepts that she is divided by history—the friend frees her, but the friendly never attempts to heal her, because he must bind himself to the history that continues to play itself out within her.

8

Shame and Love

Andrew X. Pham's Catfish and Mandala

Andrew X. Pham's 1999 memoir *Catfish and Mandala* opens with
a double dedication: "To the memory of my sister Chi, my brother
Minh, one and the same . . . if only I had learned to see without
looking." Pham explains this riddle as the narrative unfolds: over
the course of months of bicycle touring in Mexico and California,
Japan, and finally Vietnam, Pham recalls his sister's life, transformation, and untimely death. *Catfish and Mandala* intersperses its travelogue with the story of the Pham family's migration from Vietnam
to the United States; they fled by boat in 1976 and eventually made
their way to California. At every point in this story, Chi exposes
the fragility of the family. At age thirty-two, Chi committed suicide,
leaving "a silent, dark hole in our family like an extinguished hearth
no one could relight. We talk around her history, unknowingly lac-
ing her secret and our shameful failures deeper into ourselves" (29).
Chi's secret history marks the "shameful failures" of a family which
otherwise presents an image of bootstrapping success: headed by
their indomitable father, they make a swift ascent from welfare to
white-collar—all except for this eldest child.

Among Pham's darkest memories of Vietnam is a beating Chi
suffers at age eleven, at the hands of their father. Her infraction was

to trade with a beggar, dubbed by the villagers "Leper-Boy": "It was a transaction which my father had forbid. Dad said Leper-Boy might be contagious and none of us could talk to him or touch anything he touched" (56). For her crime, her father "laid her out on the living room divan and broke bamboo canes upon her, exacting the Vietnamese punishment in a cloud of blind wrath" (56). As "the Vietnamese punishment," Pham identifies caning as a fitting discipline—but his father takes it too far: "Neighbors crowded the front door, begging him to stop. Men shook their heads, women beseeched him for mercy. Yet no one crossed the threshold. It was a man's right to beat his child" (56). If Chi's transaction endangered the family, her father's vicious discipline paradoxically preserves its sanctity: "no one crossed the threshold," though, as Pham notes, they "muttered that Dad's cruelty was a curse upon our house" (56). The father's blows thus both constitute and curse the household, and Chi's treatment exposes the brutality it takes to maintain the family. In their extraordinary journey, from the shores of the village beach in a leaky boat, to eighteen months in a refugee camp in Jakarta, nine months in Louisiana under the auspices of Baptist sponsors, and finally to San Jose, Chi lurks on the edges of a family held together by a perpetual fear of contagion and flashes of paternal rage.

In the middle of the book, Pham reveals that "Chi wanted to be a boy. She was just never meant to be a girl. That simple. I had always known she was different" (189). When, in her teens, Chi began at a new school in California, she "thr[e]w away all her dresses and skirts" in favor of men's clothing: "Whether she wanted it or not, Chi had a new identity. At school, she was a *he*" (194–95). A year and a half into Chi's "new identity," her father "tried to teach her how to be a normal girl"—and when she refused this lesson, "Dad schooled his child, measuring out his love, in the way his father had taught him. He caned her" (195). At eleven, Chi was caned for contaminating the family; at sixteen, when she "sassed" (195) her father for his attempt to remake her into "a normal girl," his rage exploded again. Yet if Chi's punishment bound the family together when they were in Vietnam, her caning triggers a different response in America: "the cops came for Dad" and "Took him away in a patrol car flashing red lights" (196).[1] In the United States, the father's actions mark a dangerous Vietnameseness, and after three days of his "schooling," Chi leaves home for good, and disappears for fourteen years.

The earlier scene of caning emerged in the context of the family's escape from Vietnam, and this instance, too, revolves around a narrative of escape. The family has settled in south San Jose, down the street from the city dump and "smack in a den of poverty, alcoholism, drugs, and domestic violence" (190) that they intend to leave: "Locke Drive wasn't home, but a minefield we had to cross to get to the real America" (192). As Pham explains, "We would escape. That was the mantra of our daily lives. We were so certain we were above it all. We never thought our family might not make it through this minefield without a casualty" (192). Chi is their family's casualty, and in presenting the setting of her banishment, Pham paints a vivid portrait of poverty:

> Sometimes, I wondered why Chi's final days with us on Locke Drive did not take on a more explosive texture. I suspected it was because the flavors surrounding Dad's last quarrel with Chi were the very flavors of our lives in its absolute normalcy. It was the first time we were all under one roof living as a family, free from the appraising eyes of the church that sponsored us. Tossing in America without a net, we were learning English, we were learning about each other. Just beginning to weave the fabric of our family there in the tiny three-bedroom duplex, our halfway house to the promised land. What I remember most

were the ingredients of the everyday—the smells, the sounds, the jars and hums of an immigrant family, new to being immigrants as well as being a family. (195)

The family portrait unveiled in Chi's "final days" is uncertain and inchoate,[2] and the passage opens into a sensory tumult, riotous with clashing smells and sounds: "bulk meat stewing in fishsauce," "The neighborhood shrill with heavy metal, yelling kids" (195, 196). If the earlier scene in Vietnam marked the inviolability of the family, this one lays bare the vulnerability of their lives to the "minefield," a figurative location that ties the family back to the war that instigated their trans-Pacific crossing.

A new "normalcy" descends over the family after Chi's departure. She escapes from the juvenile detention center to say a last goodbye to her brothers and then disappears—and after she "knifed into the dark," "The police released Dad. Things returned to normal. We went to school not fully grasping the gravity of Chi's situation. Dad went to work. Mom cooked and cut hair. No one talked about it" (214). The new "normal" without Chi is easier, and Pham admits that though his dreams have been overrun by Chi, "Secretly, I was glad that she didn't come back because the court dropped the charges and Dad didn't go to jail. We would survive. There was enough to eat and, if everything went well, we would be moving away from the dump soon" (215). Recalling his sister's long absence, Pham writes, "When we did move and the months had stretched into years, we 'forgot' Chi. She slipped away from us the way our birth-language slipped from our tongue, in bits, in nuances" (215). Like the Vietnamese language, Chi can be lost and forgotten: "Her name was not spoken. It became awkward and slow when we switched back and forth between English and Vietnamese" (215). What remains of Chi is the "awkward and slow" movement between Vietnamese and English; she becomes the residue between two languages and two worlds.

Near the end of Pham's family narrative, we learn Chi's fate: "Chi survived fourteen years on the street. Once a battered teenage run-away, Chi came home at thirty-one, a post-operative transsexual. She was a man and his name was Minh" (295). While the rest of the family busily raised itself out of the slums of San Jose, Chi transformed herself into someone altogether different. Pham describes Minh as "a stout, easygoing guy with a real blue-collar aura about him that I liked" (295) and summarizes his past, from teenage run-away to professional welder:

> After Chi escaped the juvenile detention center, she ran away to San Francisco and reverted to her true self. A man. He traveled as Minh, sleeping on the street and eating out of Dumpsters until a Chinese family took him in and fed him. They found him work in a Chinatown sweatshop among ille-gal Chinese aliens. Wages were dismal, and underground life was marginal and harsh. There was the constant fear of being caught. When Minh was eighteen, he hit the road, this time as a migrant worker. Seasons later, he arrived in Montana, where he earned a living as a ranch hand, doing whatever he could find. Moving among America's illegal workforce, he learned to buy false papers and eventually bribed himself into an assembly-line job in Detroit's auto industry. (297)

Laid off from the assembly line, Minh eventually returned to California, to a Vietnamese community in Orange County, where he worked as a welder for an aerospace company in Long Beach until another layoff finally sent him "home to his lost family" (298).

Pham's affection for his new brother is matched by Minh's appre-ciation of his transformed siblings, now on their way to becoming white-collar professionals: " 'You're a big engineer now, An,' he said with genuine admiration" to Pham (296). Indeed, though *Catfish and*

Mandala presents "Chi-Minh" as the figure of transformation, Minh's homecoming reveals the extraordinary change wrought upon the rest of the Pham family during his long absence: the distance between "An" and "Andrew," the name that graces the cover of his memoir, registers Pham's own dramatic metamorphosis. In fact, the "true self" of Minh showcases the bifurcated economic status of Asians in the United States[3]—a particularly vexed division within Vietnamese American populations, alternately cast as desperate refugees and model minorities. Within the family, Minh remains a refugee trapped in the minefield, and Pham suggests that losing Chi to its dangers is in fact a condition of the rest of the family's successful crossing.

In a travelogue that pointedly dislocates the model minority's upward trajectory, *Catfish and Mandala* narrates Pham's reckoning with his family tragedy. Framed as a means of comprehending and grieving the loss of Chi as the family's constitutive absence, Pham's story defies the immigrant Bildung by renouncing white-collar security. His "two-wheeled voyage" is itself a turn away from a budding career in aerospace engineering, in favor of a peripatetic existence that suggests a counterpart to Minh's "underground life"—but in contrast to Chi's disappearance, Pham writes himself into a storied lineage. Pham's peregrinations resonate with a tradition of American vagrancy, with a global edge that corresponds to recent incarnations of the genre. Minh's wanderings, by contrast, map out the far less charted path of the "impossible person," in Mae Ngai's words, whose undocumented—not to mention transgender[4]—status renders him "a person who cannot be and a problem that cannot be solved" (5).[5] Months after Minh's homecoming, "he died the most Vietnamese of deaths, a brokenhearted suicide. His father cut him down from the ceiling while his mother and grandmother wept. And his family, who could not love him while he lived, grieved his passing. His ashes were scattered on the sea he never finished crossing" (299). In the wake of his newfound brother's death, Pham is unable to finish grieving—and he crosses back to Vietnam, where he is shattered anew by Chi's loss.

When Pham takes to his bicycle to recross the sea, he takes on the privations that Minh endured to inhabit the "most American of lives": the tourist-seeker. Indeed, Pham identifies his tribe in this role: he enjoys two episodes of blissful belonging, the first in Portland, at the beginning of his grand tour, when he shares liters of wine, poetry, and song with "A dozen souls of the fringe" (39); and the second in Hanoi, at the tail end of his ride, when he bums around "with Australians, French, Danes, Brits, Germans, and Americans just soaking up the culture, exploring the urban sprawl one district at a time" (225). In both cases, he forgets his racial and ethnic identity: in Portland, "I fall asleep on the dirty living-room carpet, thinking I belong here. I haven't talked to an Asian person in weeks. Tonight I forget I am Asian" (40); while in Hanoi, "The days pass without difficulty. I am at last among friends of similar spirit, all non-Asian, not one of them Vietnamese" (226). These happy moments "at last among friends" belong to both the beginning and end of his journey, because his very undertaking of the trip demonstrates that he is not Vietnamese but rather American—a fact that assails him throughout his travels.[6]

In reading Pham's American travelogue, this chapter traces his grief over Chi toward a buried shame: the wartime brothel for GIs run by his family. His family's disavowal of this business shuns friendly relations welcomed during the war, and Pham's revelation of it links Chi's loss with this sordid past. As he tours Vietnam, Pham laments the legacy of this wartime service economy, which he encounters as a presumed prospective client. Caught in this reversal, Pham discovers a literary model—a Vietnamese heroine who redeems such wartime transactions as instances of self-sacrifice—but this aesthetic resource offers no consolation; instead, this tale of karmic sacrifice only reopens the trauma of alliance, by unmasking it as sacrifice. From this lingering prisonhouse of wartime allegiance, I turn to two remarkable writing projects Pham took on after publishing *Catfish and Mandala*: with his father's help, he translated a wartime diary by a young, captured North Vietnamese Army doctor; and he served as amanuensis for his father's memoir. These works offer chaste and principled modes of alliance, freed from the compromised bonds and souls that Pham mourns in *Catfish and Mandala*—but on the condition that Pham relegate himself to a position behind the scenes.

It is worth noting that Le Ly Hayslip, too, claimed the privilege of the American traveler when she undertook her homecoming journey, but against her impassioned politics of friendship, Pham expresses chagrin over the legacy of Cold War alliances. And in dramatic contrast to Hayslip's healing mission, Pham's intent is to reopen old wounds with no hope or aim of resolving them. And like Lan Cao, Pham wants to divulge family secrets, but his deepest shame is degrading alliance, not the political betrayal Cao concocts. Hence, while Cao sought to revive the Cold War friendly, Pham posits a post-Cold War critique licensed by his liberation from an assimilationist narrative—which in turn lends him an American perspective that Cao's protagonists belabor and can only approximate. Hayslip put her life story front and center and Cao masked her autobiography with purifying fictions—but Pham plots his own disintegration, not only over the course of his travel memoir, in which he finds contentment when he loses himself, but also in his subsequent writerly endeavors, in which he lends his literary hand to others.

Once safely across the minefield in the New World, Pham's father lambasts refugee dependence in favor of model minority respectability. During an ill-fated family reunion in California, the conversation sours when it turns to government assistance: "Father said Vietnamese filled the ranks of the county social services with their friends and relatives, giving them special treatment, corrupting the whole system. It was his roundabout way of criticizing his sister, Huong, whom he felt relied too much on government subsidy" (253). As a rigid disciplinarian who schools his own children in "normalcy," Pham's father decries "special treatment." He critiques what he considers the abuse of the government assistance established in the late 1970s, in large part to respond to the growing numbers of Southeast Asian refugees in the United States. In her study of Vietnamese refugee families, Nazli Kibria discusses the "structure of refuge" constructed to address this population, "involving a complex configuration of policies guiding entry and settlement" through "special government-funded programs designed to aid adjustment" (12).[7] Though Kibria emphasizes the often bewildering difficulty of securing these subsidies, which rendered such assistance "a highly ephemeral and unstable resource, short-lived in its availability and subject to abrupt termination at any time" (85), Southeast Asian refugees were popularly denigrated for their access to welfare.[8] The painful family quarrel Pham recounts demonstrates how deeply this judgment has penetrated; indeed, it is those who have made it across the minefield who are the most withering in their critique of government assistance. As Nhi T. Lieu notes in her discussion of class divisions among Vietnamese Americans, "The assimilation process required them to employ one representational strategy—that of the successful model minority—to refute the other—the haunting figure of the destitute refugee" (2).[9]

At the Pham family reunion, the second generation looks on in fearful silence as the discord escalates:

My father said, "*You shouldn't abuse the system like that. There are people more needy than you.*"

Indignation swelled her eyes. *"What do you mean I shouldn't? Who are you to talk?"*

Uncle Hun butted in: *"He's your big brother. You shouldn't talk to him in that tone."*

She wasn't listening, her eyes trained on my father. Her next shot came out slowly, drawing a careful bead on the mark. *"And did I ever say anything about how you made your money?"* (253–54)

The sister's calculated riposte exposes a long-shrouded family secret. Aunt Huong cries, *"Let's get it out in the open,"* bringing the meal to a halt: "The eating stopped. Little cousins peeked in from the hallway, wondering what all the angry words were about. Grandma Pham shook her head in shame." Looking on, Pham puzzles through "Half-veiled accusations" (254) and finally, when the reunion has ended in tatters, coaxes his grandmother to divulge the secret. She tells him that his parents operated a wartime brothel that served an American military base.

When Aunt Huong poses her government subsidy in the United States against her brother's business in Vietnam, she equates one mode of dependence with the other: if she is unable to free herself from assistance, her brother's freedom is inseparable from servicing American GIs. Indeed, the continuum she insists upon between her dependence in America and his shameful trade in Vietnam bridges the divide between underclass and model minority. Listening in, Pham directs the venom of their dispute back to his lost sister: "The uncles and aunts seemed to think that our family's dysfunctionality was karmic payback for whatever my parents did way back in Vietnam. And Chi, our main casualty, was the one person no one mentioned even in the heat of it" (254). As his aunt dismantles the distinction between her failure and his father's success, Pham turns back to Chi, whose loss imposes the shadow of the underclass on the family's white-collar advancement. In the new equation Pham identifies, Chi pays dearly for the bad business that underwrote the family's escape.

Catfish and Mandala is threaded with hints of this secret. Seven brief, italicized sections entitled "Fallen Leaves" are scattered throughout the narrative and present imagistic accounts of the early days of his parents' marriage and their decision to buy "*that little tavern way out in the countryside near the American army base*" (32), glimpses of the "*truckload of big brothers*" (78) who descend in Pham's memory of the tavern, as well as his frightened experience as a four-year-old trapped in one of the forbidden rooms. The final entry makes clear the aim of the business: with his mother in the caged office of the brothel, he puzzles over the "*heaping great big blocks of bills like bricks*" that his mother orders like "*a mason laying a foundation*" (308), to which she replies, "*My son, this money will take you abroad to study. In America you will become a great engineer*" (309). Thus, when long-lost Minh finally comes home and admires his brother as a "big engineer," his words echo their mother's dream for her son—made possible not only by the "big blocks of bills" earned in the brothel but, finally, by Minh's own failures and eventual death, imagined as "karmic payback" for these profits.

Pham's childhood memories of the brothel reveal a key early contact with American soldiers:

The green army truck listed from side to side as it kicked sand into the air. The men were yelling, hollering, whooping. The truck stopped, its cloud dissipating onward. Soldiers vaulted out of its tarpaulin back like grasshoppers. Some ran straight into the big plywood house for beer, others stretched and clapped their hands in great pleasure. Giant white men with hair as gold as the chain around his mother's neck tousled An's black hair. He liked their marble eyes, the colors of sky and shallow water. He liked the way

*they tried to teach him games. They picked him up, grinning, and
said words he did not understand. They smelled strange, different,
and they moved about with a booming bigness. They planed him
through the air, rocketed him into the sky, and gently parachuted
him to the ground every time. His father didn't do that, big government official, big businessman, too busy.* (78)

In marked contrast to the first-person narrative which dominates
the book, the third-person perspective of these interludes lends
them a fictional air, thus rendering them simultaneously more distant and more immediate in sensation. The description of these soldiers bursting forth from their merrily jolting truck is flooded with
An's affection: he likes these men and their attention. The passage
parades their difference—in colors, speech, smells—as a source of
wonder. In pitting the delight of their "booming bigness" against
his father the "big governmental official," however, the passage
suggests a matching significance: his father works for the South
Vietnamese Army and so works alongside these men, even as his
wife manages the brothel that serves them. Indeed, both parents are
in the business of friendship, and An's fondness for these carefree
men arises from his parents' labors as wartime friendlies.

Yet once across the minefield, out of Vietnam, Pham's father
assails his sister for her dependence, which in turn unleashes her
vindictive exposé of his own messy alliances: neither the needy
refugee nor the model minority can extricate itself from an unequal
relation. The bitter quarrel between brother and sister trades judg-
ments, each indicting the other's bad practice—and both sides rip
the family apart. As the sister steps onto the precipice, ready to
plunge into secret depths, another brother tries to hold her back
with familial order—*"He's your big brother. You shouldn't talk to him
in that tone"*—but she simply does not acknowledge this restraint.
Just as the threshold of the family preserved in Vietnam can be

ANDREW X. PHAM'S *CATFISH AND MANDALA*

breached in the new world, the strictures of the family are no stay against the chasm that can be opened within it. The family reunion ends in total dissolution: swirling accusations of disrespect, and finally rocks hurled. This explosion reveals the ongoing, destructive effects of American assistance—as well as the proximity of the war, which continues to lie just below the surface.

The Pham family profited from the bloated service economy created by the American war. In the preface to her study of prostitution and tourism in Southeast Asia, Truong Thanh-Dam sketches the growth of the industry in Vietnam:

> Being Vietnamese, I witnessed the spread of prostitution in my adolescence in South Vietnam during the Indochina conflict. Forced urbanization campaigns, carried out for military reasons in the 1960s, uprooted millions of peasants in an effort to destroy the rural bases of communist guerrillas. Many rural women were drawn into the cities and to areas surrounding US military bases, where a service economy instantly sprung up and revolved around personal services provided to US military personnel. Brothels and sex establishments mushroomed in these areas and enriched many of their owners. The profitability of prostitution made the entrenched Confucian ethics of the society and its codes of sexual conduct almost irrelevant for many. (x)

Long after the war, the strident judgment of the younger aunt against her elder brother's past venture demonstrates the dissonance between "entrenched Confucian ethics" and this lucrative business.

The services that rose around US military bases in Vietnam were, of course, only the latest in the history of US Pacific Command, "an integrated and extremely secretive complex composed of mobile

239

forces and fixed bases over which the host states in the western, central, and south Pacific exercise merely nominal sovereignty."[10] In Korea, camptowns—hybrid US-ROK stations created to serve American military personnel—established a new breed of service labor which bore the brunt of securing transpacific relations.[11] In Vietnam, as Susan Brownmiller explains, "The American military got into the prostitution business by degrees, an escalation process linked to the escalation of the war" (93). The US military "kept its hands partially clean by leaving the procurement and price arrangement to Vietnamese civilians" (95)[12]—as in Pham's family establishment, which kept its bricks of bills within the family. The subeconomies that developed to accommodate American military personnel "had distorting effects on the larger economy and culture of the host societies,"[13] and a major legacy of American intervention in Vietnam is the distorting development of the sex trade in every region claimed for the "recreation" of American soldiers.

Cynthia Enloe's groundbreaking scholarship on women and militarization elaborated the "powerful alliance of militarism and tourism" (37) in the wake of the war in Vietnam, and Kathleen Barry, in her study of "the industrialization of sex," sketches the reach of the US military during the war in Vietnam "as Thailand and the Philippines became sites of R&R for the U.S. military. Prostitution of Vietnamese, Thai, and Philippine women during and after the Vietnam War was mobilized by degrees for the American military" (132). This intensifying growth created a "pattern of military prostitution leading to sex tourism,"[14] and after the war, at every site established for American rest and relaxation, a local army of "corrupt politicians, police, armed forces and civil servants"[15] expanded the trade as a means of enticing tourists. In Vietnam, with the adoption of a major shift toward economic liberalization in 1986, "prostitution immediately began to increase":[16] writing in the mid-1990s, Barry states that "there is a resurgence of prostitution as women are being marginalized in the development process" (138)—a development that Pham witnessed firsthand during his 1996 bicycle tour of his birth country.

II

In Pham's rediscovery of the country he fled as a child, every intimation of romance is inseparable from the taint of prostitution. When Pham arrives at a "sleepy tourist town" (126), he is captivated by a beautiful taxi dancer who bluntly explains her standing in the town. Pham notices that "people treat her differently, look at her in a way I do not like," to which Kim replies: "*'It doesn't matter,'* she says, shrugging. *'I am an untouchable in this town. People know where I work and what I do. I am like trash'*" (133). He appreciates her frankness, and when they dine out, "she insists on taking turns paying," saying *"We're friends, aren't we?"* and *"let's do it like Westerners do. Let's take turns. I don't want to be a Vietnamese girl who always waits for her male friends to pay"* (133). Kim's independence wins Pham over—yet when Kim claims that she doesn't "want to be a Vietnamese girl," she is also hinting at the larger aims of her "friendship," which she eventually spells out: *"Take me to America"* (134). Explaining that they could be married and divorced quickly at no cost to him, Kim says, *"Please, don't leave me in this life. Look at me. Look. Look at my face. I am not young anymore. I'm twenty-five. My friends have children already. There are so many young and beautiful girls at the hotel now. I won't last there much longer"* (135).

Kim's winning independence thus gives way to a desperate desire for rescue: as she explains to Pham, *"You can save me. I can save my family. And they and all my children and their children and their grandchildren will be indebted to you"* (135). When Pham declines to shoulder this burden, their meetings end. His final glimpse of

Kim is "in the company of a tall white tourist, her tiny hand looping the crook of his arm. She catches my eyes, and when her companion isn't looking, she smiles brightly at me: Friends" (135). Though Pham believes he has extricated himself through friendship, Kim's bright smile expresses the unchanged politics of their relationship: her claims for independence had always been friendly bids for rescue. Her friendship with Pham is finally not so different from her interaction with the "tall white tourist": locked within a politics of alliance created by American intervention, both Pham and his white replacement occupy the role of the powerful friend.

As he tours Vietnam, Pham continually encounters the service economy created by the circumstances of the war. Near the end of his travels, he encounters a haunting echo of Kim ensconced on "a Honda Dream, the Vietnamese Cadillac": "Hello, she says in English. Hello, I smile. She thinks I'm Japanese or Korean. How are you, she asks me. Good, I say—always glad to talk to students eager to practice their English" (331). Pham quickly discovers that she is not looking for conversation, however: "You go with me very cheap. You go. Me very cheap, very good. You go with me very cheap. Very, very cheap. I make you happy" (331). Throughout his travels in Vietnam, Pham is assumed to be Japanese or Korean—that is, a subject defined by the two preceding American interventions in the region—and this misrecognition plays up belated encounters of Cold War friendship in this period of rapid economic liberalization in Vietnam. By contrast, when he is exposed as "Viet-kieu" (an overseas or diasporic Vietnamese), he faces real hatred, as in one particularly menacing instance at a roadside hut, where he excites the ire of "three soldiers in olive uniforms" (311) whose taunts escalate into verbal assault: "*Fucking traitor. Fucking Viet-kieu. You raped the country, then you fled to America. You . . . you American pet. Now you come back rich. America pays off traitors well, don't they?*" (303). [17] Their furious envy belongs to the other side of the coin of friendship exemplified by Kim and her replica on the Honda Dream: both reignite Cold War factions—and both identify Pham as a profiteer of the war.[18]

Another acquaintance on a Honda motorbike, however, provides a literary frame for comprehending the pervasiveness of the sex trade in Vietnam. In Hue, Pham encounters a former history professor who explains, to Pham's astonishment, that Vietnam's *"national literary heroine is a prostitute"* (282):

> Taking great pains to fill the gaps in my education, the Professor explains that *The Tale of Kieu* is a story about a prostitute named Kieu, a melodramatic tragicomic poem of 3,254 verses written by an aristocratic scholar named Nguyen Du and published two hundred years ago. Every Vietnamese has read or heard at least parts of this story taught at various levels in school. (283)[19]

Nguyen Du's "supreme masterwork of Vietnamese literature"[20] deftly weaves classical Chinese learning into a tale about a virtuous girl trapped into a life of prostitution, and the Professor ties this literary figure to the people: " *'It says everything about the Vietnamese, understand-no?'* says the Professor in his lilting pedantic rambling. *'She is a prostitute. The things she has done are not commendable, great deeds. But don't you see, it is the reasons why she does these things. They are selfless acts. Sacrifices'* " (283). Her deeds are significant not because they are commendable, but rather because they are disgraceful: her disgrace is the measure of her sacrifice.

Huynh Sanh Thong's introduction to his eloquent translation of *The Tale of Kieu* charts the shifting reception of the work, from its dissemination in the 1820s, to anticolonial resistance in the 1920s, when French colonial officials attempted to use *The Tale of Kieu* to advance their interests, and all the way to the period of

American intervention. Regarding this recent history, Huynh writes: "Thoughtful Vietnamese cannot help recognizing in their country the image of a karma-cursed woman: Kieu. Between 1965 and 1975, the Washington crusade for a world safe from Soviet Russia and Red China tore asunder the warp and woof of society in South Vietnam and bred prostitution, sexual and otherwise, on a vast scale" (xxxix). Huynh concludes his introduction by delving into this identification between Kieu and Vietnam:

> To the extent that the poem implies something at the very core of Vietnamese experience, it addresses them intimately as victims, as refugees, as survivors. In the course of Vietnam's tormented history, the individual, like Kieu herself, has all too often become the toy of necessity, has been compelled to do the bidding of some alien power, to serve a master other than the one to whom he or she should owe allegiance. Beyond its literal meaning, Kieu's prostitution is interpreted as a metaphor for the betrayal of people under duress, the submission to force of circumstances. More generally, Kieu stands for Vietnam itself, a land well endowed with natural and human resources, but too often doomed to see such riches gone to waste or destroyed. And yet, despite its grim details and sordid aspects, Kieu's story conveys a message of hope for both the individual and the country: if, like Kieu, the Vietnamese accept and endure with fortitude whatever happens to them, someday they will have paid the cost of their evil karma and will achieve both personal and national salvation. (xl)

Huynh's hopeful conclusion demonstrates the power of Kieu, a literary heroine who has come to exemplify the nation under duress. In suturing an individual plight to "Vietnam itself," Kieu provides an alternative frame for comprehending the sex trade derived from a military service economy: in Huynh's evocation of a karmic economy, Kieu's endurance pays down a personal and national debt, and her suffering offers the promise of salvation on a national scale.

Evocations of karmic debt, ubiquitous in Vietnamese reckoning with its history, provide a canny resource for Vietnamese American testimonies, as in Viet Thanh Nguyen's reading of Le Ly Hayslip's appeal: "She becomes the emblematic heroine of classical Vietnamese literature—the ideal woman who retains her spiritual virtue in the face of overwhelming circumstances that deprive her of her 'chastity'" (110). Lan Cao, too, turns to the *Tale of Kieu* to redeem the seemingly negligent mother of *The Lotus and the Sword*, who is revealed to have paid the karmic debts incurred by her extended family. This redemptive spiritual economy reverses the terms of the base transactions on the street to treasure the cursed woman, but this aesthetic overlay offers Pham no consolation—in fact, karmic transactions only deepen his melancholy.

At the end of his first stop in Vietnam, when he is staying with his extended family in Saigon, Pham is overcome when he encounters a "beggar-child," in whose face he recognizes both Chi and himself (107). Deeply shaken by this child, Pham takes off on a wild search for her, and his mad chase becomes a fevered contemplation—"My Saigon was a whore, a saint, an infanticidal maniac. She sold her body to any taker, dreams of a better future, visions turned inward, eyes to the sky of the skyscrapers foreign to the land, away from the festering sores at her feet"—that opens floodgates of grief: "I wept uncontrollably, as I did when I heard my sister Chi had committed suicide—my father cutting her free from a yellow nylon rope. I had known then, as I know now, that I was weeping for her and weeping for myself because I was not there in the months before her death" (109). The wave of feeling that rises up as Pham remembers Chi's suicide reveals the impossibility of redemption: Saigon ignores its dispossessed, and the family has cast Chi away. Rendered as the casualty for the family's American privilege, Chi pays for the profits Pham enjoys—thus rerouting and short-circuiting the karmic payback that would ultimately recompense Chi and, more broadly, Vietnam.

Both the utility and insufficiency of the *Tale of Kieu* expose the political economy of friendly relations derived from the American war. To read this national fable of spiritual virtue into the military sex trade, of course, strips away the veneer of friendly relations: instead of dressing up the business, the *Tale of Kieu* insists upon its degradation as an index of the heroine's virtue. Its application in both Hayslip's and Cao's texts suggests a truth of suffering that unmasks false alliances. Yet the seduction of Kieu's hidden constancy promises a redemption that can be endlessly deferred—but, for Pham, the virtue of suffering remains incomprehensible. He never desires the selfless redemption extolled by the Vietnamese professor, and so Kieu exemplifies a Vietnamese logic that he does not share: Pham's anguish for "my Saigon" merges into the loss of Chi because he laments his distance from both.[21]

Pham binds Chi to Vietnam, and thus castigates himself for abandoning both sister and country. He is so deeply shaken when he recognizes Chi in the face of the "beggar-child" because he can see Chi's fate in this figure, who echoes the Leper Boy as well, whose contagion and difference foretold her future self. Seeing his own face in this same child, however, reveals the great transformation Pham has undergone: though he had been an abject friendly of the war, he has returned as a representative of the other side—a highly desired, yet also despised, friend. Vietnam overwhelms him because he finds himself forced to contend with his dramatically changed role in the economy of friendship. Confronted over and over again with echoes of the family business that secured his transformation, he cannot subscribe to the redemptive logic of spiritual virtue; instead, he knows all too well who benefits from friendly debasement. To Pham, Chi's "Vietnamese death" is unrelieved suffering, and it is her absolute loss that comes home to him in Vietnam.

III

Pham's subsequent writings fork into two kinds of literary endeavors: he is a prolific memoirist, and he also lends his voice to others. This second path has led him to translate and recount two untold stories of the war: the wartime diaries of a North Vietnamese Army doctor, and his father's story of his childhood in Vietnam and his service in the South Vietnamese military. These projects unfolded in tandem, and for both Pham worked closely with his father—indeed, this work was critical to healing the rift between them created by the publication of *Catfish and Mandala*.[22] The resulting works echo with the intensity of feeling Pham plumbed in his own memoir, but these texts possess a cohesion that Pham could not provide for his own story. Though these subjects endure unimaginable wartime trials, his renderings achieve a sense of balance that resonates with the conditions of their production: they are miraculous works of collaboration that could only have been ventured long after the war. Indeed, they present a post–Cold War perspective that largely eluded Pham in Vietnam, where he found himself bound by living traces of the war.

With his father's assistance, Pham translated the diaries of Dang Thuy Tram, a North Vietnamese doctor killed in the war, whose writings were saved by an American soldier in 1970 and finally returned to Vietnam in 2005. In its reclamation and return, Tram's diary pointedly marks the dissolution of Cold War divisions: Frances FitzGerald's introduction to Pham's translation details the experience of Fred Whitehurst, the former soldier who rescued the diaries from the incinerator and smuggled them home, where they were forgotten for decades, until Whitehurst shared them with his brother, another veteran of the war. The Whitehurst brothers located Tram's family in Vietnam and sent the diaries back, and the correspondence between the Whitehursts and Tram's mother and sisters blossomed into a new relation: "Rob and Fred were adopted into Thuy's family as 'sons' and 'brothers'" (xvii)—a figural adoption that clearly presents a post–Cold War counterpoint to former modes of integration reserved for friendlies.

Pham's 2007 translation of the diaries, entitled *Last Night I Dreamed of Peace*, underscores another striking continuity between former enemies. In his translator's note, he credits his father's experiential knowledge:

> I could not have made this translation without my father, Thong Van Pham. He was born in Tong Xuyen and grew up in Hanoi, not far from where Tram lived with her family. His background and knowledge of the language and culture of that time were vital to the translation of the diaries. It took us approximately five months working closely in tandem to complete the translation. (xxi)

Hence, just as the diaries connect American veterans to a North Vietnamese Army officer killed by US forces, the labor of translation bridges the political division between Pham's father, formerly an officer in the South Vietnamese Army, and this enemy doctor. And in foregrounding the close work between father and son, the note indicates a transformed relation within their family that echoes the larger, political healing showcased in the remarkable postwar career of Tram's diaries.

Historian Mark Philip Bradley describes this remarkable young woman and her writings:

> In the spring of 1967 Dang Thuy Tram, a young woman fresh out of medical school in Hanoi, arrived in the mountainous central Vietnamese province of Quang Ngai to serve as the chief physician at a thatched-roof field hospital. In this lonely and remote spot, she cared for wounded North Vietnamese and NLF soldiers. Tram kept a diary: simple notebooks of five by seven inches, dull brown with cardboard covers. The diary is full of stories about amputating limbs and trying to avoid American planes and foot patrols, which sometimes forced Tram and her colleagues to move their clinic by carrying the wounded on their backs. The diary also gives voice to her youthful optimism, to moments of self-doubt, to how much she missed her fiancé back home, and to her deep animosity towards what she calls "the American invaders." (115)[23]

Indeed, the entries are punctuated with Tram's fury against American soldiers—"The Americans are upon us like blood-thirsty devils, stealthily sinking their fangs into our bodies. Only when we have chased them all out of Vietnam will our blood stop pouring into the earth" (47)—but such sentiments clearly did not reignite old animosities for the Whitehurst brothers. In showcasing her vulnerability as a young woman longing for her family as she toils in unthinkable conditions, her writings resonated widely—with her former enemies, both American and Vietnamese, as well as with her own countrymen.

The diaries were published in Hanoi in July 2005, and "To the surprise of the book publisher, they caused an immediate sensation" (xviii). By the end of 2006, nearly a half-million copies had been sold, and the book "struck a particular chord among young readers" (xviii), making Dang Thuy Tram into a new kind of hero. Unlike "the old rhetoric of invincibility" (xviii) typical of textbook accounts of wartime heroism, Tram was captivating for her softheartedness: though the diaries evince her absolute belief in her comrades and their cause, the entries are replete with longing and disappointment. Tram repeatedly remarks upon the "jealous gossip" against her within the Party: "Some people are envious of the affection others have for me" (56). Tram inspires the devotion of several young men, whose pledges of love she describes as "the noble sentiments between people whose hearts are full of effervescent affections." Against those who "cannot and will not totally understand," Tram insists they share "a miraculous love, a love that makes people forget themselves and think only of their dear ones. With that love, people can sacrifice their lives to protect their loved ones" (86). Tram offers this "miraculous love" as a means to self-sacrifice and heroic, wartime defense.

Perhaps we may discover in Tram's love, through which "people can sacrifice their lives," a counter to the sordid business buried in Pham's family history and everywhere evident in postwar Vietnam. Tram's "noble sentiments" present a chaste love, cleansed of servitude, that binds comrades. Indeed, her pure, sisterly love ultimately transcends wartime divisions: long after her death at the hands of American soldiers, two American soldiers would become her brothers, the latest in a line of admiring men who were captivated by her sisterly charms—including the fellow northerner who fled south and all the way to the United States, who would help translate her voice for American audiences. In an entry dated August 5, 1969, Tram foretold her fate: "Perhaps I will meet the enemy, and perhaps I will fall, but I hold my medical bag firmly regardless, and people will feel sorry for this girl who was sacrificed for the revolution when she was still young and full of verdant dreams" (146). The irony that the enemy she meets will ultimately deliver her to the "people who will feel sorry for this girl" presents a nearly unimaginable expansion of her "verdant dreams."

As an actual point of connection between wartime foes, "this girl who was sacrificed for the revolution" strikingly offers opportunities for healing familial bonds. Hence, while Pham's memoir featured an implacable father whose "Vietnamese" acts of love drove away his sister, this translation is evidence of a remarkable bond: this shared endeavor unites father and son via a safe return to the war. Pham's father's past becomes newly usable in this literary labor, which prizes his Vietnamese authority in far gentler modes. And in working together to present Tram's voice, father and son intertwine two different orders of exilic experience: Tram's story returns his father to his own youth in northern Vietnam, a world he knew intimately and lost irretrievably; and Tram's availability as a pure Vietnamese sister addresses Pham's own painful longing for Chi—and, indeed, Vietnam.

If *Catfish and Mandala* presented an ultimately alienating return to Vietnam, in which Pham discovered a country deformed by the wartime economy that funded his escape, *Last Night I Dreamed of Peace* offers a healing return. In Vietnam, he only found his place among the expat community, but with this translation, he finds his way back, with his father as a guide. Translation, of course, is a well-trodden metaphor for comprehending experiences of dislocation, and Pham's labor of translating a foreign consciousness for American audiences proves not only his American fluency, but also a sympathy and even reverence for Vietnamese understanding and experience—both Tram's and his father's—that he failed to discover in his travelogue.

In the move from memoirist to translator, Pham has stepped away from the center of his writing: his own voice is subsumed under that of this hopeful revolutionary and of his father's experience. And when his own anxieties no longer form the subject of his writings, he demonstrates his ability to inhabit a perspective freed from the logic of the Cold War: imperial wars, of course, require and produce friendly translators, but just as the adoption of the Whitehursts transcended the usual terms of Cold War integration, Pham's translation offers a reprieve from this logic. The task of adopting Dang Thuy Tram's perspective dislodges Pham from his Cold War position and, crucially, requires him to attend to his father's story.

IV

The reparative literary work of *Last Night I Dreamed of Peace* belongs to a period of deep collaboration between Pham and his father, when Pham also served as his father's amanuensis to craft *The Eaves of Heaven*, a first-person account of Thong Van Pham's experiences, from his boyhood in northern Vietnam to his release from a grueling reeducation camp in 1976, the year of the family's escape. In an opening note, Pham explains his writerly role: "I have not written my father's memoir. I have lent his life stories my words. The perspectives and sentiments within are his." Pham's hand is evident throughout the text, however, especially in temporal leaps that recall the densely woven structure of his own memoir. *The Eaves of Heaven* shuttles between Thong's 1940s childhood at his family's northern estate ("the happiest years of my life" [58]), his harrowing migration to the south in the mid-1950s, the difficulty and drudgery of serving in the South Vietnamese army in the 1960s, and the 1975 fall of Saigon and its brutal aftermath. Moving back and forth between these decades, the text creates a portrait of a privileged yet deeply wounded child, who grows up in a world of bewildering political reversals.

The most compelling figure in *The Eaves of Heaven* is Thong's own father, "a devoted enthusiast of various European pleasures the colonial French made accessible to their supporters and the rich Vietnamese ruling class" (28–29). This difficult father paid an extraordinary price for his European tastes, however. In 1949, he was "captured and conscripted into service as a porter and translator for the French" (200–201): a breathtaking fall for a man who was, "in his prime, a country nobleman at large in the city with the riches of generations at his disposal" (210). The nobleman became "a colonial slave," and he returned from his captivity a "barefoot beggar" (211) who "soon succumbed to the grip of opium, the intoxicant of choice among the Vietnamese elites" (244). For the rest of his life, Thong's father would be bound to this addiction, whose oblivion he came to depend upon during the devastating journey to Saigon in 1954 and the ensuing struggle of refugee existence in the south.

Thong's own service to the US military is cast differently from his father's forced conscription to the French. Thong underwent military training to become "a lieutenant in the Army of the Republic of Vietnam," whose

> first commission was as the new commander of the Rural Development Task Force (RD), a paramilitary organization aimed at winning over the people in the countryside. I was chosen based on my college education, because RD commanders must also work with advisors from the U.S. Agency for International Development (USAID). (108)

Thong's service allied Vietnamese and US Special Forces units: "In addition to my Rural Development duties, I also served at the front as a liaison officer at a Vietnamese Special Forces camp established and assisted by U.S. Special Forces" (164). His military service shadowing US intelligence and special operations, however, would ultimately become a source of betrayal and imprisonment. As Saigon fell, "Our trusted American allies never came" (230), and as he watched white foreigners allowed entry into the American embassy before clamoring Vietnamese crowds, "I had never felt so much envy toward foreigners as I did at that moment. Since I was a teenager, I could never escape the feeling that they glided on some other plane above us; their dignity, living standards, and privileges thriving in another stratum beyond our reach" (233). As a teenager, the foreigners that glided above were French; and as a decommissioned officer, he watched in chagrined disbelief as his American allies left him at the mercy of the enemy.

Thong endured "Seven months of psychological torture, brainwashing, brutal imprisonment, starvation, physical abuse, and hard labor" (295) in a reeducation camp, during which he managed never to betray his intelligence work for the Americans. Upon his release,

> I caught a glimpse of myself in a shop window and saw the image of my father decades earlier looking back at me—the shadow of a man the French had released, the emaciated body, the sun-charred face, the cracked lips, the sunken red eyes, wrinkles as deep as scars. Barefoot and penniless, we were equally impoverished across a generation. (294)

This passage marks the single instance in which Thong sees his father in himself, in a text which is otherwise at pains to distinguish Thong from his playboy father. This instance, too, underscores their difference: though both suffer for their military service, it was Thong's victorious countrymen, not colonial occupiers, who tortured him. Hence, unlike his father during the French occupation, Thong is not a slave, but rather a principled—albeit abandoned—friend who is tortured for his loyalty, thus magnifying the distinction between father and son.

Near the end of the book, however, we discover an obscured echo between them: in 1949, back in Hanoi after his conscription by the French, Thong's father converted the family villa into an inn "serving French expatriates, merchants, and soldiers on leave" (242), a business which quickly devolved into a brothel. While his father "constructed a comfortable new life" (244) from its proceeds, Thong and his cousin Tan were charged with operating the inn. The young men were "ashamed of our family's business": "We ran a modest inn, but the soldiers had turned it into a whorehouse" (272). *The Eaves of Heaven* makes no mention of the inn that Thong himself later bought near the American military base, but this late revelation clearly recalls the business unveiled in the bitter family feud in *Catfish and Mandala*. The inn for French soldiers is a prelude to the one for Americans; each establishment has been tailored to suit an occupying military power—and the striking omission of this second brothel shields both Thong and his American clientele.

The Eaves of Heaven thus excises the taint of dependence that fractures the larger Pham clan in the United States and torments Pham when he returns to Vietnam. So much of the book is a meditation on a difficult father by a son who struggles to understand him—and as Thong wrestles with the ghost of his father, Pham has found a way of composing and managing his own father by lending him his words. With this book, which Pham presents in his opening note as "the distillation of years of collaboration," Pham rescues his father from imperial servitude in favor of principled friendship: while his grandfather was forever damaged by his conscription to the French, his father is not a servant to the Americans, but rather a friend who remains loyal despite being discarded.

Back in *Catfish and Mandala*, however, Pham presented his father in a moment of difficult rumination, in which Thong compares his own conduct to his father's. Saying, "I should have been more like an American father. They know how to cherish their children," he blames himself for Chi's loss—"I shouldn't have beaten her like that. I was wrong" (320)—and goes on to diagnose his failings as part of a vicious cycle: " 'My father was violent. I was an abused child,' Father said. 'He was abusive. And . . . I was abusive' " (321). This admission devastates Pham: "I wished with all my might that he hadn't said it. For him, it was too much. He was a man of the old world, given to the old ways, the harsher values. He wasn't American, not like me" (321). As a counter to this unbearable remorse, Pham presents his father's life story in striking miniature:

> He was an intellectual, the quintessential Vietnamese, a man given to passion and mountainous determination. He was a poet, a tireless, award-winning translator of French verse. He was enamored with classical guitar music. And although I never knew it during my school years when he was discouraging me from becoming a painter, he was himself a fair artist. All this in a man whose life was a mad saga: the first son of an abusive aristocrat, a teenager who lost his mother, a war and famine survivor, a refugee from the North Vietnamese Communists, a ditchdigger, a star academic, a disobedient son who wedded his beloved, a civic official, a soldier, an officer in the Nationalist Army, a government propagandist, a teacher of mathematics, a successful businessman, a prisoner in the labor and reeducation camp, an escapee from Communist Vietnam, a penniless refugee in America, a janitor, a college student, a programmer, a software engineer. Amid his travails, his daughter ran away, became a man, came home fourteen years later, and, at last, committed suicide. (321–22)

The "mad saga" of a privileged life thrown into disarray by war is the stuff of *The Eaves of Heaven*, which stops short of the American chapter of his father's life. The late trajectory from penniless refugee to software engineer, however, lends a recognizable conclusion to an otherwise tumultuous catalogue. But if Thong's life finds a resolution in America, Chi's did not. Indeed, just as his treatment of Chi matches him to his difficult father, the concluding sentence devoted to Chi's life undoes his late, hard-won rise.

The Eaves of Heaven both frees Thong from the sins of his father and retrieves him from American standards. In walking a fine line between these ends, Andrew Pham has lent his voice to tell a largely unheard experience: that of the South Vietnamese soldier. As Yen Le Espiritu notes in *Body Counts*, this figure has been "erased from almost all historical accounts of war" (108); and in her argument for commemorating South Vietnamese war dead in order to complicate the so-called "good refugee," Espiritu strikingly reveals, "In truth, I had not intended to write this chapter," explaining that it was when she "happened upon my uncle's headshot" online that she felt called "to follow the photograph, not knowing where it might lead, but trusting the journey" (116). Espiritu traces her uncle's image to a set of moving and largely unseen commemorations of his military leadership "to show that anticommunist practices are not necessarily or only about propping up U.S. ideas of assimilation and empire" (137), and the extraordinary collaboration of *The Eaves of Heaven* offers us a human portrait of becoming South Vietnamese against a heartbreaking legacy of imperial occupation. How to be anticommunist without being an apologist for empire is, of course, a central concern of the friendly, and Pham's loving, writerly assistance for his father quiets the clamor of divisive friendship that tore the family apart in *Catfish and Mandala*.

The fact of their collaboration in both *The Eaves of Heaven* and *Last Night I Dreamed of Peace* transports political alliances into healing modes underwritten by a significantly post–Cold War largesse. Both texts set aside Cold War logic, whether in converting the suffering enemy into an angel of mercy, or in expurgating a

shameful example of neocolonial alliance. The reunions that stem
from and sustain these works rise above sordid love and break a
cycle of abuse. In *Catfish and Mandala*, delving into these secrets
launched a nightmare metamorphosis from friendly to friend—
and mired Pham within his grief. His subsequent—and far less
tumultuous—returns[24] to past Vietnams are facilitated by his
father's assistance and, critically, by keeping himself in the background. Pham's collaborative works portray subjects longed for by
the melancholy Vietnamese American—whose own role remains
cast within belated scenes of Cold War integration.

Conclusion

I would like to conclude by returning to Asian America's foundational epic and its famous underworld descent: the graphic account of the torture that a young Maxine inflicts upon another Chinese American girl—who is the mirror image of herself—in Maxine Hong Kingston's *The Woman Warrior*. In particular, a critical bit of historical context interests me: in setting the stage for this encounter, Kingston writes,

> We were chasing one another through the playground and in and out of the basement, where the playroom and lavatory were. During air raid drills (it was during the Korean War, which you knew about because every day the front page of the newspaper printed a map of Korea with the top part red and going up and down like a window shade), we curled up in this basement. Now everyone was gone. The playroom was army green and had nothing in it but a long trough with drinking spigots in rows. (174)

The war deeply colors this scene: the newspaper map of the Korean peninsula, with its red shade pulled up and down, renders the school basement an army green. Cornering the girl in the lavatory, Maxine declares, "You're going to talk," and then elaborates: "I'm going to make you talk, you sissy-girl" (175). In this basement air raid shelter, her menacing tones echo military interrogation, and so much of this devastating scene is conditioned by Korea: not only does Maxine take on the demonized role of the Chinese interrogator, but the resemblance between these two girls recalls the structure of civil war, in which the identity between sides sparks inhuman brutality. Maxine's subsequent fate is strangely fitting as well: bedridden with a mysterious illness, she becomes a recluse for eighteen months, during which "Nothing happened" (182). A peculiar conflict and a strange paralysis; little appreciable change, but the order of things has been utterly shaken.

Maxine punishes this too-quiet girl because

> People told how *they* had tried *their* best to be friendly. *They* said hello, but if she refused to answer, well, they didn't see why they had to say hello anymore. She had no friends of her own but followed her sister everywhere, although people and she herself probably thought I was her friend. (173)

Maxine indicts her for unfriendliness, and in forcing her to talk, she undertakes to school this child in friendly conduct. In her increasingly desperate attempts to force speech out of this unresponsive subject, however, Maxine loses herself. Sobbing, her own voice echoing against the walls of the lavatory, Maxine ultimately fears that it is she who would "have to confess" (181) for her behavior. She is both interrogator and prisoner, because she has attacked a friend for not being friendly enough—an ensnaring contradiction that drives her to engage in enemy behavior, which then threatens Maxine herself with a potential future injunction "to talk." In this dizzying encounter, wartime relations govern a friendship between two girls to reveal the coercion at the heart of alliance: to insist on friendliness always risks nullifying the relation, and, in the case of this key instance, its participants as well. It is my contention that attending to the political overtones of this famous scene helps to account for its strange magnification: in concert with the more apparent significance of this moment for Maxine as a major rupture in her own development of what she terms "personality" when she berates the quiet girl, the war in the newspapers shades her conduct.

Asian America has been particularly implicated by the operations of wartime allegiance, a defining fact of existence that Kingston foregrounds in the closing section of *China Men*, her companion volume to *The Woman Warrior*: at the opening of this section, entitled "The Brother in Vietnam," Kingston declares, "There has always been war, whether or not I knew about it" (264). And in turning to one brother's experience during Vietnam, Kingston examines the plight of the Asian American friendly. She presents her brother's reasoning behind his decision to enlist in the Navy, despite his dismay at the war:

> In a country that operates on a war economy, there isn't much difference between being in the Navy and being a civilian. When we ate a candy bar, drank grape juice, made a phone call, put money in the bank, cleaned the oven, cooked it, ran a computer, drove a car, rode an airplane, sprayed with insecticide, we were supporting the corporations that made tanks and bombers, napalm, defoliants, and bombs. (284)

And because the war fuels every American activity, he resolves to "be a Pacifist in the Navy" (285), a decision that Kingston curiously anchors with the following news:

> When the new Secretary of Defense called the Chinese "the enemy of the world" and predicted all-out nuclear war before 1970, the brother stopped reading the newspapers. There

wasn't any news; it would be news if the war ended. The news didn't change; only the numbers kept going up. (285)

Like the newspaper map of Korea in *The Woman Warrior*, this news provides a historicized portrait of political enmity that is, interestingly, not news. There has always been war, and so the "news didn't change"—war is old news for Asian America, whose standing has always been determined by the US-Asian relationship, itself conditioned by wartime politics that date back at least to the annexation of the Philippines at the turn of the twentieth century.

This war, however, secures the brother's friendship: though China is the enemy of the world, the Chinese American soldier discovers that he has been deemed friendly. This wary young man—a schoolteacher before and after the war, who laments the ignorance of his impoverished students shipped off to Vietnam and discovers even more desperate cases among his fellow sailors—ultimately finds himself grateful for war: when he clears a security check for a promotion, " 'Thank you. Thank you. I got something good out of the Navy,' the brother blurted. 'I'm getting something good out of the Vietnam war' " (299). He considers the ramifications of this security clearance:

The government was certifying that the family was really American, not precariously American but super-American, extraordinarily secure—Q Clearance Americans. The Navy or the FBI had checked his mother and father and not deported them. Maybe that grandfather's Citizenship Judge was real and legal after all. So Uncle Bun's defection to Communism didn't matter, nor Father's gambling, nor Great Uncle's river piracy, second-story work, and murder. . . . The government had not found him un-American with divided loyalties and treasonous

inclinations. . . . While his services were needed for the unde-
clared American-Vietnam war, the family was safe. (299)

China Men is made up of portraits of these fractious and wayward
men—communists, gamblers, pirates—and in this closing section,
the brother's service wipes the family slate clean. The brother is both
profoundly relieved and disquieted by the clearance he secures in
Vietnam: the family is safe—but only while his services are needed.
The good of war is political safety meted out in return for service,
and Kingston's insistence that there has always been war, coupled
with her brother's collapsing of the distinction between military
and civilian, renders this *quid pro quo* an ongoing, deep-seated, and
disturbingly beneficial structure.

In tracing Cold War logic back into these ur-texts of Asian
American literature, my concluding gesture aims to demonstrate
what we may discover when we attend to the wartime friendly.
Reading across these two instances in Kingston's paired, epic foundation, we may comprehend the shaping force of Cold War powers
of division and incorporation. Asian American studies has been at
the forefront of what has been termed the "transnational turn" in
American studies, and my focus on the Cold War friendly provides a
periodizing and politicizing lens. US cultural studies has expanded
its framework beyond the domestic sphere to put renewed focus on
complex movements between nations and continents; Cold War
studies, too, has turned in the early twenty-first century from a
longstanding focus on domestic demonization to consider global
integration. By layering together these critical insights, my study of
Cold War transnationalism has examined proto-American subjects
forged by the integrating forces of US-Asian wartime relations—
and in featuring the making of Asian Americans out of these distant battlefields, *Cold War Friendships* has uncovered structures of

incorporation by turns subtle and insistent, in masked and forthright efforts of political alliance.

Interestingly, between *The Woman Warrior* and *China Men*, Korea provides a backdrop for demonization while Vietnam offers safety—a seeming reversal of the usual sense of these wars. But the peculiar risks of Korea and the surprising opportunities of Vietnam are entirely in keeping with the experience of the Asian friendly, whose capacity for bad behavior or good reward are determined by wartime strictures, in which friendlies find themselves policing each other and currying favor with neocolonial agents. And though it would be easy to discount such uneasy acts of friendliness—indeed, Asian American literary studies has long favored more satisfying acts of enmity figured as political resistance—this study has instead explored the formidable complexity of initiating, registering, and sustaining political alliances. I have attended to the formal contours of these representations to reveal maneuvers that are not merely instances of bad faith or false consciousness; instead, my readings have delved into the friendly's knowing self-positioning. The friendly is all too aware of the determining forces of Cold War division and integration; and though she risks her integrity—as both Maxine and her brother do in their acts of interrogation and service—her gestures of alliance recalibrate vectors of great power politics in order to ensure her own place within a global order.

Asian American studies is a wartime formation: it arose out of the antiwar movement of the late 1960s, and Vietnam haunts the works of its literary pioneers—as we have seen in Kingston's writing, both in this concluding discussion and in my reading of *The Fifth Book of Peace* in Chapter 6. The curiosity of the Cold War's longstanding contest instituted a mode of liberal integration whose contradictions became particularly evident in the hot wars in Korea and Vietnam; and though such liberal ideologies have long been discredited, these Cold War subjects act in their service. *Cold War Friendships* has examined the ways in which the new Americans born out of these unpopular skirmishes remade themselves into subjects capable of an integration whose political risks they knew all too well. And in attending to literary performances of Cold War friendship, my readings have aimed to reveal novel strategies for maintaining selves that rely on political attachment not only at the expense of their integrity but, ultimately, in order to preserve it.

In leading with representations of the Korean War, my oblique return to the Cold War consensus of the 1950s unveiled a series of typologies for the friendly: the allied soldier, foreign student, and war orphan. All three types rendered themselves legible through attachment, and yet the three mainstream fictions I considered ultimately stranded their protagonists in their attempts to express the affection, and even love, necessary to consolidate their place in the United States. Indeed, reading across these novels, I unearthed a disheartening trajectory: even as these figures grew younger and more promising—from soldier, to student, to child—nevertheless their powers of attachment were progressively weakened. If Richard Kim's South Korean soldier outfitted himself for a new trans-Pacific attachment in 1964, the 1998 revisionist history of the Korean War in Susan Choi's romance sought to shelter the foreign student in the American South, despite his having been betrayed by his American friends during the war; and by the time of Chang-rae Lee's 2010 portrait of an indomitable war orphan, the requisite innocence of this friendly simply became inconceivable. With the diminishing hopes of these protagonists, however, comes a developing story of this formerly unnarratable war: a decade after the Korean War, Kim landed a bestseller by transcending it, but fifty years later, Lee's Korean War is itself enduring. Indeed, in the mind of his ever-youthful orphan June, the war remains an ongoing and strangely exhilarating run—which paradoxically insists upon the tantalizing integration of the Cold War even as the attainment of this promise remains forever at bay.

In framing Vietnam with Korea, my study has reconsidered this American trauma within the continued promise of liberal integration. Revisionist histories of Korea have insisted upon the continuity of these two wars, but the ongoing cultural and aesthetic juggernaut of Vietnam in the American imagination has neglected this political and formal inheritance. Yet Vietnamese American accounts of the war have always insisted on a profound attachment between the United States and South Vietnam—even as they registered the betrayal of their erstwhile friends. And while in Korea, wartime friendship militarized relations of servitude—as elaborated in Chapter 1—in Vietnam, such relations took on a new intimacy, in large part because of the narrowed possibilities of alliance—as explained in Chapter 5, which examined the American Special Forces officer as the single agent of attachment in this conflict. For abandoned Vietnamese allies, this troubled agent was their only ticket to the United States, and, upon arrival, these discarded friends faced the excruciatingly difficult labor of reviving a wounding affection.

In striking contrast to the elaborate fictions of the Korean War, Vietnam's friendlies seem to tell more heartfelt tales, but these testimonials are deeply charged acts of persuasion. In her 1989 and 1993 autobiographies, Hayslip remade herself into a humanitarian in the service of a healing relation between the United States and Vietnam—and while skeptical readers have cast doubt on her purported political innocence, her bid for friendly recognition reframed the war to replace the wounded American GI with the Vietnamese refugee at its center. Indeed, the arguments for friendship evinced in these texts are far less invested in soul-baring than they are in demonstrating political and ethical fitness for allegiance. Both Lan Cao's fictionalized 1997 memoir and Andrew Pham's

1999 travelogue-cum-memoir promised to reveal secrets of infidelity, only to detach themselves from these revelations. In both cases, shameful family secrets served to distinguish good friends from bad—and both look back to the war to restore the category of the Cold War friend.

Part I of this study, devoted to narratives of the Korean War, traced a hardening figuration, in which a war orphan ultimately becomes a calculating friendly; by contrast, the Vietnamese American memories of war in Part II are portraits of vulnerability. In pointed distinction to the highly stylized literary renderings of Part I, these works each possess a utilitarian air—albeit in unreliable modes—whether as self-help, diary, or travel guide, and even as my inquiries have exposed the politics of friendship that conditioned these expressions, it has been my aim to respect them. Hence, by considering the complex overtures of the friendly in the wake of both wars, this study has both advanced a harder look at forms of political collaboration in overwrought narratives of the Korean War, and taken seriously the feeling pronouncements advertised in Vietnamese refugee testimony. Finally, in measuring the appeal of liberal integration by and for precisely those figures least attractive to the Cold War consensus—that is, friendlies in proxy wars meant to remain in the periphery—*Cold War Friendships* has read attachments that are, in fact, perverse in their sincerity. "Sincerity," of course, was the key term of the early Cold War, and a primary ingredient in a political consensus that demanded affection for an economic system. My readings have contemplated expressions of longing for the "free world" by subjects conscripted into proxy warfare, not merely to expose the politics of Cold War friendship, but rather to register significant acts of self-making calibrated to vaunted liberal aims at once licensed and limited by these two deeply unpopular wars.

NOTES

Introduction

1. Keyssar discusses the film's "superficially disguised" allusions to Vietnam: "Altman noted in a 1983 interview that in the original cut of M*A*S*H there was not one reference to Korea: '. . . they said you have to put in the titles that it was Korea. That's when we put in the statement of Eisenhower's'" (57).

2. Keyssar cites this scene as one of the film's "more aggressive allusions to Vietnam" (58), along with the opening images of helicopters, which, as she puts it, "for spectators who watched late sixties television news . . . signal the war in Vietnam" (57).

3. Weis uses this phrase in her assessment of the film, which echoes feminist critics of the film at the time of its release: "While the film's aesthetic achievements remain impressive, its simplistic attitudes have dated it embarrassingly. Its politics, other than its diatribe against the absurdity of war, seem puerile. The surgeons who are its heroes express themselves in the mode of frat-party antics. Altman seems not only to condone but share their adolescent view of women" (312).

4. Weis 313. She further notes that "Variety regularly wrote articles tracing M*A*S*H as a unique phenomenon that in rerun could 'attract and hold an audience at any time of the day'" (313).

5. Budd and Steinman 68. Their article traces a critical shift over the course of the show's long run: "Originally, at least in part, a displaced way of thinking about Vietnam, of remembering it, M*A*S*H quickly became a way of forgetting it, a pacification of memory" (69).

NOTES

6. Diffrient cites Peggy Herz, from her 1975 *All about* M*A*S*H, the first published book about the show (1).

7. Diffrient, quoting from a 1981 *New York Times* article (96). Diffrient emphasizes Alda's "status as the ideal, nonthreatening New Man of the 1970s and early 1980s" (94).

8. Diffrient underscores this phrase, particularly with regard to "Hawkeye's paternalistic affection" (11).

9. In a recent interview, Kieu Chinh recalls Alda's personal kindness—and she also reveals that a possible recurring role on the show as Hawkeye's love interest was quashed by negative responses from Alda's fans.

10. Diffrient notes the more well-known Asian American actors featured over the years on the show, including Pat Morita and Philip Ahn, among many others (117–19), and he mentions the recurring appearance of Kellye Nakahara as an Asian American nurse (48).

11. Budd and Steinman discuss this phrase (62).

12. The OED dates the first usage of the noun plural form to 1861, from a New Zealand collection of private papers which distinguished "friendlies" among the Maori. The use of "friendly" in military contexts—to modify troops and artillery—dates back more recently, to 1925.

13. Barnet 37.

14. Barnet 36. Barnet characterizes the two sides as those "who manage foreign relations—the National-Security Managers—and the Revolutionaries, who guide insurgent movements" (36). Considering both the US and Soviet leadership as "National-Security bureaucrats," Barnet explains that for both imperial powers, "the Cold War conferred a manageable unity upon the landmass of Asia, Africa, and Latin America" (41). Reinhold Niebuhr noted in his 1959 *The Structure of Nations and Empires*, "The curious fact that the two nations which have achieved imperial power condemn imperialism for different reasons has led to some serious confusions" (20).

15. Westad examines the shared and contested lineage between the United States and the Soviet Union: "Locked in conflict over the very concept of European modernity—to which both states regarded themselves as successors—Washington and Moscow needed to change the world in order to prove the universal applicability of their ideologies, and the elites of the newly independent states proved fertile ground for their competition" (4).

16. Cumings muses over these axes in *Chapter 4 of Korea's Place in the Sun* (185–236).

17. Mao excoriated both superpowers and held China up as a model of "continuing revolution" for the Third World. Mao characterized US imperialism as "the main enemy of the people of the world" (Chang 169), and in the face of a growing movement toward détente between the superpowers, Mao "accused the Soviet Union of selling out world revolution" (Lüthi 347).

18. Chen 2.
19. Westad 112.
20. Barnet 37.
21. Westad 39.
22. In his explication of NSC-68, a security statement drafted in 1950, John Lewis Gaddis explains containment policy as a determination that "the United States would, in effect, 'draw the line,' defending all future targets of Soviet expansion, but without any attempt to 'liberate' areas already under Moscow's control" (21).
23. Hegel 112.
24. Wittfogel claims to pursue an analysis of Oriental despotism that corrects "Marx's retrogressions in analyzing Asiatic society" (387). Wittfogel insists that Marx's neglect of the Asiatic mode blinded him and ultimately justified Stalinist despotism.
25. Gordon Chang calls attention to the significance of anti-Asian sentiment in the progress of the Cold War in *Friends and Enemies*: "There is one factor that has not been given sufficient attention in understanding U.S. policy toward Beijing and Moscow in the 1950's. Prejudice against Asians permeated the entire top levels of the administration. Exclamations of racial fear, mistrust, and disdain often intruded into discussions of policymakers" (170).
26. In his famous response to a reporter's question about "the strategic importance of Indochina" in a 1954 news conference, Eisenhower responded by emphasizing "the possibility that many human beings pass under a dictatorship that is inimical to the free world" and the "broader considerations that might follow what you would call the 'falling domino' principle. You have a row of dominoes set up, you knock over the first one, and what will happen to the last one is the certainty that it will go over very quickly" (Williams, *America in Vietnam: A Documentary History* 156).
27. Schmitt 27.
28. Parikh, *An Ethics of Betrayal* 3.
29. See Belletto and Grausam for an overview of this critical turn in Cold War cultural studies; see also Belletto's *No Accident, Comrade* for a compelling recent reading of key figurations in Cold War American literature.
30. Klein 11.
31. In a study of Asian Americans who rose to prominence during the Cold War, Cindy I-Fen Cheng discusses "The belief that Asian Americans were direct extensions of people in Asia, regardless of place of birth or length of stay in the United States" (4) in the Cold War era.
32. Allan Punzalan Isaac explains that "instead of the full protection of citizenship," US Nationals were "legal placeholders of not-quite-belonging in the U.S. imperium" (37). In an analysis of anticolonial Filipino American aesthetics, Sarita Echavez See argues that "Filipino American desires for

belonging and home surprisingly lead to the disintegration rather than the consolidation of the American empire" (xxx).

33. Analyzing portrayals of Japanese in the United States during the Pacific War, John Dower writes, "Subhuman, inhuman, lesser human, superhuman—all that was lacking in the perception of the Japanese enemy was a human like oneself" (9).

34. See Robert G. Lee's *Orientals* for a reading of Chinatown as a Cold War theater for assimilation (145–79), as well as Cheng's discussion of Jade Snow Wong's career as Cold War ambassador (85–115).

35. As Dudziak notes, she is paraphrasing Randolph Bourne. Dudziak's critique of wartime as a "state of exception" positions itself against Giorgio Agamben (4)—though it should be noted that Agamben's *State of Exception* opens by establishing "the essential contiguity between the state of exception and sovereignty" (1). It is also worth noting that when Agamben turns to American history, he focuses on internment: "The most spectacular violation of civil rights (all the more serious because of its solely racial motivation) occurred on February 19, 1942, with the internment of seventy thousand American citizens of Japanese descent who resided on the West Coast (along with forty thousand Japanese citizens who lived and worked there)" (22).

36. Christopher Lee's introduction elaborates the shift in the field that has "reinforced a narrative in which the essentialist foundations of Asian American Studies unravel under the pressure of subsequent critiques" (5). His rehearsal of this genealogy settles on the "idealized critical subject" of Asian American literature as "a compromised, albeit powerful, figure for Asian American Studies" (22)—which resonates with my endeavor to read the power of compromised figuration in the vexed case of the friendly.

37. Victor Bascara's study of the dominance of the model-minority myth spells out of the significance of pairing incorporation and assimilation for Asian American cultural politics (12).

Chapter 1

1. McMahon, *The Cold War* 51.

2. Walter LaFeber notes the serendipity of Korea's civil war for US aims: containment "was a policy in search of an opportunity. That opportunity arrived on June 25, 1950 when, as [U.S. Secretary of State] Acheson and his aides later agreed, 'Korea came along and saved us'" (100).

3. See Stueck for the international dimensions of the war and Jager for a recent reconsideration of the war and its legacy for both the United States and Korea.

4. Casey cites and discusses this speech, 209.

5. Quoted in Cumings, *The Origins of the Korean War*, vol. 1, xx.

6. As in Stueck's thesis: "In its timing, its course and its outcome, the Korean War served in many ways as a substitute for World War III" (3).

7. Quoted in Higgins 145. Higgins reads the contradiction of this "best known of his many attacks on limited war" by turning to MacArthur's own proposal for a limited war against China (145).

8. Truman in fact did not coin the term, but rather acceded to a reporter's characterization of the war as a "police action" during a press conference.

9. Of course, local services spring up around occupying armies wherever they are stationed, and Korean houseboys, as we saw with the faithful Ho-John in Hornberger's *MASH* (see Introduction), were ubiquitous—in Kahn's words, "Almost every tent or hut occupied by a bunch of United Nations soldiers had a Korean houseboy" (146).

10. Charles K. Armstrong writes, "In theory a liberated country, South Korea (the American zone south of the thirty-eighth parallel) was treated by the US. more like an occupied enemy country" (73). Lloyd C. Gardner notes the "political difficulties" of US military "efforts to achieve a gradual transfer of power to Korean civil authorities" against "a storm of protest from nationalist political leaders who wanted the immediate eradication of the last vestiges of Japan's forty-year rule" (14). See Stueck and Yi for a recent account of the soured relations between US military occupiers and domestic leaders in the aftermath of Japanese imperial rule in South Korea.

11. Hye Seung Chung notes that "As one of the two first Korean War feature films exhibited in American theaters (along with *Korea Patrol* [1951]), *The Steel Helmet* generated fierce controversy, demonstrating not only the difficulties of representing the first Hot War of the Cold War but also the precarious relationship between the industry and the Department of Defense" (125).

12. Susan L. Carruthers explains that "Metaphors of enslavement played a crucial role in transforming the Soviet Union and China from courageous wartime allies into barbarous foes implacably opposed to the 'free world.' This cold war vision of a globe fractured between good and evil—half free, half slave—drew on a peculiarly American tradition of configuring any infringement of liberty as 'slavery' and any such challenge as an existential threat to national survival that required total annihilation" (5).

13. Chung notes that in South Korea, *Battle Hymn* has become a television staple and "remains the best-known Hollywood Korean War film" (141).

14. SooJin Pate reads the proliferation of orphanages in Korea as a demonstration of "militarized humanitarianism" (21–40). Hess's orphanage was one of the "more than 400 Korean orphanages [that] had been built or repaired by American servicemen" by the 1960s (32).

15. Quoted in Chung 143.

16. Pate explains that such entertainment was an "all too common sight": "In most of the performances, the girls dress in *hanbok* (Korean traditional dress) while singing and dancing traditional Korean folk songs" (57).

17. These children were sponsored by the Christian Children's Fund, which raised funds by offering figural "adoptions" to American donors (Klein 153). One of the children flown to Hollywood, however, was actually adopted by an American family: Hess's beloved "Chu," played by Jung Kyoo Pyo, became Sam Friar (Chung 163–64). See Chapter 4 for a discussion of Korean War adoptions.

18. Geoffrey A. Wright reads *Pork Chop Hill* as "the defining film on the violence and political uncertainty of the Korean War" (unpaginated online journal; page 5 of 21) and provides an overview and account of the paucity of Korean War films.

19. Thomas Borstelmann notes that "the domestic civil rights movement and what might be called the international civil rights movement of anticolonialism moved on parallel tracks" (46).

20. Mary L. Dudziak in *Cold War Civil Rights* explains that "one of President Truman's most important civil rights accomplishments was initiating desegregation of the armed services. Discrimination and segregation in the military were particularly galling to people of color who risked their lives to protect the nation yet were not treated equally even during their military service. When troops traveled to foreign lands, other nations were directly exposed to American racial practices" (83).

21. It is worth noting that the Korean orphan would have experienced the recent occupation, and Japanese imperialism and Korean nationalism sparked clashes in diasporic communities.

22. Cited in Casey 20.

23. Another rare technicolor movie devoted to the war is *The Bridges at Toko-Ri* (1954), a striking portrayal of a man in a gray flannel suit—that quintessential bourgeois subject of midcentury—who finds himself in Korea. The film, which concludes with the protagonist's death in a desolate trench, presents a stern lecture on the dark reality and necessity of the war. See May for a reading of this film and an account of the corpus of Korean War movies.

24. Hunter 4.

25. See Charles S. Young for a full account of POWs in Korea and the battle over repatriation. POWs made headlines throughout the Korean War, notably including an infamous kidnaping of an American General by North Korean prisoners, which novelist Ha Jin took as the subject of his 2004 novel *War Trash*.

26. Michael Rogin notably dubbed *The Manchurian Candidate* the "most sophisticated movie of the cold war" (252). In their monograph devoted to the film, Matthew Frye Jacobson and Gaspar González explain that "*The Manchurian Candidate* will repay nearly any amount of critical attention that one is willing to pour into it" (xiv).

27. Jacobson and González detail the film's remarkable reception and influence, including its withdrawal in the wake of JFK's assassination.

28. This restriction is especially noteworthy in the context of the film's liberal treatment of African American soldiers.

Chapter 2

1. "Plenary Lecture," 24–25 (ellipsis in original).

2. In the words of John Foster Dulles's 1950 address to the South Korean National Assembly: "The American people welcome you as an equal partner in the great company of those who make up this Free World, a world which commands vast moral and material power and resolution that is unswerving" (87–88).

3. Christine Hong's reading of the novel explains that *The Martyred* "offers a fictionalized account of UN rollback that obscures the U.S. agenda" (153); Hong's analysis underscores the "strategic value of fiction" (146) in concealing and revealing such political agendas.

4. Armstrong 74.

5. Bruce Cumings reads these overlapping axes: "The Korean problem was what we would now call a Third World problem or a North-South problem, a conflict over how best to overcome the deviltries of colonial rule and comparative backwardness. In the Cold War milieu of the time, however, it was always seen by Americans as an East-West problem" (*Korea's Place in the Sun* 209).

6. Grayson provides an overview of Christianity in Korea from the initial reception of Catholicism in Korea in 1777, to nineteenth-century persecution of Catholicism, to the arrival of Protestantism in the late nineteenth century and its subsequent flourishing.

7. Chung-shin Park 4.

8. Chung-shin Park explains that, "the religious community, which was allowed to function when all political and social organizations and activities were banned, served as a forum for political discussion, a political training ground, and a clearinghouse for political information in early colonial Korea" (4–5).

9. Timothy S. Lee explains that "there was an indisputable link between Korean evangelicalism and religious establishments in America; the communists saw that link as a channel through which the United States, an imperial power, sought to delay the liberation of the Korean proletariat" (62). Lee notes that "by the time the war ceased, upwards of 40 percent of northern evangelicals, or 80,000 of them, had fled southward" (68). It is worth noting that Kim Il Sung, the North Korean leader, grew up in a Christian family; Soviet alliance

separated him from his mother's faith, but Christianity's American ties drove the Northern regime's persecution of Christian leaders. Chung-shin Park argues against the "facile" view "that Christian idealism and Marxist materialism were irreconcilable": "It would be closer to the truth to say that the ideological dichotomy was a result of social and political conflict ... Kim himself was born into a devoted Christian family and was raised in strong Christian surroundings" (165).

10. Led by Syngman Rhee, whom Timothy S. Lee describes as "a Methodist elder who on August 18, 1948 became the first president of the Republic of Korea. Backed by USAMGIK [the United States Army Military Government in Korea] and the rightist regime, southern evangelicals became active in national politics" (66).

11. Timothy S. Lee writes that "8,000 of the 50,000 citizens of P'yongyang had professed to be Christians by 1909, earning for their city the title 'Jerusalem of Korea'" (23).

12. Chong Bum Kim portrays this influential minister: "Considered by some to be the 'father of Korean Christianity,' Kil played a central role in the growth and expansion of Protestantism in its early stages. ... The revivalist tradition, of which he was one of the pioneers, has become a permanent feature of Korean church life" (150).

13. Timothy S. Lee explains that the "missionaries wanted some qualitative proof that their labor was bearing authentic fruits, that the Koreans were truly being converted" (14).

14. An admiring reading of Kim's fiction by Robert J. Goar in 1980 suggests that Shin could not be a "genuine atheist" (455).

15. See Armstrong for an account of the policies of the occupation of Pyongyang by South Korean forces.

16. Along with the allusion to *The Plague*, *The Martyred* strikingly recalls Miguel de Unamuno's 1930 short story *San Manuel Bueno, martir*. Unamuno's story depicts an unbelieving priest who collects disciples similar to secondary characters in Kim's novel: Hann echoes Unamuno's fool Blasillo and Park resembles Lazaro, the doubter who becomes a passionate acolyte when San Manuel confides in him. Mario J. Valdes reads Unamuno and Kim together to argue that "the common theme of these two novels—the courage to continue living in the face of nothingness—is at once one of the most contemporary expressions of man in literature and thought, through Existentialism, and also one of the most ancient, through Stoicism" (379).

17. Camus's rebel, who understood that "Rebellion in itself is moderation" (301), came under heavy critique in light of his critical paralysis with regard to Algeria—when the dashing revolutionary of World War II was branded a disappointing moderate. The problem of Camus's antirevolutionary rebel provides a critical lens for understanding *The Martyred*'s complex loyalties.

Heinz Fenkl's Introduction to the Penguin edition of *The Martyred* astutely reads Camus and Kim together: "like Camus, Kim is able to move beyond nihilism by embracing and transcending the many enigmas portrayed in *The Martyred*" (xvi).

18. From Walsh's review.

19. James Kyung-Jin Lee 30. Lee notes that Kim's biography shares some features of his novel: Kim's "maternal grandfather, a fiercely devout Christian minister, was taken prisoner by Communist forces and shot" and Kim later "joined the South Korean military, and served as an ROK English-language liaison officer to the U.N. forces for the rest of the war" (31).

Chapter 3

1. Choi explains in a 2003 interview that "The scene literally at the end of the book, where Chuck returns to his family and is mistaken for a beggar by his mother, was something I'd written at Cornell in different form—and the very beginning, where Chuck is leaving Seoul, was also written at Cornell." In a 2005 interview, she discusses her decision to write fiction based on her father's recollections: "The things he told me were so sketchy that I had to fictionalize to fill in, and I liked the freedom that fiction gave me. I wish that I had taken better notes, or kept the notes I took. The novel and the real version of his life are now confused with each other, and it's unsettling. I've rewritten our family history, unintentionally."

2. In "Writing the Borderline Subject of War in Susan Choi's *The Foreign Student*," Crystal Parikh reads Chuck's "abject freedom": "The moment of Chang's abandonment/freedom that closes the novel inaugurates radically new affiliations with those others who will define him. This is not, I argue, an American freedom, made possible by United States intervention and Chang's integration in the South. Rather it is a freedom that originates in the destructive violence that has unmade and remade him entirely. The narrative of assimilation is, in this respect, only an epilogue to this world-shattering violence" (58).

3. Reading the rapprochement of postcolonial and Asian American discourses, Victor Bascara discusses the slogan: "Originally invoked by and for immigrants to England from its former colonies, that slogan erupts at the convergence of Asian American cultural politics and the emergence of U.S. imperialism" (xxiv–xxv).

4. Reading Chuck's incorporation into Chicago's Little Tokyo, Kim explains that his "assimilation to this American interethnic community thus recapitulates the re-education that Koreans underwent when their country was forcibly integrated into the Japanese empire" (569).

5. Cieslak 21.

6. Klein discusses "a whole new subset of travelers" in the postwar era, which significantly included American "educators and students" (105).

7. Wilson 5, 16.

8. Quoted from http://eca.state.gov/fulbright/about-fulbright/history/j-william-fulbright/j-william-fulbright-quotes.

9. John W. Gardner 637.

10. Cieslak discusses the history of students from China and Japan, whose first graduates date back to the 1850s (6–7). A cursory look at Asian American writers who came to the United States as university students reveals a wide-ranging set of artists: the modernist poets José Garcia Villa and Yone Noguchi, the midcentury fiction writers Bienvenido Santos, Lin Yutang, and C.Y. Lee, and contemporary novelists such as Mohsin Hamid.

11. Kim recalls his barber's perennial greeting: "So, what are you studying these days?" ("Plenary Lecture" 23). When he returned to Korea in 1966, Kim encountered "resentful reaction" from "those who were not as lucky as he was": "I know lots of students who went to America. Like you. . . . Every kid I know wants to get out" (Eleana Kim 68).

12. John A. Gardner 643.

13. John A. Gardner writes, "In thinking about the living circumstances of the foreign student it is necessary, of course, to face candidly and realistically the problem of racial discrimination. . . . The Communists could wish for nothing better than a steady stream of youngsters returning from the United States embittered by humiliating experiences of discrimination" (644).

14. My reading builds upon Jodi Kim's argument for comprehending the Korean War as an "active production of Cold War knowledge" (150).

15. It is worth noting the particular significance of the Underwood typewriter for Korean students: Horace Grant Underwood, a Presbyterian missionary in Korea, led the Christian college in Seoul that would become Yonsei University (which presently features the Underwood International College). His missionary efforts were financed by his brother, John Thomas Underwood, founder of the Underwood Typewriter Company. Choi's naming of Underwood in this instance further ties Chuck to a modern history of American intervention in Korea.

16. Cieslak notes, "Religious groups probably play a larger role in the community contacts of foreign students than any other group. The same zeal that prompts them to send missionaries to foreign lands prompts their interest in foreign students here. And the majority of foreign students are churchgoers" (151).

17. See the Introduction for a discussion of these analogies.

18. Arguing that the Korean War "was a civil war, a war fought by Koreans, for Korean goals," Cumings invokes a story by Ambrose Bierce set during the

Civil War to dramatize the heartbreak of fratricidal war ("The Korean War" 274–75).

19. Daniel Y. Kim observes that, "in her critical approach to the American policies that led to the war and exacerbated its violence, Choi seems to have drawn from the account that Bruce Cumings put forward in his landmark two-volume study, *The Origins of the Korean War*" (559).

20. In "Writing the Borderline Subject of War in Susan Choi's *The Foreign Student*," Parikh considers the 1955 "birth of the Non-Aligned Movement (NAM) at the Asian African Conference in Bandung, Indonesia," which "emphasized the need for the post-colonial and decolonizing societies to remain neutral with respect to the bipolarity of the Cold War" as a context for understanding Chuck's desire, which "exceeds liberal, possessive rights" (63). Jodi Kim argues for his nonalignment in this instance (158) and offers a larger argument for *The Foreign Student* as a translation of the Korean War.

21. In her 2003 interview, Choi explains that "Katherine was never meant to be such a principal character; she was originally meant to be just one of many people Chuck meets in the U.S."

22. In a discussion of "white miscegenous desire" (17) in *Sexual Naturalization*, Susan Koshy explains that "the exoticism of the Asian woman was associated with her identification with extraterritorial sexual license" (18).

23. "Charlie" names both the Asian servant and the "VC" in Vietnam, identified in military parlance as "Victor Charlie" and then just as "Charlie." That the foreign student is named Chuck, of course, hints at his eventual replacement of Charles Addison.

24. "Princely" is a repeated clue to the true identity of the terrorist in the novel, and its application to Lee reveals how the foreign student appears to a fellow student. Choi suggests resonances between Chuck and Lee, as in their shared appreciation of the hush of campus in summer, and it is also tempting to read the telos of both of these works as the imminent arrival of the mixed-race daughter (more than a wink to Choi herself) that concludes the latter novel. Choi's fourth novel, *My Education* (2013), returns to campus in a narrative that is strikingly freed from the historical constraints of her previous work, though its mixed-race protagonist faintly recalls the awaited daughter of *A Person of Interest*. In addition, the exhilarating love triangle of *My Education* recalls the Chuck–Katherine–Charles Addison formulation. Colleen Lye reads *A Person of Interest* alongside the case of Wen Ho Lee to uncover the "novel's historicization of the racial subject's naïveté" (265). Considering Choi's protagonist against Wen Ho Lee's late racialization reveals what Lye terms an Asian American reading practice (266). Patricia Chu reads Choi's second novel, *American Woman* (2001), as neither mainstream nor within the parameters of Asian American studies in order to examine its fictional

portrait of Wendy Yoshimura in the context of state biopolitics. Both articles underscore the historicist work of Susan Choi's fiction, and particularly, its usefulness as a lens for reconsidering Asian American subject formation.

Chapter 4

1. Quoted in Arissa Oh 171. Oh writes, "Korean orphans captured the American imagination from the moment the Korean War erupted in 1950. Photographs and articles in newspapers and mass-market magazines like *Life, Collier's,* and *Look,* as well as on newsreels and radio programs, showed Americans a ruined Korea . . . Juxtaposed on the devastation were the faces of orphaned Korean children . . . In almost every human-interest story about the Korean War, these 'waifs,' 'urchins,' and 'moppets' figured prominently" (164).
2. Arissa Oh 171.
3. As Eleana J. Kim puts it, "As depoliticized figures of humanitarianism, Korean orphans provided opportunities for intimate diplomacy through international adoption" (76).
4. In "The Korean War, the Cold War, and the American Novel," an overview of and argument for Korean War literature, Steven Belletto reads the "textbook US Cold War version of the war" (68) presented in *Native Speaker.* Belletto exposes Lee's protagonist as a "good Korean" who "embod[ies] the darker sides of US power" (69).
5. In a 2010 interview upon the novel's publication, Lee explained, "I'd always wanted to write something about the Korean War because of my heritage. My father lost his brother during the war, and I fictionalized that episode, which was told to me very briefly without much detail" (Gilmore).
6. James Wood's review essay of *The Surrendered.*
7. SooJin Pate argues for the continuity between orphan and war bride in her reading of the gendering of Korean War orphans, 41–71.
8. Cho 14, 23.
9. Caroline Chung Simpson discusses popular representations of the Japanese war bride as "the gracious and hardworking middle-class housewife" as "an early form of the Asian American model minority" (151).
10. Susan Zeiger notes that while in the 1960s "as many as 11,000 Korean military wives came to live in the United States, Korean brides were all but invisible in American culture. . . . It was instead the Korean military prostitute who drew the attention, albeit muted, of the American public" (211).
11. See Moon's groundbreaking scholarship on the political labor of camptown prostitutes.
12. June thus never undertakes the metamorphosis "from orphan to adoptee" detailed by Pate in her reading of the Korean orphan as an emblem of

neocolonial relations. Indeed, by marriage in lieu of adoption, June seems to displace the unequal alliance that Pate examines—which is not to say that she eludes such a relation, but that the slippage between these roles in the narrative closely follows the novel's desire to upend and ultimately reverse the unequal alliance between orphan and GI.

13. Journalist I.F. Stone significantly challenged "the validity of Tokyo Headquarter's [i.e., MacArthur's] favorite nightmare, the Chinese 'horde'" (214) in order to indict US provocation.

14. The novel implies that this prisoner may be June's brother, thus suggesting a comparison between two kinds of friendlies, the allied soldier and the orphan—and the desperate soldier is less convincing than the canny orphan.

15. The title of Sokolsky's 1932 study, part of a flurry of books devoted to the 1931 "Manchurian incident," when Japanese forces attacked the Manchurian railroad in an effort to expand their empire into the mainland. Sokolsky runs through the modern history of conflict in Manchuria: "Once Japan and Russia have fought in that corridor; twice Japan has fought China for it; once Russia and China have fought over the control of one of its railroads" (1).

16. Louise Young 22.

17. Klein 152. Klein explains the fundraising campaign by Dr. J. Calvitt Clarke, the founder of the Christian Children's Fund, who "appealed to prospective American donors by representing their relationship with the children they sponsored as one of 'adoption'" (152).

18. Eleana J. Kim 45. Kim writes, "The metonymic association of the United States with 'heroic saviors' took material form in American newspaper images that portrayed servicemen arriving at airports after the end of their tours of duty in Korea—with young Korean boys, or mascots, in tow. These reports, first appearing in 1952, described how Korean boys and girls were adopted by the GI's parents and sometimes by the soldier himself" (51).

19. Pearl S. Buck examines their plight: "Can we be responsible for these half-American children? In a sense, I suppose we are more responsible than the people of other countries, and for two reasons: first, we are a mixed people and many of our citizens are Oriental, thus providing more potential adoptive families; second, an unknown number of these children are fathered by Americans living and working abroad as military and other personnel" (149). Buck's own Welcome House played a significant role in placing mixed-race children born in America. See Klein for a discussion of Buck's adoption efforts.

20. Arissa Oh explains, "Observers of the orphan situation in Korea concurred with the United Presbyterian Mission of Korea's opinion that 'Korean

society massively rejects the mixed-blood' and that a mixed-race child faced 'a radically impossible situation'" (163). Relief organizations emphasized this difficulty to American audiences, making it "unsurprising that Western observers believed that the only solution for GI babies was to find homes for them outside Korea" (164).

21. Dong Soo Kim writes that "what was originally started as a critical rescue mission in Korea has now become a permanent institution of child welfare services on an international level" (7).

22. Pate provides an overview of Holt's operations (101–25), including the telling detail that Holt proclaimed that "he chose four girls and four boys who '[weren't] so attractive' and were the 'least fortunate'" (105) for his own family. Caroline Ceniza Choy contextualizes Holt's enterprise and those of other "charismatic individuals who popularized international and transracial adoption in the United States in the mid-twentieth century," (75) including Pearl Buck, Josephine Baker, and Jane Russell, within broader social service efforts in the period (75–103).

23. Spoken by Senator Neuberger, who championed Holt's efforts in Congress (quoted in Arissa Oh 175).

24. Arissa Oh 175.

25. Buck goes on to write: "It is not a method approved by orthodox agencies, since it means that parents cannot see the child whom they adopt, and if they do not like the child there is no one responsible for its return. The child must stay in the home unwelcome and therefore unhappy. The hard fact was, however, that the proxy method was the only one approved by the Korean government, which at that time was anxious to get the half-American children out of Korea as quickly as possible. Any other method was interminably slow and children often grew too old or died in orphanages before they could get to their American families" (157–58).

26. Eleana J. Kim notes, too, that the GI baby "presented a possible weapon that the communists could seize upon in the ideological battle to discredit the United States and its cold war expansionism" (48). Pate's overall claim for reading the Korean adoptee as an emblem of neocolonial relation that exceeds the specific frame of the Korean War elaborates the significance of this figure.

27. Mark C. Jerng discusses adoption in *A Gesture Life*, which he reads as a mode of mediating between the "narrative drives" of minority assimilation in the United States and traumatic World War II memories that "coexist uneasily within this text" (193). The formal work of adoption in this reading permits a core oscillation that resonates with my claim for Sylvie's function in *The Surrendered*—which also underscores the plain yet key fact that there are no adoptions in the later novel.

28. Quoted from Lee's 2010 interview.

Chapter 5

1. To borrow from Christian Appy's recent *American Reckoning*, whose overview of six decades of American accounts of the war provides a piercing assessment.

2. In addition to the recent scholarship in Asian American studies that I engage throughout Part II, historians Mark Philip Bradley in *Vietnam at War*, Mark Atwood Lawrence in *The Vietnam War*, and Lien-Hang T. Nguyen in *Hanoi's War* significantly incorporate Vietnamese experiences of the war, which is the subject of anthropologist Heonik Kwon's *Ghosts of War in Vietnam*.

3. The novel uses this key term in French to express colonial engagement. Vigot, the French inspector who suspects Fowler's involvement in Pyle's death, is particularly critical of Fowler's studied detachment, insisting "You're *engagé*, just like the rest of us" (138).

4. Steven J. Whitfield identifies the origins of "the quiet American": "The phrase itself came from Philby, who described the CIA's leading agent in Iran, Kermit Roosevelt (T. R.'s grandson), as 'the quiet American'" (69).

5. Richard Drinnon encapsulates Greene's American reception, citing *The Christian Century*: "American reviewers of *The Quiet American* could hardly believe 'the malice toward the United States that controls the novel'" (417).

6. The film's Pyle is played by Audie Murphy, the most decorated GI of World War II. Whitfield portrays Murphy's postwar celebrity: "He was probably the nation's most remarkable infantryman ever, an unassuming, unaffected yet haunted hero cursed thereafter by trying to fulfill Hollywood's idea of a hero" (66).

7. Drinnon notes that "the United States furnished 'financial support' for Trinh Minh Thé, the Cao-Dai Third Force terrorist responsible for the street bombings Graham Greene incorporated in his novel" (422).

8. In *The Limits of Empire*, Robert J. McMahon provides a portrait of Diem: "The son of a court official in the imperial city of Hue, the Catholic Diem was a Vietnamese rarity: a French-speaking aristocrat with strong credentials as both a nationalist and an anticolonialist" (76). Bradley depicts Diem's American career: "From 1950 to 1953 he lived in Maryknoll seminary in New Jersey and came to impress a number of influential American political figures, including Cardinal Spellman, Senator John Kennedy, Supreme Court Justice William O. Douglas, and Senate Majority leader Mike Mansfield" (81).

9. Marilyn B. Young discusses American responsibility for the execution, which took place in early November: "Three weeks later, Kennedy was dead, assassinated. 'We had a hand in killing him,' Johnson told Hubert Humphrey, gesturing at a portrait of Diem. 'Now it's happening here'" (102).

10. Jim Neilson discusses the "notion that *The Quiet American* encapsulated all that was important about the Vietnam War": in the mid-1970s, "critics

started to reappraise *The Quiet American,* moving from accusations of anti-Americanism to an appreciation of the novel's forecasting of American actions in Vietnam" (76–77).

11. Marita Sturken has explored the power of these iconic images as "a kind of talisman": "the photographs of Kim Phuc, General Loan, and the My Lai massacre possess the capacity to conjure the entire war" (93).

12. George W. Bush notably returned to *The Quiet American* in his 2007 speech to the Veterans of Foreign Wars national convention, when he cited Alden Pyle as "a symbol of American purpose and patriotism—and a dangerous naiveté," only to redeem Pyle and to argue for extending his "dangerous naiveté" to Iraq.

13. John Hellmann explains that "Lederer had just retired after serving eight years as special assistant to the Pacific commander-in-chief, while Burdick was a professor of political science at Berkeley" (3).

14. Drinnon 374.

15. Slotkin 447. Slotkin discusses the significance of the "thought-experiments" offered by fictional works like *The Ugly American*: "Some of these thought-experiments were in several respects more accurate than the policy papers and counterinsurgency manuals in their understanding of the logic and anticipation of the future course of counterinsurgency" (447).

16. Slotkin argues against this perception: "But it was a serious mistake to see the Lansdale/Magsaysay partnership as a tutelary one. In fact, Lansdale and Magsaysay worked effectively because the relationship was balanced; and Magsaysay, as both a native leader and an expert on his own political culture, shaped the objectives and overall course of policy" (442).

17. Marilyn B. Young notes, "American analysts compared the unhappy effort of the French to recolonize Vietnam with the exemplary American decolonization of the Philippines" (43).

18. Stern toured NGOs in the 1950s and reportedly "tested the script on people in Southeast Asia and discarded ideas that were clever but unworkable for helping people" (Ball).

19. Bradley notes a striking instance of this sort of partnership: the Viet Minh forged "a relationship with members of the US Office of Strategic Services (OSS) who were posted to southern China and northern Vietnam in early and mid-1945. Indeed, for a time Ho [Chi Minh] became OSS Agent 19, or Lucius, and reported regularly on Japanese troop movements in Vietnam" (35).

20. Renny Christopher argues that *The Ugly American* "remains the most politically complicated American film about U.S. involvement in Vietnam, and Okada's Deong is still the most fully realized Asian character to appear in any such film" (201). The film's staging of Sarkhanese resistance, too, strikes a realist, documentary tone that breaks through this otherwise middling

picture. Albert Auster and Leonard Quart note "the airport demonstration riot that greets MacWhite's survival": "The images and action convey a chilling sense of Third World anti-Americanism" (20). One performance in particular stands out: the prime minister of Sarkhan, a weary sophisticate who critiques both American intervention and native resistance, was played to perfection by the future prime minister of Thailand, where the filming took place. *The New York Times* review of *The Ugly American* describes his performance: "His firm and impassioned indignation at the obtuseness of the American, tempered by a fragile but magnificent oriental dignity and grace, intrudes again a strong dash of illusory realism into the film" (Crowther). Thailand was an American ally that became a playground for American soldiers during the war: in *The Limits of Empire*, McMahon notes that the "preference of R&R-bound GIs serving in Vietnam for the bright lights, nightclubs, and massage parlors of Bangkok had, moreover, in conjunction with the permanent U.S. military presence in the country, been pumping another $200 million per year into the Thai economy ever since the mid-1960s" (172).

21. The opening of the film cites an earlier speech of Deong's, notably from the 1955 Bandung conference: "The United States has again taken up the cudgel of colonialism. I warn America: our multitudes are pledged as one man, one voice, one heart to resist the imperialist tide to the end and beyond the end."

22. John Hellmann writes that Moore's book "reportedly induced so many enlistments of young men hoping to become Green Berets that the Selective Service was able to suspend draft calls during the first four months of 1966" (53).

23. From the back flap of *The Green Berets*.

24. Taylor cites David Halberstam's cynical appraisal, 38.

25. Shelby L. Stanton explains that these assignments grew out of "early American efforts to beef up President Diem's regular army, the ARVN, by forming a wide variety of paramilitary, or nonregular, groups to render an armed presence at the village level" (38). Colorful examples of these nonregular groups include juvenile delinquents and "the 'Fighting Fathers,' a group of Catholic priests who raised sizable armed contingents to fight the Viet Cong" (45).

26. As Colonel George C. Morton, "the first commander of those valiant officers" of the Special Forces, puts it in Stanton's preface, his soldiers "forfeited career advancement to serve in the Special Forces" (x).

27. Moore has obviously lumped together North Vietnamese troops with the southern resistance.

28. Stanton notes this history: "Since the French had generally protected the Montagnard land (*Pays Montagnard Sud*) from the Vietnamese, the tribesmen liked Caucasian people. During the First Indochina War, the French had used, with some success, this trust to employ guerrilla bands" (39).

29. John Wayne's poorly received 1968 Hollywood version of *The Green Berets* is a throwback to 1950s-era Cold War westerns—and in a seeming nod to Korean War conventions, it notably features an orphan. It is worth noting, however, resonances between Wayne's beloved Rangers and the Green Berets, as well as between his "Injuns" and the mountain tribes of Southeast Asia. Slotkin discusses both the "special mystique" of ranger units (454) and their "complex identification with the Indians, whose character as natives marked them as the original and quintessential 'Americans' but whose character as 'savages' marked them as the ultimate enemy" (455).

30. Stanton explains that, "In the wake of South Vietnam's total defeat . . . Special Forces fell in such disfavor that the country's unconventional warfare capability nearly disappeared during the late 1970s" (293).

31. Hellmann discusses the image of Michael, *The Deer Hunter*'s protagonist, in Vietnam: in headband and war paint, he is "a Green Beret Ranger in an advance reconnaissance unit, and both his appearance and his professional identity link him to the tradition of Indian fighters who used Indian skills, became like Indians, to protect the community from Indians" (179).

32. Reading Coppola against Conrad, Garrett Stewart argues that "Conrad's epoch of colonization, with the idealism, hypocrisy, and greed that spawned it and the delusions of European moral grandeur that ennobled its rhetoric, has atrophied in Coppola's film beyond mere political expediency to urges so violent and atavistic that they have left articulation itself behind" (468).

33. Along with *Apocalypse Now* and *The Deer Hunter, Coming Home* (1978) formed the triumvirate of cinematic events that shaped the genre in the late 1970s.

34. Marilyn B. Young writes, "Those who fought the war were disproportionately poor, badly educated, and black" (319), products of dramatic enlistment efforts: "Between 1966 and 1972, a special Great Society program—Project 100,000—scooped up over 300,000 young men previously considered ineligible for the military because of their low test scores"—a program which "had the advantage of avoiding the politically unpleasant alternative of requiring students or reservists to do the same" (319–20).

35. H. Bruce Franklin significantly examines the ways in which "The POW myth exerts surprising power on levels of American society from top to bottom" (7) with a special emphasis on *Rambo*, which "helped make the MIA religion not only a distinctive feature of American culture but also a lucrative market" (156).

36. Auster and Quart describe the effort: "In November 1982, a former Green Beret colonel, James B. Gritz, and a group of his followers were foiled in their attempt to launch a raid into Laos intended to free the Americans reported to be held captive there. The raid, whose most noteworthy achievement was its theatricality, was hardly diminished by the fact that it was partially financed

by two Hollywood stars, William Shatner (*Star Trek*) and Clint Eastwood (*Dirty Harry*), both of whom wanted the rights to the story should the raid prove successful" (99).

37. As Appy puts it, "The *real* postwar POWs were not former American bomber pilots withering away in bamboo cages, but Vietnamese who had served in the South Vietnamese military or worked for the American-backed government" (250).

Chapter 6

1. Leslie Bow explains the significance of the film: "This is why Oliver Stone's film, *Heaven and Earth*, can still be compelling as a positive discourse that has ironically ignored Vietnamese presence in Vietnam; its initial focus on Le Ly as subject distances it from prior representations of the Vietnamese as voiceless, fleeing peasants, although it may also admittedly aestheticize and subordinate them to a lush, panoramic landscape" (132).

2. Duncan's inside look at the Green Berets revealed training in torture methods: "Our own military teaches these and other even worse things to American soldiers. They then condemn the Viet Cong guerrillas for supposedly doing those very things" (14).

3. In Stone's DVD commentary to *Heaven and Earth*, which is largely a diatribe against critics of the film, he makes a passionate case for the film's authenticity by emphasizing Hayslip's involvement.

4. Bow expresses this critique: "Thus her text offers a caveat to generalizing the political function of Third World women's *testimonio*; in its portrayal of naturalized gender values that purport to be transnational, her text exemplifies the ways in which women's life stories potentially collude with what some might view as neocolonialism" (117).

5. The structure of the first book was likely influenced by her coauthor, particularly in light of the linear narration of the second book, which was coauthored by Hayslip's son. For the first book, Hayslip first enlisted her son—then a teenager—as her scribe, but when their efforts failed to interest publishers, she determined to find a collaborator. In her only mention of Jay Wurts, Hayslip describes him as "a man about my age but with a very 'old soul'—a person who, in my opinion at least, had seen enough karmic cycles to understand what my story was about, feel what I had felt, and live those feelings on paper" (*Child* 300). Bow addresses his invisibility: "Who the hell is Jay Wurts? At the end of the text, Wurts is identified as a former Vietnam War Air Guard pilot but otherwise his participation as coauthor goes unremarked." Bow goes on to explain that "Wurts was responsible for much of the narrative crafting of what was initially a three-hundred-page manuscript" (133).

6. Viet Thanh Nguyen examines Hayslip's "representative account of how she as an individual is caught up in the forces that bind the United States and Vietnam" to argue that "this attempt at representation is clouded by her attempt at reconciliation, which is expressed twice, once at the end of each volume" (116). My reading considers the effects of this intertwining of representation and reconciliation.

7. Shawn Frederick McHale explains that Vietnamese Buddhists "selected freely from Pure Land and Zen Buddhism, and showed little interest in defining adherence to a particular sect or school. In terms of popular devotional practice, most Vietnamese Buddhists followed a simple version of Pure Land doctrine" (146), which "focuses on prayer and faith, not on rigorous textual study, mastery of Tantric techniques, or meditation practice. The rewards of faith are not achieved in this world" because all "are born into endless cycles of death and rebirth" (147).

8. From Merton's foreword, x.

9. In *The Lotus Unleashed*, Robert J. Topmiller examines "the Buddhist challenge to the South Vietnamese government" in order "to demonstrate the importance of Buddhist efforts to end the war and to create a neutralist government" (x).

10. Sister Chan Khong discusses her early frustration with Vietnamese Buddhism: considering that "though Catholics are in the minority in our country, they take care of orphans, the elderly, and the poor," she asks her Buddhist teacher, "Why don't Buddhists do anything for the poor and hungry?" (15). Later, when she meets Thich Nhat Hanh, she describes his response to this dilemma: "If I liked to help poor people, I could be enlightened by this work. I did not have to divide my time between merit work and enlightenment work" (26).

11. Thomas presents his numbed experience of the war: "During my tour in Vietnam I was directly responsible for the deaths of many, many people. But after the horrors of basic training, and after my childhood of abuse and neglect, I didn't recognize what I was doing as killing people. The enemy was simply the enemy, not human" (15).

12. Lifton writes, "In December of 1970 I helped initiate a program of weekly 'rap groups' at the New York office of the Vietnam Veterans Against the War . . . and met regularly with one of those groups over a period of two years" (18).

13. Kingston links her experience of the fire's devastation to the war: "I'm not crazy . . . People who've been there, who saw . . . the Long plain and Hue after the firefights, compared our fire to war" (14).

14. In *Being Peace*, Nhat explains "the two promises": "compassion, or love, and understanding. They are the essence of the Buddha's teaching" (88).

15. As Kingston puts it, "Yes, women are sanctuary; women bring soldiers home. But also women need to hear war stories" (247–48).

16. In a 2008 interview, Hayslip describes the "brother-sister relationship" between her two books and two humanitarian foundations: the books present the "global war problem," while the foundations nurture damaged bodies. Hayslip emphasizes, too, the pragmatic necessity of her first foundation as a means of returning to Vietnam in the midst of the US embargo.

17. Like Hayslip, Thich Nhat Hanh made a highly publicized pilgrimage to Vietnam. Exiled since 1966, he returned in 2005 at the invitation of the Vietnamese government. John Chapman explains that the government's "main reason for inviting Thich Nhat Hanh was probably to display to the international community the existence of freedom of religious belief in Vietnam, hoping thereby to facilitate its integration into the world economic system, and thus increase economic growth and strengthen its legitimacy" (298).

18. Edwin A. Martini argues that "As the Vietnamese war for national independence reached an end in the spring of 1975, a new phase of the American war against Vietnam began" (2). Martini engages "a more expansive definition of warfare in order to identify and name many of the more insidious and invisible aspects of violent relations between nations—economic, cultural, and environmental—that often go unnoticed" to suggest that "If war, as Karl von Clausewitz claimed, is the continuation of politics by other means, is the inverse not also true? Is politics not the continuation of war by other means, particularly in a case such as that of the United States and Vietnam after 1975, when the policies followed by the United States seem to bear more than a passing resemblance to those enacted during the military phase of the war?" (10).

19. Bradley notes interpretations of Vietnam's economic liberalization: "Some observers have argued that the history of post-war Vietnam demonstrates that North Vietnam may have won the war but lost the peace. Revisionist historians in the United States go even further, arguing that the embrace of the market and the rise of a liberal capitalist economic order in Vietnam reveal that the United States in fact won the American war in Vietnam" (179).

20. Oliver Stone in particular helped clear the way, as Hayslip notes: "Three days after he had asked to see plans for the Mother's Love Clinic and background information about East Meets West, he donated a check for the amount needed to finish our work. Just as miraculously, as if triggered by this first domino, we received our license from the State Department to build our clinic and our waivers to the 1942 Trading with the Enemy Act. Brick by brick, the wall that had isolated my old from my new country was coming down" (*Child* 359).

Chapter 7

1. Kakutani concludes her review by praising Cao's "impressive debut," which has "joined writers like Salman Rushdie and Bharati Mukherjee in mapping the state of exile and its elusive geography of loss and hope."

2. From Cao's 2005 interview with Miranda Kossoff, in which Kossoff emphasizes "Cao's cinematic recall of her childhood."

3. Clare Stocks examines Thanh's "inextricable links with the land" in order to argue that "Thanh's mythic distortions, erasures, and unspeakable silences testify to the difficulties of narrating both a personal and national history" (99).

4. Seung Ah Oh reads "the power dynamics among women in this scene" to examine "the ways in which Mai's brief interaction with the manager's girlfriend anticipate her more obvious collusion with Aunt Mary's white American domesticity" as well as "Thanh's exclusion from the interaction" (83).

5. Catton 17. Catton explains, "The Ngos proposed to develop a cultural synthesis for Vietnam by drawing upon a doctrinal import from Europe called Personalism," which "drew upon Catholic humanism" (41).

6. I follow popular convention in identifying Tran Le Xuan as Madame Nhu. In official correspondence, she signed her name as Madame Ngo Dinh Nhu.

7. Jacobs 88, 89. Jacobs's language echoes—and does not critique—the journalism of the era.

8. Jacobs 172. Howard Jones discusses Madame Nhu's twenty-two-day American tour, which was replete with speaking engagements and interviews. Despite being asked to "quiet down" by South Vietnam's new ambassador to the United States, she became "a hot new item" in the popular press, and Kennedy's "administration found it impossible to parry the rapier-like remarks of its Vietnamese visitor" (385).

9. The title of *Life*'s 1957 portrait of Diem.

10. Madame Nhu opens her letter to the editor "With reference to your gratuitously and unnecessarily insulting editorial on Aug. 9."

11. Jones 423.

12. Michele Janette suggests "that Thanh's final letter is a red herring, offering false closure and specious security, and that rather than unveiling an 'authentic' truth, the novel urges us to see discursive formations" (54–55).

13. Cao divulges this information in her interview with Kossoff.

14. Thomas K. Adams writes, "The Montagnards responded to the fair treatment and respect accorded them by developing deep and lasting ties of loyalty to the Special Forces men who lived and worked among them, following local customs, and often risked, sometimes losing, their lives in defense of the villages" (85). See Chapter 5 for a discussion of Green Berets in Vietnam.

15. Kodosky xiv, 149, 144, 145, 188.

16. Janette argues, "With its classic pathos, replete with small boy, baby animal, and wailing mother, this tale invites skepticism. Rather than a truthful tale, this one again seems tactical. As a metonym for the war, the colonel's story offers a replacement for *The Deer Hunter*'s nihilistic, absurd roulette game. It counters the sadistic imagery of the Vietnamese in *The Deer Hunter* with one of compassion and tragedy" (68).

17. From Pauline T. Newton's interview, 177, 178.

18. *Everything You Need To Know about Asian American History* follows the format of Himilce Novas's 1994 *Everything You Need To Know about Latino History*; both are published by Plume.

19. For example, Cao's 2007 article "Culture Change" argues that "culture matters to law and development. The observation, that culture matters, and the proposal, that it be examined and evaluated, run counter to the tradition of public and private international law" (1).

20. In his reading of Cao's novel, Te-Hsing Shan notes that "*Everything You Need To Know about Asian-American History* serves as a significant subtext to *Monkey Bridge*" (22).

21. Cao's acknowledgments cites "excellent books on the war in Vietnam," all notably pitched along the lines of the cited title by Mark Moyar, *Triumph Forsaken* (387).

22. Friedman 187.

Chapter 8

1. Nazli Kibria notes the "widespread concern" among the Vietnamese refugee community "that the intervention of the law into family life detracted from the authority and rights of parents to discipline their children as they chose" (132), citing "situations in which school or police officials directly intervened in conflicts between children and their family elders, often in response to complaints of physical abuse made by children" (147).

2. Kibria emphasizes that for Vietnamese refugees, "their migration to the United States was not the first but rather one of several relocations experienced by themselves or their families in recent times" (38); as a result, Vietnamese families in the United States often create a "more fluid and flexible model of kinship" (44).

3. In *Asian American Women and Men*, Yen Le Espiritu explains, "In the post-1965 era, the economic status of Asian Americans has bifurcated, showing some great improvements but also persistent problems. Today's Asian Americans both join whites in the well-paid, educated, white-collar sector of the workforce (albeit as 'proletarianized' professionals) *and* join Latino immigrants in lower-paying service and manufacturing jobs" (65).

NOTES

4. Minh also resonates with the "ghostly presence" of queer diasporic figures discussed by David Eng, notably in his reading of Monique Truong's 2003 novel *The Book of Salt*. Eng examines the figure of the disappearing Indochinese as a demonstration of "how the conceptual category of queer diaspora ... brings together dissonant desires with the political, thereby forcing a crisis in historicism" (1483). In *Catfish and Mandala*, we may identify a similar role assigned to Minh within the realm of the Pham family: his dissonant desires at once threaten, and ensure the progress of, the family.

5. Minh belongs to a raced underclass born out of the bipolar order of postwar minoritization in the US, which Aihwa Ong traces back to the "racial logic" that "has always lain like a serpent in the sacred ideal of American citizenship" (10). Ong explains that "The tendency to frame ideas about immigrants in terms of a bipolar racial order has persisted, and newcomers are located along the continuum from black to white" (11), and she notes that the experience of Southeast Asian refugees in particular has been rendered "analogous to those of African American urban migrants, including imposed labels of stigmatization—underclass, welfare mother, shiftless men" (19).

6. Delores B. Phillips analyzes Pham's unsettled stomach in the novel to argue that "the country itself seems to sicken him as he travels through it, and the spectacle of his illness becomes a central trope of his struggle to reconcile himself to his homeland" (68).

7. Kibria explains that this "structure of refuge" allows "access to the welfare system (Aid to Families with Dependent Children, Supplemental Security Income, Medicaid, food stamps) on the same means-tested basis as citizens" (12–13).

8. Pointing out that "The vast majority of immigrants in the United States, both in the past and today, have not had access to such government aid programs," Kibria suggests that "The eligibility of refugees for government assistance has perhaps contributed to the rather lukewarm reception that U.S. society has accorded Vietnamese refugees" (13). James M. Freeman puts it more starkly: he poses the personal narratives presented in his collection of Vietnamese American experiences against perceptions of refugees as "welfare sponges" (10).

9. In tracing the origins of this "haunting figure," Lieu marks a dramatic about-face in the popular American imagination: with Saigon's fall, "media representations of Vietnamese people transformed overnight from enemies who were largely indistinguishable from U.S. allies to asylum-seeking refugees desperately in need of a place of settlement" (4). Further, Lieu notes that this transformation from enemy to "destitute refugee" served a key ideological aim: namely, to create "hypervisible images of the state-dependent refugee" ultimately "forgets America's imperialist past" (21).

10. Bello 14.

11. See Moon's discussion of camptown prostitutes as "personal ambassadors" in *Sex Among Allies*. Jin-Kyung Lee's *Service Economies* demystifies the "miracle" of South Korean development by reading the critical "necropolitical labor" (7) of prostitutes and others as constitutive of South Korean modernization.
12. Brownmiller goes on to explain that the US military "controlled and regulated the health and security features of the trade" (95)—a pattern that developed widely throughout the Pacific.
13. Bello 15
14. Barry 132.
15. Lim 11.
16. Barry 137.
17. Isabelle Thuy Pelaud pairs two interactions between Pham and veterans of the war, one American, the other Vietnamese. In Mexico, Pham encounters Tyle, an anguished American veteran, and later in Vietnam, he discusses Tyle with Uncle Tu, a Vietnamese veteran who has lost everything in the war but offers "*to welcome him like a brother*" (267). Pelaud notes, however, that Uncle Tu's conciliatory speech makes it "apparent that a man like Pham is absent. Those who matter are the Vietnamese and the American GIs," and as a result, "Instead of allowing him a center stage of his own, the two men see in Pham a bridge, a trigger of memory and a ghost of their past" (225).
18. Heonik Kwon's *The Other Cold War* argues for the "decomposition of the cold war"—and not its so-called end—by considering the "other places" where "people had to live the cold war as part of their everyday lives and in their most immediate, intimate domains" (6). His particular attention to Vietnam and Korea as sites that demonstrate "the enduring effects of bipolar conflicts on local social and cultural processes" (9) resonates with Pham's experiences in Vietnam.
19. Huynh explains that Nguyen Du "did not invent the story himself but borrowed it from another source. It was, in fact, a Chinese prose novel" (xx), which Nguyen significantly condensed "into a spare poem of 1,627 couplets" (xxi). Huynh elaborates the significance of the poem for Vietnamese literature: "By triumphantly rescuing Vietnamese poetry from the stranglehold of classical Chinese, Nguyen Du performed for the vernacular what Dante had once done for Italian, liberating it from its position of subservience to Latin" (xxi).
20. Huynh xx.
21. In her reading of *Catfish and Mandala*, Anita J. Duneer argues that, "In identifying Chi with Vietnam, Andrew subverts the role of a victimized Vietnam. He sees Chi's rejection of the female side of her identity as a stand for independence, an end to a legacy of colonial oppression and self-sacrifice" (211), while noting that "in leaving her family, Chi ironically affirms her

Vietnameseness; she goes to San Francisco to live among other Asians" (212). My reading is less sanguine about Chi's independence.

22. Pham's website mentions this rift and emphasizes the literary labors both he and his father undertook to heal it (http://andrewxpham.com/work).

23. Bradley's brief mention of Tram's "fiancé" simplifies a complex relation. The entries are filled with her frustrated longing for an "M." who seems not to have returned her affections.

24. It is worth noting that Pham presently resides in Southeast Asia and is primarily a memoirist, whose other works include autobiographical essays and a culinary tour of the region.

WORKS CITED

Adams, Thomas K. *US Special Operations Forces in Action: The Challenge of Unconventional Warfare.* London: Frank Cass, 1998. Print.

Agamben, Giorgio. *State of Exception.* Trans. Kevin Attell. Chicago: U of Chicago P, 2005. Print.

Anderegg, Michael. "Hollywood and Vietnam: John Wayne and Jane Fonda as Discourse." *Inventing Vietnam: The War in Film and Television.* Ed. Michael Anderegg. Philadelphia: Temple UP, 1991. 15–32. Print.

Armstrong, Charles K. "The Cultural Cold War in Korea, 1945–1950." *The Journal of Asian Studies* 62.1 (2003): 71–99. Print.

Apocalypse Now. Dir. Francis Ford Coppola. United Artists, 1979. Film.

Appy, Christian. *American Reckoning: The Vietnam War and Our National Identity.* New York: Viking, 2015. Print.

Atanasoski, Neda. *Humanitarian Violence: The U.S. Deployment of Diversity.* Minneapolis: U of Minnesota P, 2013. Print.

Auster, Albert, and Leonard Quart. *How the War Was Remembered: Hollywood and Vietnam.* New York: Praeger, 1988. Print.

Ball, Linda. "Stewart Stern and *The Ugly American*." *Slackerwood.com.* 26 October 2009. Web. 14 April 2011. <http://www.slackerwood.com/node/881>.

Barnet, Richard J. *Intervention and Revolution: America's Confrontations with Insurgent Movements Around the World.* New York: New American Library, 1972. Print.

Barry, Kathleen. *The Prostitution of Sexuality.* New York: NYU P, 1995. Print.

Bascara, Victor. *Model-Minority Imperialism.* Minneapolis: U of Minnesota P, 2006. Print.

Battle Hymn. Dir. Douglas Sirk. Universal, 1957. Film.

Belletto, Steven. *No Accident, Comrade: Chance and Design in Cold War American Narratives*. New York: Oxford UP, 2012. Print.

———. "The Korean War, the Cold War, and the American Novel." *American Literature* 87.1 (March 2015): 51–77. Print.

Belletto, Steven, and Daniel Grausam. "Introduction." *American Literature and Culture in an Age of Cold War: A Critical Reassessment*. Ed. Steven Belletto and Daniel Grausam. Iowa City: U of Iowa P, 2012. 1–14. Print.

Bello, Warren. "From American Lake to a People's Pacific." *Let the Good Times Roll: Prostitution and the U.S. Military in Asia*. Ed. Saundra Pollock Sturdevant and Brenda Stoltzfus. New York: The New Press, 1992. 14–21. Print.

Benedict, Ruth. *The Chrysanthemum and the Sword: Patterns of Japanese Culture*. Cleveland: Meridian-World, 1969. Print.

Bhabha, Homi K. *The Location of Culture*. London: Routledge, 1994. Print.

The Bridges at Toko-Ri. Dir. Mark Robson. Paramount, 1954. Film.

Borstelmann, Thomas. *The Cold War and the Color Line: American Race Relations in the Global Arena*. Cambridge, MA: Harvard UP, 2001. Print.

Bow, Leslie. *Betrayal and Other Acts of Subversion: Feminism, Sexual Politics, Asian American Women's Literature*. Princeton: Princeton UP, 2001. Print.

Bradley, Mark Philip. *Vietnam at War*. New York: Oxford UP, 2009. Print.

Brown, Wendy. *Politics Out of History*. Princeton: Princeton UP, 2001. Print.

Brownmiller, Susan. *Against Our Will: Men, Women and Rape*. New York: Simon and Schuster, 1975. Print.

Buck, Pearl S. *Children for Adoption*. New York: Random House, 1964. Print.

Budd, Mike, and Clay Steinman. "*M*A*S*H* Mystified: Capitalization, Dematerialization, Idealization." *Cultural Critique* 10 (Autumn 1988): 59–75. Print.

Bundeson, Lynne. "Vietnam: One Woman's Story." Rev. of *When Heaven and Earth Changed Places*, by Le Ly Hayslip. *Los Angeles Times* 25 June 1989. Web. 18 June 2015.

Butler, Judith. *Frames of War: When Is Life Grievable?* London: Verso, 2009. Print.

Cao, Lan. "Culture Change." *Virginia Journal of International Law* 47 (2007): 357–412. Print.

———. Interview by Miranda J. Kossoff. "Visiting Law Professor Lan Cao's Vietnam Memories Turned into Praised Work of Fiction." Bowie State University. 10 February 2005. Web. 21 June 2011. <http://www.bowiestate.edu/academics/english/freshcomp/lcarticle.htm>.

———. *The Lotus and the Storm*. New York: Penguin, 2014. Print.

———. *Monkey Bridge*. New York: Penguin, 1997. Print.

Cao, Lan, and Himilce Novas. *Everything You Need To Know about Asian American History*. New York: Plume, 1996. Print.

Carruthers, Susan L. *Cold War Captives: Imprisonment, Escape, and Brainwashing*. Berkeley: U of California P, 2009. Print.

Casey, Steven. *Selling the Korean War: Propaganda, Politics, and Public Opinion in the United States, 1950–1953.* New York: Oxford UP, 2008. Print.

Catton, Philip E. *Diem's Final Failure: Prelude to America's War in Vietnam.* Lawrence: UP of Kansas, 2002. Print.

Chang, Gordon H. *Friends and Enemies: The United States, China, and the Soviet Union, 1948–1972.* Stanford: Stanford UP, 1990. Print.

Chapman, John. "The 2005 Pilgrimage and Return to Vietnam of Exiled Zen Master Thich Nhat Hanh." *Modernity and Re-enchantment: Religion in Post-Revolutionary Vietnam.* Ed. Philip Taylor. Lanham, MD: Rowman & Littlefield, 2007. 297–341. Print.

Chen, Jian. *Mao's China and the Cold War.* Chapel Hill: The U of North Carolina P, 2001. Print.

Cheng, Cindy I-Fen. *Citizens of Asian America: Democracy and Race during the Cold War.* New York: NYU P, 2013. Print.

Cho, Grace M. *Haunting the Korean Diaspora: Shame, Secrecy, and the Forgotten War.* Minneapolis: U of Minnesota P, 2008. Print.

Choi, Susan. *The Foreign Student.* New York: Harper Perennial, 1998. Print.

———. "Foreword." *The Martyred.* By Richard E. Kim. New York: Penguin Books, 2011. xiii–xvi. Print.

———. Interview by H. Y. Nahm. "Susan Choi, Shadow Novelist." *Goldsea. com.* 2003. Web. 28 January 2011. <http://goldsea.com/Personalities/Choisusan/choisusan.html>.

———. Interview by Istar Schwager. "Susan Choi Discusses Her Writing." *CreativeParents.com.* 2005. Web. 28 January 2011. <htttp://www.creative-parents.com/SusanChoiinterview.html>.

———. *My Education.* New York: Penguin, 2014. Print.

———. *A Person of Interest.* New York: Viking, 2008. Print.

Chong, Sylvia Shin Huey. *The Oriental Obscene: Violence and Racial Fantasies in the Vietnam Era.* Durham: Duke UP, 2012. Print.

Chow, Rey. *The Age of the World Target: Self-Referentiality in War, Theory, and Comparative Work.* Durham: Duke UP, 2006. Print.

Choy, Caroline Ceniza. *Global Families: A History of Asian International Adoption in America.* New York: NYU P, 2013. Print.

Christopher, Renny. *The Viet Nam War / The American War: Images and Representations in Euro-American and Vietnamese Exile Narratives.* Amherst: U of Massachusetts P, 1995. Print.

Chu, Patricia E. "The Trials of the Ethnic Novel: Susan Choi's *American Woman* and the Post-Affirmative Action Era." *American Literary History* 23.3 (Fall 2011): 529–54. Print.

Chuh, Kandice. *Imagine Otherwise: On Asian Americanist Critique.* Durham: Duke UP, 2003. Print.

Chung, Hye Seung. *Hollywood Asian: Philip Ahn and the Politics of Cross-Ethnic Performance.* Philadelphia: Temple UP, 2006. Print.

Cieslak, Edward Charnwood. *The Foreign Student in American Colleges.* Detroit: Wayne State UP, 1955. Print.

Crowther, Bosley. "Rev. of *The Ugly American.*" *The New York Times* 12 April 1963. Web. 14 April 2011.

Cumings, Bruce. "The Korean War: What Is It that We Are Remembering to Forget?" *Ruptured Histories: War, Memory, and the Post-Cold War in Asia.* Ed. Sheila Miyoshi Jager and Rana Mitter. Cambridge, MA: Harvard UP, 2007. 266–90. Print.

———. *Korea's Place in the Sun: A Modern History.* New York: Norton, 2005.

———. *The Origins of the Korean War: Liberation and the Emergence of Separate Regimes, 1945–1947.* Vol. 1. Princeton: Princeton UP, 1981. Print.

Dang, Thuy Tram. *Last Night I Dreamed of Peace.* Trans. Andrew X. Pham. New York: Harmony Books, 2007. Print.

The Deer Hunter. Dir. Michael Cimino. Universal, 1978. Film.

Derrida, Jacques. *The Politics of Friendship.* Trans. George Collins. London: Verso, 2005. Print.

Diffrient, David Scott. *M*A*S*H.* Detroit: Wayne State University Press, 2008. Print.

Dower, John W. *War without Mercy: Race and Power in the Pacific War.* New York: Pantheon, 1986. Print.

Drinnon, Richard. *Facing West: The Metaphysics of Indian-Hating and Empire-Building.* Minneapolis: U of Minnesota P, 1980. Print.

Dudziak, Mary L. *Cold War Civil Rights: Race and the Image of American Democracy.* Princeton: Princeton UP, 2000. Print.

———. *Wartime: An Idea, Its History, Its Consequences.* New York: Oxford UP, 2012. Print.

Dulles, John Foster. "To Save Humanity from the Deep Abyss." *The Korean War.* Ed. Lloyd Gardner. New York: Quadrangle Books, 1972. 84–92. Print.

Duncan, Donald. "The Whole Thing Was a Lie!: Memoirs of a Special Forces Hero." *Ramparts* (February 1966): 12–24. Print.

Duneer, Anita J. "Postpositivist Realism and Mandala: Toward Reconciliation and Reunification of Vietnamese and American Identities in Andrew X. Pham's *Catfish and Mandala.*" a/b: *Auto/Biography Studies* 17.2 (December 2002): 204–20. Print.

Eng, David L. "The End(s) of Race." *PMLA* 123.5 (October 2008): 1479–93. Print.

Enloe, Cynthia. *Does Khaki Become You?: The Militarisation of Women's Lives.* London: Pluto Press Limited, 1983. Print.

Espiritu, Yen Le. *Asian American Women and Men: Labor, Laws, and Love.* Thousand Oaks, CA: Sage Publications, 1997. Print.

———. *Body Counts: The Vietnam War and Militarized Refuge(es).* Oakland: U of California P, 2014. Print.

Fenkl, Heinz Insu. "Introduction." *The Martyred.* By Richard E. Kim. New York: Penguin Classics, 2011. xvii–xxxii. Print.

First Blood. Dir. Ted Kotcheff. Orion, 1982. Film.

FitzGerald, Frances. "Introduction." *Last Night I Dreamed of Peace.* By Dang Thuy Tram. New York: Harmony Books, 2007. v–xix. Print.

Franklin, H. Bruce. *M.I.A. or Mythmaking in America.* Brooklyn: Lawrence Hill Books, 1992. Print.

Freeman, James M. *Hearts of Sorrow: Vietnamese-American Lives.* Stanford: Stanford UP, 1989. Print.

Friedman, Andrew. *Covert Capital: Landscapes of Denial and the Making of U.S. Empire in the Suburbs of Northern Virginia.* Berkeley: U of California P, 2013. Print.

Gaddis, John Lewis. *Strategies of Containment: A Critical Appraisal of American National Security Policy during the Cold War.* New York: Oxford UP, 2005. Print.

Gardner, John W. "The Foreign Student in America." *Foreign Affairs* 30.4 (July 1952): 537–650. Print.

Gardner, Lloyd C. Introduction. *The Korean War.* Ed. Gardner. New York: Quadrangle Books, 1972. 3–27. Print.

Goar, Robert J. "The Humanism of Richard Kim." *The Midwest Quarterly* 21 (January 1980): 450–69. Print.

Grayson, James Huntley. "A Quarter-Millennium of Christianity in Korea." *Christianity in Korea.* Ed. Robert E. Buswell Jr. and Timothy S. Lee. Honolulu: U of Hawai'i P, 2006. 7–25. Print.

The Green Berets. Dir. John Wayne. Warner Brothers, 1968. Film.

Greene, Graham. *The Quiet American.* New York: Penguin, 1996. Print.

Hayslip, Le Ly. *Child of War, Woman of Peace.* With James Hayslip. New York: Anchor Books, 1993. Print.

———. Interview. *VietnamAnon.blogspot.com.* YouTube, 31 March 2008. Web. 18 June 2015. <https://www.youtube.com/watch?v=ilgTWHaSBfk>.

———. *When Heaven and Earth Changed Places.* With Jay Wurts. New York: Plume, 2003. Print.

Heaven and Earth. Dir. Oliver Stone. Warner Brothers, 1993. Film.

Hegel, G. W. F. *The Philosophy of History.* Trans. J. Sibree. New York: Dover, 1956. Print.

Hellmann, John. *American Myth and the Legacy of Vietnam.* New York: Columbia UP, 1986. Print.

Higgins, Trumbull. *Korea and the Fall of MacArthur: A Précis in Limited War.* New York: Oxford UP, 1960. Print.

Hong, Christine. "Pyongyang Lost: Counterintelligence and Other Fictions of the Forgotten War." *American Literature and Culture in an Age of Cold War.* Ed. Steven Belletto and Daniel Grausam. Iowa City: U of Iowa P, 2012. 135–62. Print.

Hooker, Richard. *MASH.* New York: William Morrow, 1968. Print.

Hunt, Michael H., and Steven I. Levine. *Arc of Empire: America's Wars in Asia from the Philippines to Vietnam.* Chapel Hill: U of North Carolina P, 2012. Print.

Hunter, Edward. *Brain-washing in Red China: The Calculated Destruction of Men's Minds*. New York: The Vanguard Press, 1953. Print.

Huynh, Sanh Thong. "Introduction." *The Tale of Kieu*. By Nguyen Du. Trans. Huynh. New Haven: Yale UP, 1983. xix–xl. Print.

Isaac, Allan Punzalan. *American Tropics: Articulating Filipino America*. Minneapolis: U of Minnesota P, 2006. Print.

Jacobs, Seth. *Cold War Mandarin: Ngo Dinh Diem and the Origins of America's War in Vietnam, 1950–1963*. Lanham, MD: Rowman & Littlefield, 2006. Print.

Jacobson, Matthew Frye, and Gaspar González. *What Have They Build You to Do?* The Manchurian Candidate *and Cold War America*. Minneapolis: U of Minnesota P, 2006. Print.

Jager, Sheila Miyoshi. *Brothers at War: The Unending Conflict in Korea*. New York: Norton, 2013. Print.

Janette, Michele. "Guerrilla Irony in Lan Cao's *Monkey Bridge*." *Contemporary Literature* 42.1 (Spring 2001): 50–77. Print.

Jerng, Mark C. *Claiming Others: Transracial Adoption and National Belonging*. Minneapolis: U of Minnesota P, 2010. Print.

Jin, Ha. *War Trash*. New York: Vintage, 2005. Print.

Jones, Howard. *Death of a Generation: How the Assassinations of Diem and JFK Prolonged the Vietnam War*. New York: Oxford UP, 2003. Print.

Kahn, E. J., Jr. *The Peculiar War: Impressions of a Reporter in Korea*. New York: Random House, 1951. Print.

Kakutani, Michiko. "The American Dream with a Vietnamese Twist." Rev. of *Monkey Bridge*, by Lan Cao. *New York Times* 19 August 1997: C13. Print.

Keyssar, Helene. *Robert Altman's America*. New York: Oxford UP, 1991. Print.

Khong, Chan. *Learning True Love: How I Learned and Practiced Social Change in Vietnam*. Berkeley: Parallax Press, 1993. Print.

Kibria, Nazli. *Family Tightrope: The Changing Lives of Vietnamese Americans*. Princeton: Princeton UP, 1993. Print.

Kieu, Chinh. "Interview." *Asians on Film*. July 2011. Web. 9 March 2012. <https://www.youtube.com/watch?v=efMD9Fs8SGw>.

Kim, Andrew Eungi. "Political Insecurity, Social Chaos, Religious Void and the Rise of Protestantism in Late Nineteenth-Century Korea." *Social History* 26.3 (2001): 267–81. Print.

Kim, Chong Bum. "Preaching the Apocalypse in Colonial Korea: The Protestant Millennialism of Kil Son-ju." *Christianity in Korea*. Ed. Robert E. Buswell Jr. and Timothy S. Lee. Honolulu: U of Hawai'i P, 2006. 149–66. Print.

Kim, Daniel Y. "'Bled In, Letter by Letter': Translation, Postmemory, and the Subject of Korean War: History in Susan Choi's *The Foreign Student*." *American Literary History* 21.3 (Fall 2009): 550–83. Print.

Kim, Dong Soo. "A Country Divided: Contextualizing Adoption from a Korean Perspective." *International Korean Adoption: A Fifty-Year History of Policy and*

Practice. Ed. Kathleen Ja Sook Bergquist et al. New York: The Haworth Press, 2007. Print.

Kim, Eleana J. *Adopted Territory: Transnational Korean Adoptees and the Politics of Belonging.* Durham: Duke UP, 2010. Print.

Kim, Jodi. *Ends of Empire: Asian American Critique and the Cold War.* Minneapolis: U of Minnesota P, 2010. Print.

Kim, Richard E. *The Martyred.* New York: Pocket Books, 1965. Print.

———. "Plenary Lecture." *Asian Voices in English.* Ed. Mimi Chan and Roy Harris. Hong Kong: Hong Kong UP, 1991. 23–32. Print.

Kingston, Maxine Hong. *China Men.* New York: Vintage, 1989. Print.

———. *The Fifth Book of Peace.* New York: Knopf, 2003. Print.

———. *The Woman Warrior.* New York: Vintage, 1989. Print.

Kinney, Katherine. *Friendly Fire: American Images of the Vietnam War.* New York: Oxford UP, 2000. Print.

Kirsch, Robert R. "Korean War Story Deserves To Be Classed as Great Novel." Rev. of *The Martyred,* by Richard E. Kim. *Los Angeles Times* 23 February 1964: C14. Print.

Klein, Christina. *Cold War Orientalism: Asia in the Middlebrow Imagination, 1945–1961.* Berkeley: U of California P, 2003. Print.

Kodosky, Robert J. *Psychological Operations American Style: The Joint United States Public Affairs Office, Vietnam and Beyond.* Lanham, MD: Rowman & Littlefield, 2007. Print.

Koshy, Susan. "The Fiction of Asian American Literature." *Yale Journal of Criticism* 9 (1996): 315–46. Print.

———. *Sexual Naturalization: Asian Americans and Miscegenation.* Stanford: Stanford UP, 2004. Print.

Kwon, Heonik. *Ghosts of War in Vietnam.* New York: Cambridge UP, 2008. Print.

———. *The Other Cold War.* New York: Columbia UP, 2010. Print.

LaFeber, Walter. *America, Russia, and the Cold War, 1945–1975.* New York: John Wiley and Sons, 1976. Print.

Lawrence, Mark Atwood. *The Vietnam War: A Concise International History.* New York: Oxford UP, 2010. Print.

Lederer, William J., and Eugene Burdick. *The Ugly American.* New York: Norton, 1999. Print.

Lee, Chang-rae. *The Surrendered.* New York: Riverhead, 2010. Print.

———. "Interview by Jennifer Gilmore." *The Rumpus.* 11 March 2010. Web. 29 March 2015. <http://therumpus.net/2014/03/the-rumpus-interview-with-chang-rae-lee-2/>.

Lee, Christopher. *The Semblance of Identity: Aesthetic Mediation in Asian American Literature.* Stanford: Stanford UP, 2012. Print.

Lee, James Kyung-Jin. "Best-Selling Korean American: Revisiting Richard E. Kim," *Korean Culture* (Spring 1998): 30–39. Print.

Lee, Jin-kyung. *Service Economies: Militarism, Sex Work, and Migrant Labor in South Korea*. Minneapolis: U of Minnesota P, 2010. Print.

Lee, Robert G. *Orientals: Asian Americans in Popular Culture*. Philadelphia: Temple UP, 1999. Print.

Lee, Timothy S. *Born Again: Evangelicalism in Korea*. Honolulu: U of Hawai'i P, 2010. Print.

Lieu, Nhi T. *The American Dream in Vietnamese*. Minneapolis: U of Minnesota P, 2011. Print.

Lifton, Robert Jay. *Home from the War: Vietnam Veterans: Neither Victims nor Executioners*. New York: Simon and Schuster, 1973. Print.

Lim, Lin Lean. "The Economic and Social Bases of Prostitution in Southeast Asia." *The Sex Sector: The Economic and Social Bases of Prostitution in Southeast Asia*. Ed. Lin Lean Lim. Geneva: The International Labour Office, 1998. 1–28. Print.

Lowe, Lisa. *Immigrant Acts: On Asian American Cultural Politics*. Durham: Duke UP, 1996. Print.

Lüthi, Lorenz V. *The Sino-Soviet Split: Cold War in the Communist World*. Princeton: Princeton UP, 2008. Print.

Lye, Colleen. "The Literary Case of Wen Ho Lee." *Journal of Asian American Studies* 14.2 (June 2011): 249–82. Print.

McHale, Shawn Frederick. *Print and Power: Confucianism, Communism, and Buddhism in the Making of Modern Vietnam*. Honolulu: U of Hawai'i P, 2004. Print.

McMahon, Robert J. *The Cold War: A Very Short Introduction*. New York: Oxford UP, 2004. Print.

———. *The Limits of Empire: The United States and Southeast Asia Since World War II*. New York: Columbia UP, 1999. Print.

The Manchurian Candidate. Dir. John Frankenheimer. United Artists, 1962. Film.

Marshall, S. L. A. *Pork Chop Hill: The American Fighting Man in Action, Korea, Spring, 1953*. New York: William Morrow, 1956. Print.

Martini, Edwin A. *Invisible Enemies: The American War on Vietnam, 1975–2000*. Amherst: U of Massachusetts P, 2007. Print.

Maslin, Janet. "A Woman's View of Vietnam's Horrors." Rev. of *Heaven and Earth*. *The New York Times* 24 December 1993: C1, C22. Print.

Masuda, Hajimu. *Cold War Crucible: The Korean Conflict and the Postwar World*. Cambridge, MA: Harvard UP, 2015. Print.

May, Lary. "Reluctant Crusaders: Korean War Films and the Lost Audience." *Remembering the "Forgotten War": The Korean War through Literature and Art*. Ed. Philip West and Suh Ji-moon. Armonk, NY: East Gate, 2001. 110–36. Print.

Moon, Katharine H. S. *Sex Among Allies: Military Prostitution in U.S.-Korea Relations*. New York: Columbia UP, 1997. Print.

Moore, Robin. *The Green Berets*. New York: Crown Publishers, 1965. Print.

Neilson, Jim. *Warring Fictions: American Literary Culture and the Vietnam War Narrative*. Jackson: UP of Mississippi, 1998. Print.

Newton, Pauline T. *Transcultural Women of Late-Twentieth-Century U.S. American Literature: First-Generation Migrants from Islands and Peninsulas*. Burlington, VT: Ashgate, 2005. Print.

Ngai, Mae M. *Impossible Subjects: Illegal Aliens and the Making of Modern America*. Princeton: Princeton UP, 2004. Print.

Ngo Dinh Nhu, Madame. "Letter." *New York Times* 14 August 1963: 32. Print.

Nguyen, Mimi Thi. *The Gift of Freedom: War, Debt, and Other Refugee Passages*. Durham: Duke UP, 2012. Print.

Nguyen, Viet Thanh. *Race and Resistance: Literature and Politics in Asian America*. New York: Oxford UP, 2002. Print.

Nhat Hanh, Thich. *Being Peace*. Ed. Arnold Kotler. Berkeley: Parallax Press, 1987. Print.

———. *Vietnam: Lotus in a Sea of Fire*. New York: Hill and Wang, 1967. Print.

Niebuhr, Reinhold. *The Structure of Nations and Empires*. New York: Charles Scribner's Sons, 1959. Print.

Oh, Arissa. "A New Kind of Missionary Work: Christians, Christian Americanists, and the Adoption of Korean GI Babies, 1955–1961." *Women's Studies Quarterly* 33.3&4 (Fall/Winter 2005): 161–88. Print.

Oh, Seung Ah. *Recontextualizing Asian American Domesticity: From Madame Butterfly to My American Wife!* Lanham, MD: Rowman & Littlefield, 2008. Print.

Ong, Aihwa. *Buddha is Hiding: Refugees, Citizenship, the New America*. Berkeley: U of California P, 2003. Print.

Osborne, John. "The Tough Miracle Man of Asia." *Life* 13 May 1957: 156–76. Print.

Parikh, Crystal. *An Ethics of Betrayal: The Politics of Otherness in Emergent U.S. Literatures and Culture*. New York: Fordham UP, 2009. Print.

Parikh, Crystal. "Writing the Borderline Subject of War in Susan Choi's *The Foreign Student*." *Southern Quarterly* 46.3 (Spring 2009): 47–68. Print.

Park, Chung-shin. *Protestantism and Politics in Korea*. Seattle: U of Washington P, 2003. Print.

Pate, SooJin. *From Orphan to Adoptee: U.S. Empire and Genealogies of Korean Adoption*. Minneapolis: U of Minnesota P, 2014. Print.

Pelaud, Isabelle Thuy. "Catfish and Mandala: Triple Vision." *Amerasia Journal* 29.1 (2003): 221–35. Print.

Pham, Andrew X. *Catfish and Mandala: A Two-Wheeled Voyage through the Landscape and Memory of Vietnam*. New York: Picador, 1999. Print.

———. *The Eaves of Heaven: A Life in Three Wars*. New York: Harmony Books, 2008. Print.

Phillips, Delores B. "Quieting Noisy Bellies Moving, Eating, and Being in the Vietnamese Diaspora." *Cultural Critique* 73 (Fall 2009): 47–87.

Pork Chop Hill. Dir. Lewis Milestone. United Artists, 1959. Film.

The Quiet American. Dir. Joseph Mankiewicz. United Artists, 1958. Film.

The Quiet American. Dir. Phillip Noyce. Miramax, 2002. Film.

Riesman, David, with Reuel Denney and Nathan Glazer. *The Lonely Crowd: A Study of the Changing American Character.* New Haven: Yale UP, 1950. Print.

Rogin, Michael. *Ronald Reagan, the Movie and Other Episodes in Political Demonology.* Berkeley: U of California P, 1987. Print.

Schlesinger, Arthur M. *The Vital Center: The Politics of Freedom.* Boston: Houghton Mifflin, 1949. Print.

Schmitt, Carl. *The Concept of the Political.* Trans. George Schwab. Chicago: U of Chicago P, 2007. Print.

See, Sarita Echavez. *The Decolonized Eye: Filipino American Art and Performance.* Minneapolis: U of Minnesota P, 2009. Print.

Shan, Te-Hsing. "Crossing Bridges into the Pasts: Reading Lan Cao's *Monkey Bridge.*" *Chang Gung Journal of Humanities and Social Sciences* 3.1 (April 2010): 19–44. Print.

Shipler, David K. "A Child's Tour of Duty." Rev. of *When Heaven and Earth Changed Places,* by Le Ly Hayslip. *New York Times* 25 June 1989. Web. 18 June 2015.

Simpson, Caroline Chung. *An Absent Presence: Japanese Americans in Postwar American Culture, 1945–1960.* Durham: Duke UP, 2002. Print.

Slotkin, Richard. *Gunfighter Nation: The Myth of the Frontier in Twentieth-Century America.* New York: Atheneum, 1992. Print.

Sokolsky, George E. *The Tinder Box of Asia.* Garden City, NY: Doubleday, Doran, & Company, 1932. Print.

Stanton, Shelby L. *Green Berets at War: U.S. Army Special Forces in Southeast Asia, 1956–1975.* Novato, CA: Presidio, 1985. Print.

The Steel Helmet. Dir. Samuel Fuller. Lippert, 1951. Film.

Stewart, Garrett. "Coppola's Conrad: The Repetitions of Complicity." *Critical Inquiry* 7.3 (1981): 455–74. Print.

Stocks, Claire. "Bridging the Gaps: Inescapable History in Lan Cao's *Monkey Bridge.*" *Studies in the Literary Imagination* 37.1 (Spring 2004): 83–100. Print.

Stone, I. F. *The Hidden History of the Korean War.* New York: Monthly Review Press, 1952. Print.

Stueck, William. *The Korean War: An International History.* Princeton: Princeton UP, 1995. Print.

Stueck, William, and Boram Yi. "'An Alliance Forged in Blood': The American Occupation of Korea, the Korean War, and the US-South Korean Alliance." *The Korean War at Sixty: New Approaches to the Study of the Korean War.* Ed. Steven Casey. London: Routledge, 2012. 15–47. Print.

Sturken, Marita. *Tangled Memories: The Vietnam War, the AIDS Epidemic, and the Politics of Remembering.* Berkeley: U of California P, 1997. Print.

Taylor, Mark. *The Vietnam War in History, Literature, and Film*. Tuscaloosa: U of Alabama P, 2003. Print.

Thomas, Claude Anshin. *At Hell's Gate: A Soldier's Journey from War to Peace*. Boston: Shambala, 2004. Print.

Topmiller, Robert J. *The Lotus Unleashed: The Buddhist Peace Movement in South Vietnam, 1964–1966*. Lexington, KY: UP of Kentucky, 2002. Print.

Truong, Thanh-Dam. *Sex, Money, and Morality: Prostitution and Tourism in Southeast Asia*. London: Zed Books, 1990. Print.

The Ugly American. Dir. George Englund. Universal, 1963. Film.

Valdes, Mario J. "Faith and Despair: A Comparative Study of a Narrative Theme." *Hispania* 9.3 (1966): 373–80. Print.

Van Fleet, James. "The Truth about Korea." *Life* 18 May 1953: 156–72. Print.

Walsh, Chad. "Another War Rages Within." Rev. of *The Martyred*, by Richard E. Kim. *New York Times* 16 February 1964: BR1. Print.

Weis, Elisabeth. "*M*A*S*H* Notes." *Play It Again, Sam: Retakes on Remakes*. Ed. Andrew Horton and Stuart Y. McDougal. Berkeley: U of California P, 1998. 310–26. Print.

Westad, Odd Arne. *The Global Cold War: Third World Intervention and the Making of Our Times*. New York: Cambridge UP, 2007. Print.

Whitfield, Stephen J. "Limited Engagement: *The Quiet American* as History." *Journal of American Studies* 30.1 (1996): 65–86. Print.

Williams, Randall. *The Divided World: Human Rights and Its Violence*. Minneapolis: U of Minnesota P, 2010. Print.

Williams, William Appleman, Thomas McCormick, Lloyd Gardner, and Walter LaFeber, eds. *America in Vietnam: A Documentary History*. Garden City, NY: Anchor Press, 1985. Print.

Wilson, Howard E. *Universities and World Affairs*. New York: Carnegie Endowment for International Peace, 1951. Print.

Wittfogel, Karl A. *Oriental Despotism: A Comparative Study of Total Power*. New Haven: Yale UP, 1964. Print.

Wong, Sau-ling Cynthia. *Reading Asian American Literature: From Necessity to Extravagance*. Princeton: Princeton UP, 1993. Print.

Wood, James. "Keeping It Real." Rev. of *The Surrendered* by Chang-rae Lee. *The New Yorker* 15 March 2010. Web. 29 May 2015.

Wright, Geoffrey A. "Acknowledging Experience: *Pork Chop Hill* and the Geography of the Korean War." *War, Literature, and the Arts* 23.1–2 (2011). Web. 15 May 2015.

Wright, Richard. *The Color Curtain: A Report on the Bandung Conference*. Cleveland: The World Publishing Company, 1956. Print.

Young, Charles S. *Name, Rank, and Serial Number: Exploiting Korean War POWs at Home and Abroad*. New York: Oxford UP, 2014. Print.

Young, Louise. *Japan's Total Empire: Manchuria and the Culture of Wartime Imperialism*. Berkeley: U of California P, 1998. Print.

Young, Marilyn B. *The Vietnam Wars, 1945–1990*. New York: HarperPerennial, 1991. Print.

Zeiger, Susan. *Entangling Alliances: Foreign War Brides and American Soldiers in the Twentieth Century*. New York: NYU P, 2010. Print.

INDEX